The Philosophy of Evolution

The Philosophy of Evolution

U.J. JENSEN

Professor of Philosophy,
University of Aarhus, Denmark

and

R. HARRÉ

Lecturer in the Philosophy of Science
and Fellow of Linacre College,
University of Oxford

ST. MARTIN'S PRESS · New York

© 1981 The Harvester Press Ltd

All rights reserved. For information, write:
St. Martin's Press, Inc., 175 Fifth Avenue, New York, NY 10010
Printed in Great Britain
First published in the United States of America in 1981

ISBN 0-312-60670-2

Library of Congress Cataloging in Publication Data

Main entry under title:

The Philosophy of evolution.

Papers based on a symposium held at the Institute of
Philosophy, University of Aarhus, Denmark.
Includes index.
1. Evolution—Congresses.   I. Jensen, Uffe Juul.
II. Harré, Romano.
B818.P47   1981   573.2   81-9409

ISBN 0-312-60670-2   AACR2

Contents

Preface

THE philosophical problems that stem from the wide use of evolutionary concepts and models in many different fields have rarely been looked at as a whole. The idea for a comprehensive study of the uses of these concepts began in a seminar jointly given by us (U. J. Jensen and Rom Harré) in Oxford in 1976. In the course of our meetings we realized that the breath and depth of the problems we encountered suggested a cooperative effort to bring in experts in several fields. We were fortunate to be able to realize this project in an international symposium at the Institute of Philosophy, in the University of Aarhus, Denmark, on the occasion of the fiftieth anniversary of the founding of the University. We are particularly grateful to the Faculty of Humanities of Aarhus University, to the Danish Research Council for the Humanities and to the Jubilaeumsfond of the University for supporting the symposium financially.

We would also like to thank members of the staff of the Institute who played an invaluable part in planning and running the symposium, and particularly to Hans Fink and Jörgen Ringgård, who with ourselves formed the planning group for the meeting.

With the exception of the contributions by Peter Ruben and Peter Beurton, all the contributors have in some measure reworked and rewritten their contributions, partly in the light of the discussions at the symposium. This volume is not, therefore, to be read as the proceedings of that symposium but as an independent work which developed out of many discussions of which the symposium itself was only one.

U. J. Jensen
R. Harré
Aarhus and Oxford, 1980

Introduction: Preconditions for Evolutionary Thinking

U. J. Jensen*

1. Discourses on evolution

1. FOR more than a hundred years there have been many interweaving but continuous discourses involving the topic of evolution in the science and philosophy of the West. 'Discourse' seems to be a more appropriate term than discussion.[1] To talk about discourses does not presuppose a common theoretical framework or a common understanding of the way the problem presents itself. There has been an incessant conversation. Changing theoretical approaches, philosophical presuppositions and metaphysical proclamations have played a part. There has been no united effort to identify a common goal, but questions and viewpoints presented in one discourse have created the background for new discourses. It would be absurd to attempt to reveal a *common essence* in these. There is no such thing as the *concept of evolution* more or less adequately elucidated by, for example, Morgan and Whitehead, Monod and Engels. However, there is a close relationship between continuous discourses about evolution. Discourses descend from other discourses forming one of the most viable species of our cultural, scientific ecology.

2. The discourses on evolution that make up that cultural species have certainly been characterized by longevity and fecundity. But to the experimental and theoretical minded biologists of the eighties they may appear as an artificial collection of intellectual monsters. Biology is nowadays a first-rate experimental and theoretical science. Is it even possible from this advanced observation post to describe with accuracy the borderline between scientific and metaphysical reflections on the evolution of nature and the nature of evolution? Or is it

* I should like to thank Rom Harré for having read and commented on this paper in a very constructive way.

1

even true that contemporary biology is a descendant of the evolution discourses of the past?

3. *Thomas Hunt Morgan*, one of the founders of experimental biology, did not hesitate to offer answers to these questions. It was the main purpose of his book *The Scientific Basis of Evolution* to 'insist that the study of evolution has become sufficiently advanced to rest our case for its acceptance on the same scientific procedures that have led to the great advances in chemistry and physics'.[2] Morgan is up against strong opponents. In the first part of the century even eminent philosophers and scientists proposed general philosophical theories of evolution. He must face widespread opinions of 'scientists, metaphysicians and philosophers'. The division of the opponents is not accidental. The first two categories are not taken very seriously. Morgan, however, cannot just ignore Whitehead 'the great mathematician and philosopher'. Morgan battles for a biology based on methods and results of the physical sciences. But Whitehead in a way expresses the exact opposite view: the biological concept of an organism is vitally important for physicists and trancends their traditional, narrow point of view, enshrining ideas about inert and unstructured matter. The biologist may be flattered—Morgan admits—when told that he is engaged in the elucidation of something that extends beyond the farthest star (as stated by the mathematician and astronomer Jeans in *The Mysterious Universe*).[3] But he will not accept the suggestion that the riddle of the universe can be solved by metaphysical (non-experimental-science) means. The scientific biologist returns from this metaphysical extravaganza to his experimental business: 'Impressed by these great ideas, but left still in doubt, the working biologist will return to his shop to see whether there be not some safer way of finding out about living things and their evolution.'[4]

4. The distinction between a scientific and a philosophical approach to evolution is—to Morgan—a distinction between an analytical, experimental approach and a holistic, speculative approach. Philosophers put a burden, a duty, on biologists: search for a final solution to your problems. If a biologist cannot manage this he will be criticized. But, Morgan regrets, 'it is unfair to put this burden on the pure mechanist.'[5] From Morgan to Monod the defence of the experimentalist against philosophy is

a vigorous fight against finalism and speculative holism. There *is* still a battlefield for such an effort. The light of speculative and metaphysical evolutionism was turned on again at the end of the seventies. Dark days called forth thoughts with the greatness of revelation. Gregory Bateson published *Mind and Nature: A Necessary Unity*;[6] Lyell Watson speculates in *Lifetide*[7] on the place of our mind in the evolution of nature. S. Moscovici has suggested a dialectical interplay of culture and biology in *Society against Nature*.[8]

5. Philosophers of the past may have put an unfair burden on biologists. In spite of this, contemporary biologists should not let philosophy of today suffer for the sins of the fathers. Vitalism and finalism are no longer at issue in the borderland between biology and philosophy. This does not imply, however, that the other antagonist in the unfruitful struggle between vitalism and mechanism has won the fight and that all the biological sciences are safely mechanist. Mechanicism and reductionism in their various forms are philosophical positions just as vitalism and finalism are. They are not just *the method* of biology. They get their philosophical flesh and blood from the negation of vitalism. They presuppose a philosophical nominalism sharpened in the critique of the idealist tradition which has distorted scientific thinking in various ways since Plato.

6. Eminent biologists have tried to fight the inclination to present reductionism as *the* method of the biological sciences. *Ernst Mayr*, one of the greatest evolutionary biologists of this century, has led the way; however, the struggle has been difficult. How can you fight reductionism without relapsing into vitalism and finalism? Mayr consoles himself with the thought that vitalism has been dead for thirty years. But biologists still suffer from the dead hand of the past when the only alternatives available are vitalism and mechanism. Even Mayr has to argue from Authority. He quotes Simpson: 'Insistence that the study of organisms requires principles additional to those of the physical sciences does not imply a dualistic or vitalistic view of nature'.[9] Biological processes obey the laws of physical science. This conclusion gives vitalism the deathblow. Reductionism is rejected by the argument that 'complex biological systems have numerous properties that one simply does not find in inanimate matter'.[10] Fighting reduc-

tionism is resisting the philosophical principle that a system is
nothing more than its constituents. The strife between reductionism and biological anti-reductionism is not a controversy
about the universal applicability of experimental and statistical
techniques in biology. But are there not strong methodological
reasons in favour of the philosophical position of reductionism?
Is all our scientific progress—including in biology—simply not
due to reductionistic moves? We get knowledge about systems
by getting knowledge about their parts. If this is reductionism,
then is reductionism not quite acceptable to the Darwinian
naturalist? He changes our perspective from wholes and
essences to living varieties of nature.

7. Darwinism implied a rejection of essentialism. Darwin
has, according to Mayr, a well-defined philosophical basis, an
understanding of which is a prerequisite for the understanding
of the evolutionary process. It was no accident that two 'English
amateurs', Darwin and Wallace, found the solution to the
problem of evolution. The Germans had their professionals,
but—Mayr explains—continental philosophy was dominated
by essentialism.

A different kind of thinking had developed in England:
populational thinking, based on opposite assumptions to essentialism. 'It claims that only individual phenomena have reality
and that every endeavour to infer from them to an essence is a
process of abstraction.'[11] But does that not imply that the anti-
reductionist cannot get a foothold in the history of biological
research? The Darwinian revolution seems—as to its philosophical content—to be a *nominalistic* critique of essentialism.
Isolated quotations from the *Origin of Species* seem to confirm
such an impression. In a famous passage Darwin remarks that
he looks at 'the term species as one arbitrarily given, for the sake
of convenience, to a set of individuals closely resembling each
other'.[12] What is the Darwinian *populational thinking* so vigor-
ously advocated by Mayr and his students? In many contexts it,
and the Darwinian concept of the species, is presented as a
position transcending nominalism as well as essentialism. Mayr
directly criticizes the numerical taxonomist for 'the demonstrably false claim that groups in nature are the product of the
human mind (or of the computer!) rather than of evolution'.[13]

8. Groups (populations, species) have reality. Is that more

than a simple repetition in biological terms of the philosophical principle that a system is more than the sum of its parts? The naturalists do not mean simply to make philosophical proclamations; they appeal to our knowledge of biological facts. They want to stress that species are a kind of collective entity. Each species is a reproductive community. It plays a highly specific role in the household of nature. To the nominalist this might seem to be nothing but metaphors. But can it not be expressed in a less figurative way?

Mayr tries to express the case in terms of the notion of species, which is a relational concept. It is compared to the word 'brother'. 'Like the word brother (which has only meaning in relation to other sibs), the species concept does not refer to an intrinsic property but to the relation of a species population to others. The relation being that of reproductive isolation.'[14] Mayr stresses the point which was crucial in Ghiselin's presentation of the innovatory character of Darwin's revolution in metaphysics. When we face the complexity of nature nominalism falls short. 'It overlooks the significance of relational properties, so that it may treat communities as families as if they were just as much abstractions as the class of red books.'[15] Have the naturalists steered clear of the Scylla of essentialism and Charybdis of nominalism? The tough-minded experimental biologist will feel a bit uneasy about all the metaphysical navigation. He is usually proud of having experimental tools more reliable than the metaphysical tools of the naturalist. Brothers are of course related in specific ways, but they are also characterized by similarity in genetic make-up.

9. The naturalists have never been quite happy about staggering between nominalism and a kind of relational holism or collectivism. So they have tried to adapt their metaphysical interpretation to their biological presuppositions (e.g. there is nothing over and above individuals). Species are also individuals. This point of view might appear counterintuitive, but only because of our essentialistic heritage. Species are chunks of the genealogical nexus.[16] The members of a species are then really *parts* of the *individual species*. We only understand that point when we understand proper distinctions between *taxon* and *category*. The taxon, *Homo sapiens*, is an individual (of which Ronald Reagan is a part). The taxon is a *member* of the

class (category) of species. Any species-taxon is an individual. The species category is a class.

Defenders of the species-as-individuals thesis are in doubt. 'Perhaps the distinction between individual and class is too crude', says Hull.[17] Some hybrid category might be more appropriate ('complex particulars' or 'individualized class'). Hull will let the scientific evidence be the judge in the metaphysical strife: '. . . from the point of view of evolutionary theory with its strong principle of heredity, species must be interpreted as individuals'. What is the force of the 'must'? In which ways do scientific theories impose metaphysical commitments upon us? The anti-metaphysical attitude of Morgan and the experimentalists should be kept in mind. Why not simply throw down the metaphysical weapons and stick to the facts?

10. The naturalists and their philosophical escort take part in several interrelated discourses. One is related to the old and indispensable taxonomic praxis. Another is the continuous story about the phylogeny of the species. Since the time of Aristotle these discourses have had their special philosophical ring. Contemporary versions have been summed up above. Several contributions to this volume (Hull, Beurton, Toulmin and Harré) are closely connected and are directly or indirectly related to the themes discussed above. The objective is to describe the conceptual or categorial structure of evolutionary explanation and understanding. But is listening to the philosophical discourses of the naturalists really any help? Is it not simply closing ones eyes to the revolution in contemporary biology? Discourses on evolution seem to have been replaced by a marvellous scientific edifice, a theory of the mechanism of evolution. Perhaps the conversation has to stop when the mirroring of our genetic construction (and the genetic construction of other species) becomes still more reliable. The contributions mentioned above bear witness to the transition phase characterizing contemporary biology. The Synthetic Theory of Evolution and the understanding of genetics are the indispensable starting points of any reflection on evolution today.

11. But how do we get into that edifice—already lauded by its servants? It did not rise out of nothing. Does it still reverberate

to the discourses of its constructors? Mayr warns us not to forget the history.[18] He tells us that a peculiar myth developed in biology by the middle of the fifties: that evolution is a purely genic phenomenon; a change from generation to generation of gene frequences in populations. Taking that for granted, mathematical populational genetics can be seen as a precondition for understanding evolution. Mayr tries to show that key concepts of the contemporary synthesis (not only natural selection but also e.g. genetic drift, isolating mechanics and geographic variations) are rooted in ideas of pre-genetic biology.

2. *Mirroring the genetic machinery*

12. The edifice of recent biology was named a long time ago: the Modern Synthesis[19] or the synthetic theory of evolution. Various discourses now take place at a common location. Distinct enterprises have become coordinated. But there is much uncertainty about the structure of this edifice. Two connected pillars were, however, seen by everyone: evolution as a two-stage phenomenon, and the production of variations and the sorting out of the variants by natural selection—a unity of Mendelism and Darwinism. Whatever the biologist is doing he has to inscribe his results on these pillars. As Francois Jacob said: 'whatever his speciality whether he deals with organisms, cells or molecules, every biologist today sooner or later has to interpret the results of his investigations in the light of the theory of evolution'.[20]

13. The constructors—Dobzhansky, Mayr, Huxley, Simpson and Stebbings—have had dignity conferred upon them: *their* publications constitute the research programme of modern biology.[21] The precise structure and function of synthetic theory is a matter of controversy and interpretation. But is synthetic theory really a *theoretical* edifice? Estimated according to the canons of much contemporary philosophy of science, the edifice is built on sand, and does not seem to fit the standard of hypothetic-deductive theory-building. Instead of exchanging the old metaphysical burdens (discussed by Morgan) for new methodological burdens, we should try to understand the real function of synthetic theory.

In the light of contemporary successful molecular biology an answer is at hand concerning the status of synthetic theory. It is not the real theoretical edifice of biology but only a stage in the transition from separated biological discourses to the theory mirroring the real mechanism of evolutionary change. We can get an impression of that *successor theory* of the future when inspecting populational genetics. Hardly anyone would claim that we have the real theoretical edifice at present, but we can get a glimpse of its beauty. The educated will see the crude concepts of the naturalistic area replaced by a more exact conceptual structure, and the talk about evolution replaced by estimation of gene frequencies. Genes are really nothing but DNA sequences. In the end the biological edifice is built on chemical knowledge.[22]

14. Mayr has, as already mentioned, protested against those who would eliminate evolutionary biology in favour of population genetics. He agrees that we are still far from a complete understanding of almost any of the more specific problems of evolution, but he still emphasizes the importance of *evolutionary* biology.

Many others have pointed to the problems in shifting to the discourse of genotypes. Lewontin even talks about an *epistemological* paradox.[23] Evolutionary genetics must be concerned with evolutionarily significant genetic change. The first task of such a science is the description of the genetic composition of populations. But then we encounter a paradoxical situation between what we wish to measure and what we can measure. Mendel's work has shown us that the possibility of enumerating discrete genotype classes depends on whether the substituting of one allele for another at a locus leads to sufficiently large change in phenotype. Lewontin reminds us that Mendel was successful because he chose his characters very carefully (namely those which allowed individuals to be unambiguously classified into a small number of classes).

There is, however, a striking contradistinction between the discreteness of genotypic classes and 'the quasi-continuous nature of the phenotype differences that are the stuff of evolutionary change'. We are reminded of the following insight which implies what Lewontin calls an epistemological paradox, 'the substance of evolutionary change at the phenotypic level is precisely in those characters for which individual gene substitutions make only slight differences as compared with variation produced by the genetic background and the environment'.[24] So Lewontin concludes that what we can measure is by definition uninteresting and what we are interested in is by definition unmeasureable.

15. If one takes the problem of evolutionary change seriously, how attractive is the idea of (a future) genetic theory mirroring the mechanism of evolution? First of all, there is still not such an edifice from the roofs of which nature can be inspected. It is not even easy to imagine what it would look like. So the advocates of truly mirroring genetic reality must, for the time being, become poets and metaphysicians. They cannot show us the actual theory. However, they try to give us a vision of the mirror, which will reflect genetic reality.

Richard Dawkins has, in a clear and beautiful way, opened (or reopened) a metaphysical gene discussion in *The Selfish Gene*. He sums up his position in very simple words: 'We are survival-machines—robot vehicles—blindly programmed to preserve the selfish molecules known as genes'.[25] Dawkins is not pretending to build a new theoretical edifice for biology. He has a much more modest end in view: to tell us, laymen, scientists, and philosophers, what Darwinism is really about. He does not argue from outside (from some speculative chemico-genetical position). Dawkins is an ethologist. So in a way he has the same starting point as the Mayrian naturalists presented above: real living nature subject to the mechanism of natural selection. Our knowledge of that fact is due to Darwin. But, says Dawkins, 'the full implications of Darwin's theory have yet to be widely realized'.[26] He is aware that his interpretation is not uncontroversial among biologists; to some it 'may sound as an extreme view'.[27]

16. In his contribution to this book Hull points out correctly that Dawkins has committed an act of metaphysics. It is precisely his metaphysical commitments which are of interest for our discussion. His metaphysical interpretation of the concept of gene will—if acceptable—pave the way for a new understanding of the biological sciences of the future. We are then *already on our way to* a mirroring of the chemico-genetical mechanism which turns the wheel of nature. Animals, plants, bacteria, and viruses are survival machines, survival machines

for a special kind of entity: genes. Genes are replicators. Replicators are an amazing kind of molecule: molecules which have the incredible property of being able to create copies of themselves.[28]

17. Today we know the structure of the replicators for which we are survival machines: molecules of a specific kind (DNA). Individual organisms have a transitory existence, but the genes are *eternal*. According to Samuel Butler, the chicken is the egg's way of making another egg. Organisms are the gene's way of making new genes. Genes live for ever. In a way they are like diamonds, but only in a way. An individual diamond has an enduring existence (as an unchanging pattern of atoms). The gene lives eternally as copies of itself.

Metaphysics is almost as difficult a business as biology. A new metaphysical basis for presenting biology is put forward by Dawkins, but it contains some dialectical tensions. We are told that we are survival machines for the eternal—or at least longliving—genes. We understand that genes are very strange things: 'what I have done is to define a gene as a unit which, to a high degree, approaches the ideal indivisible particulateness'.[29] But how do we trace the history of such *things*? What are the criteria of identity for genes? 'It is not easy, indeed it may not even be meaningful, to decide where one gene ends and the next begins.'[30] Dawkins maintains that this does not matter to his purpose.

18. Such a pragmatism is, however, unacceptable in metaphysical matters. A heavy metaphysical burden is put on the concept of gene by Dawkins. His whole presentation presupposes this category of *individual* but durable entities. We cannot renounce a more precise characterization of such a fundamental category. However, it is not only a question of metaphysics. There is among biologists a general agreement that the old bean-bag conception of genes (as individual entities related directly to phenotypic characters) is wrong. A leading biologist, *Stephen Gould*, characterizes the gene-machine metaphor as strictly *nonsensical*.

An individual is not decomposable into independent bits of genetic coding. The bits have no meaning outside the milieu of their body, and they do not directly code for any bounded piece of morphology or any specific behavior. Morphology and behavior are not rigidly built by battling genes; they need not be adaptive in all cases.[31]

So there *is* a case for Dawkins to defend. Those eternal genes seem very elusive. So occasionally Dawkins changes to the DNA discourse. One of the strange things about genes is their metaphysical duality. They are presented as *productive* (copying) entities; and at the same time they are the bearers of the structure, the essence, which determines the *value* of all their products? Changing to the DNA discourse this dialectical peculiarity seems to dissolve. The replicating DNA molecules are really not very permanent. Their life is short 'perhaps a matter of months, certainly not more than one lifetime'.[32] But in the form of copies of itself '*it*' can live for a hundred million years. According to his own presentation, Dawkins needed some *permanent entities*, but they cannot be molecules. He baptized the category: the longliving genes. But listening to his DNA discourse, one gets the impression that there are really no permanent entities. He exhibits an old philosophical endeavour —seeking the unity of the concrete and the universal. It is strange, but in spite of our DNA discourse and the glittering biological edifice of the future Dawkins is caught in the same metaphysical problems as the founders of genetics and one of the founders of our philosophy, Aristotle.

19. Dawkins points out that his central idea about evolution was 'foreshadowed by A. Weismann in pre-gene days at the turn of the century—his doctrine of the "continuity of the germ-plasm"'.[33] The Danish geneticist, Wilhelm Johannsen, who coined the word 'gene' not only foreshadowed the idea. In his book, *Arvelighed* (Heredity), he directly presented the 'eternal-seed' idea as the basic idea of the theory of heredity.[34]

20. Johannsen knew very well the history of science and of philosophy. He stressed the importance of taking that history into account: he finds the roots of modern genetic understanding in Greek thinking, in *Aristotle*. Aristotle fought against the Hippocratean view. According to Johannsen that view is very close to the pangenesis theory defended by Darwin. So the opposition between a Darwinian synthesis and a Mendelian genetics was foreshadowed in the Greek controversy between Aristotelians and Hippocrateans. Darwin characterized

Linnaeus and Cuvier as schoolboys in comparison with Aristotle.
But then it makes a sad impression, says Johannsen, that Darwin
did not know the Aristotelian critique of Hippocrates. Extract-
ing the moral of that story, Johannsen says: do not neglect
the history of science.

21. But what was so important in Greek speculation on the
generation of organisms, so important that, according to
Johannsen, it held the whole basis of the modern theory of
heredity? Johannsen summarizes the Aristotelian position.
Seed is in a way refined blood. United with the raw materials
from the mother an embryo is produced. The moving principle
of the seed penetrates the material. But, stresses Johannsen,
Aristotle also uses the word 'seed' in a broader sense. The seed is
now that which is united through fertilization (what we call the
fertilized egg). By the supply of nutrition the material develops.
It becomes a youngster and eventually an adult. But not all the
seed has been used; there is a residue of seed material from
which comes the new individual. It is not surprising that the
seed of the new individual is just as the original seed (in the same
way as the painter often makes use of paint left over from a
previous job). The seed not only makes the various organs of the
offsprings, but also makes quite directly the seed of the
offspring. *The seed of the offspring is a direct continuation of the
seed of the parents.* From generation to generation there is an
unbroken 'continuity of seed'. This is the reason why the
offspring can be similar to the parents.[35] Johannsen is not a man
of extravagant ideas, and we should listen when he exclaims:
'This idea is of genius. Aristotle comes straight to the point. His
ideas have become the leading principles in contemporary
research. What a pity that the Hippocratean theory and not the
Aristotelian seed theory exerted an influence on biology'.

22. The metaphysical problems which Dawkins has to face
are very close to the problems in Johannsen's Aristotelianism.
Saying that the seed (or gene) is *the same* t_1 and t_{nb} two times
separated perhaps by hundred of years, means within the
Aristotelian framework (presented by Johannsen) that the seed
at t_n is a *material part* which was already present in the seed at
t_1. The seed t_n is not only *the same kind* of seed as the seed t_1,
there is not only a *similarity* between the seed t_1 and the seed t_n,
there is *identity*. Seed is of course a strange kind of thing. We do

not just come up against it. If we picked up a small portion, how should we decide if it was *one and the same individual seed* as was present at some earlier time in history (picked up by another observer) or if it was only *an individual seed of the same kind* very similar to the first?

23. In the case of ordinary particulars we have rather simple means for solving such problems. We can trace the individual in space and time. My desk is one and the same desk as that sold by auction in Copenhagen on 10 May 1972 at a price of 1000 D.kr. I can map its route from Copenhagen to my Aarhus domicile. Hardly anyone—neither Aristotle, Johannsen nor Dawkins—would say that the lasting seed, gene or whatever we might call it is a material particular in *that* sense. What matters is not material identity, but in one way or another structural or formal identity. The Aristotelians offer another ontological category—a strange hybrid of the individual and the universal.

Two desks can be of the same colour, but what does that imply? It implies that they have the same kind of material fine-structure. Such fine-structure, when perceived by us, is classified as a specific kind of colour. Two things having the same colour would then, ontologically speaking, imply similarity in material structure (there would be no point in distinguishing between one and the same structure and similar structure). (The same problem emerges in the attempt to apply the replicator idea to the field of socio-cultural evolution (see Harré, this volume)).

24. From the Aristotelian point of view advocated by Johannsen this would hardly be satisfactory. To Aristotle 'the white' is *in* the table. White is a scattered universal. All the whites are not just similar structures; they are one and the same *white*. It is remarkable that Johannsen's Aristotle directly compares the seed with paint. My door and my table have the same colour. The identity is not just a matter of similar fine-structure. They have one and the same colour. How do we decide? Not just by looking or by looking at some hidden fine-structure. The same paint was used for my table and for my door. The colour which is now *in* my table and in my door was in the paint. But are we then not just saying that it is the same material used at various occasions? The problem is that

'same material' is ambiguous as used here. If we mean 'same fine-structure', similarity of structure will be sufficient for securing identity. However, that would not be enough for securing sameness of colour in the Aristotelian sense. Material similarity would probably secure colour of the same kind or almost similar colours; 'one and the same colour' (a scattered particularized universal) is different from that.

25. It is not surprising that Johannsen finds the Aristotelian categories useful as an ontological framework for the theory of heredity. The units of heredity were conceived of as particulars of a very peculiar kind. They were transmitted from organism to organism. They were particulate and indivisible (as were Aristotelian colours). Their existence was not dependent upon the existence of this or that organism with its specific material structure. Dawkins adopts this category for his theory of the lasting genes. But because he does not make the ontological peculiarities of the category clear, he does not really face the tension and contradiction between the Mendelian (Johannsen) conception of genes as *indivisible* and *unitary* particulars (concrete universals) and the dynamic and structural complexity of the DNA-replicator system.

3. *Revealing the reification of abstractions*

26. Our excursus into the roots of the gene-machine metaphysics leads us back to one unavoidable question: why does Dawkins—as do so many others—stick to 'the ideal of indivisible particulateness' of the genes? This question is not only of central importance to the philosophy of genetics and biology. Psychologists and philosophers of psychology have retained an ideal of the indivisible particulateness of experiences.[36] Philosophers and practitioners of medicine have for centuries interpreted diseases as disease entities, units as particulate and indivisible. In our view the ontological ideal is a consequence of a systematic misinterpretation of the classificatory character of certain terms.

27. What are we specifying when attributing an IQ to an individual? Are we specifying a particulate state of intelligence —Something the individual *has* as he *has* his genes, pains and diseases? Attributing an IQ to an individual presupposes a

standard of classification. Having IQ is being able to solve such-and-such problems in such-and-such a way. Attribution of IQ presupposes such standards or model descriptions. But the attribution presupposes a *fixation* of the individual. The individual here at that specific time *has* IQx, we say. We are abstracting from the individual as a changing, evolving entity, and then applying the abstraction as a fixed concrete property. What are the relations between the continuously developing person, the individual fixed under specific experimental conditions and the IQ specified under these conditions? Adopting the part-whole metaphysics now dominating the philosophy of biology, we should say the following: the IQ is a part of the individual; the individual is a part of the evolving person (conceived of as a lineage of time-slices).

28. The ontological hierarchy sketched above is a product of a very old and dangerous philosophical habit: reifying abstractions, not taking into account that the abstractions are established under specific experimental conditions and for quite specific purposes. The abstractions are not things out there to be placed in the right hierarchy of parts and wholes. They are dependent upon human intervention and the application of standards.

The history of taxonomy provides us with very instructive examples of reifications. The whole typological (or essentialistic) tradition ignored the role of standards in the process of classification. Classifying an organism is not revealing its inner nature. A specimen is selected and used as standard for a specific class. Saying that an object belongs to the class in question is not saying that it has the same essence as the other members, but neither is it saying that it is an ontological part of some ontological whole. Relative to the selected standard the object belongs to such and such a class of objects. It is an empirical question as to how that common classification is to be *explained*. There might or might not be a common material essence.

29. Our remarks on the taxonomy of intelligence-states and organisms may seem uncontroversial. However, there are very relevant lessons to be learnt for discussion about a genetic edifice mirroring the mechanisms of evolution.

Quite often the history of genetics is presented as progressive or accumulating. Mendel discovered genes (though calling them factors), and gradually the inner parts of that whole have been revealed. Layer-cake metaphors or machine-metaphors are, however, inadequate. They draw a veil over the classificatory or experimental character of the original concept of genetics. The famous biologist, L. J. Stadler, in 1954 presented reflections which illuminate the point.[37] Fundamental concepts of genetic analysis have been wrongly interpreted. Experimental concepts have been interpreted as if they specified inner (hypothetical) mechanisms. According to Stadler, such a confusion underlies the idea that the frequency of gene mutation may be greatly accelerated by X-ray treatment. According to this hypothesis, experimental treatment would produce 'a change in the constitution of a unit of genetic material, producing a new gene with altered gene action'. However, experiments did not validate such an interpretation. Was then 'gene mutation' an empty term? Not at all. It had a fixed experimental meaning: 'Gene mutation was identified in experiments by the occurrence of a mutant character inherited as if it were due to change in a gene'.

30. Stadler pleads for operationalist definitions of the experimental concept in genetics.

The essential feature of the operational view point is that an object or phenomenon under experimental investigation cannot usefully be defined in terms of assumed properties beyond experimental determination but rather must be defined in terms of the actual operations that may be applied in dealing with it.

Now there seems to be some confusion in this operationalist manoeuvre. What is the object (phenomenon) under experimental investigation? Stadler seems to imply that it is 'the mutant gene', something abstract waiting for definition. This is of course misleading. Some organic system is made the object of experiment, an individual fixed under specific conditions. The whole system (and not some inner, hidden part) is attributed the state 'being mutant' or 'having a mutant character', though some 'inner part' may play a role within that totality that could be played by no other. Saying that the attribution presupposes the specific experimental conditions is not 'reducing' genetic predicates to behavioural predicates. It is pointing out that the specified state is not some inner structure revealed by experimental scrutiny but a public state of the system experimentally produced, of which the inner structure is a necessary but not a sufficient condition. Hence we may not infer a *particular* inner structure from a genuine public state.

Taking the reification of the classificatory, experimental concepts seriously provokes strong metaphysical reactions. Richard Goldschmidt simply concluded that genes do not exist although he was not denying the existence of genetic material. The complex character of cellular activity could not be analyzed into particulate phenomena generated by individual genes. He introduced a 'dynamic' or 'continuum' model of the genetic material.[38]

Goldschmidt's ideas have not been confirmed by contemporary molecular biology. Whatever his contribution to genetics may be, he has contributed to the philosophical critique of the ontological framework of particulars presupposed in early genetics. Piaget has undertaken a similar kind of philosophical intervention. He applies the insights gained by Mayr, Darlington and Waddington, interpreting 'the genetic system and the genome itself as relational totalities which are both the products of a protracted growth and the centre of coadaptations and varied regulations'.[39]

31. We have repeatedly alluded to the Rortyan terminology of discourses, mirrorings and edifications. Darwinian discourses were partly replaced by the edifying discourse of genetics. The Rortyan vocabulary still seems appropriate. Rorty stresses that '. . . edifying discourse is *supposed* to be abnormal, to take us out of our old selves by the power of strangeness, to aid us in becoming new beings'.[40] Genetics (especially in the man-as-gene-machine interpretation) seems to play exactly such a role.

32. However, to Rorty 'edifying' is an honorific title. Typically edifying discourses are not mirroring at all. He criticizes the 'Platonic-Aristotelian view that the only way to be edified is to know what is out there (to reflect the facts accurately—to realize our essence by knowing essences)'.[41] He defends the hermeneutical point of view that 'the quest for truth is just one among many ways in which we might be edified'.

In so far as genetics (in the reductionist interpretation) wants to provide a master-vocabulary which permits commensuration of all biological discourses, it should certainly not be called a Rortyan edifying discourse. On the contrary, it is then rooted in a tradition deeply influenced by the epistemology of the West. The idea of the master-vocabulary goes together with an idea of the universe 'made up of very simple, clearly and distinctly knowable things'. Knowledge of the essences of such things then provides the master-vocabulary.

The Rortyan framework is, after all, illuminating in our case. The idea of the unified genetic theory of the future mirroring the machinery of evolution is, as argued above, rooted in an idea of genetic material as clearly and distinctly knowable things, the genes.

33. However, Rorty's critique of truth-seeking (mirroring) enterprises is to some degree misplaced. It is really directed against a *special* kind of truth-seeking and mirroring, one which reifies or hypostatizes its own abstractions—philosophers and scientists ignoring the preconditions of their own activity, presenting their theoretical products as if they reveal the essence of things. Rorty makes this point very clear in his critique of the Cartesian roots of the mirroring enterprise. Cartesian dualism itself is a consequence of a hypostatizing of universals. The Cartesian dualist has 'stopped talking about pains as states of people or properties predicated of people and started talking about pains as particulars, a special sort of particular whose nature is exhausted by a simple property'.[42]

34. To criticize the mirroring tradition rooted in western epistemology does not mean reducing truth-seeking *in general* to a dubious and subordinate role in human life. Truth-seeking of the kind criticized by Rorty has been (and is constantly) an impediment to understanding the world as changing and evolving. Essentialism was for centuries an obstacle to evolutionary thinking. Gene-machine reductionism may today be an obstacle to an evolutionary understanding. However, neither of these is the *biological* theory. They are specific philosophical interpretations of biological conceptions, of the *kind* so intensively criticized by Rorty.

The biological conceptions themselves have to be understood on the basis of practical, experimental contexts in which they have been established. Human beings have established them in the ongoing fight to extend our mastery over nature. Understanding the preconditions for evolutionary thinking involves reflecting on our situation in the world as working, experimenting beings. If we neglect that elementary fact we shall be clasped by the tentacles of reified abstractions.

35. How can we apply our lessons from biology in other areas of research? Is there such a thing as an evolutionary approach which can be applied within fields such as psychology, social science, and perhaps even philosophy?

The key to comprehension of the concept of evolution is understanding the role of *standards* in our classifying and isolating objects and systems in our natural and cultural surroundings. *We* select or isolate a standard (for example a flower or a system under controlled conditions) from its complex and changing conditions. The real reason why this practice is necessary is the existence of changing and evolving surroundings (otherwise the application and refinement of concrete standards would be superfluous, the Aristotelian nous would have been sufficient)— the mere possibility of being able to select standards (to be applied in representing kinds of—for example—organisms, diseases, cultures and theories) also reveals another important aspect of the concept of evolution. In any sub-realm of nature or culture relatively stable structures are established under given conditions. In nature there are species, in society there are groups, classes and modes of life, in science there are communities. No single mechanism governs change and stability of units within different sub-realms. Perhaps, the various mechanisms are not even analogous. In any sub-realm concrete theoretical analysis must reveal the mechanisms determining change, development and evolution. No general philosophical theory can perform that task. Thus, in taking an evolutionary approach to our natural and cultural surroundings we are not constructing a scientific esperanto or master-vocabulary out of evolutionary metaphors. Neither is it simply—in a rortyan manner—letting the conversation go on, letting new discourses blossom. It is instead reflection on the kind of concrete conditions which any classificatory or experimental representation has to *abstract* from.

Notes

1 We have adopted the Rortyan way of presenting our changing culture and science as interrelated discourses. See his *Philosophy and the Mirror of Nature*, Princeton, 1979.
2 London, 1935, p. vii.
3 New York, 1930.
4 Morgan, *ibid.*, p. 14.
5 *ibid.*
6 London, 1979.
7 London, 1979.
8 (English translation.) The Harvester Press, Hassocks, Sussex, 1976.
9 G. G. Simpson, Biology and the Nature of Science. *Science*, vol. 139, pp. 81–8.
10 Mayr, 'Basic Concepts of Evolutionary Biology', reprinted in *Evolution and the Diversity of Life*, London, 1976, p. 357.
11 *ibid.*, p. 12.
12 Quoted from the Everyman's Library Edition, 1971, p. 59.
13 'Theory of Biological Classification', reprinted in *Evolution and the Diversity of Life*, *op. cit.* p. 429.
14 *ibid.*, p. 480.
15 T. Ghiselin, *The Triumph of the Darwinian Method*, Berkeley, 1969.
16 *ibid.*, pp. 85–6. See also his 'A radical solution to the species problem', *Systematic Zoology*, vol. 23, pp. 536–44.
17 Hull, 'Are Species really individuals?', *Systematic Zoology*, vol. 25, 1976, p. 190.
18 'Where are we?', reprinted in *Evolution and the Diversity of Life*, *op. cit.*, p. 307.
19 Julian Huxley, *Evolution, the Modern Synthesis*, London, 1942.
20 *The Logic of Life* (English translation), New York, 1973, p. 14.
21 Dobzhansky, Ayala, Stebbings and Valentine, *Evolution*, Freeman, 1977, p. 17.
22 Kenneth F. Schaffner, 'The Watson-Crick Model and Reductionism', *Brit.J.Phil.*, vol. 20, 1969, pp. 325–48.
23 R. L. Lewontin, *The Genetic Basis of Evolutionary Change*, Columbia, 1970, p. 20.
24 *ibid.*, p. 23.
25 Dawkins, Oxford, 1976.
26 *ibid.*, p. 1.
27 *ibid.*, p. 12.
28 *ibid.*, p. 16.
29 *ibid.*, p. 35.
30 *ibid.*, p. 23.
31 *Ever since Darwin*, London, 1979, p. 269.
32 *ibid.*, p. 37.
33 *ibid.*, p. 12.
34 *Arvelighed: I historisk og eksperimentel belysning*, Copenhagen, 1917.
35 *ibid.*, pp. 13–14.
36 See my 'Conceptual Epiphenomenalism', *The Monist*, vol. 56, 2, 1972.
37 'The Gene', *Science*, vol. 120, 1954, pp. 811–9.
38 See his 'Different Philosophies of Genetics', *Science*, vol. 119, 1954, pp. 703–10.
39 See his *Biology and Knowledge* (translated from French), Chicago, 1971, p. 91.
40 Rorty, p. 360.
41 *ibid.*
42 *ibid.*, p. 30. See also my *Conceptual Epiphenomenalism*, *op. cit.*

PART I

Evolution in a Biological Context

1 Units of Evolution: A Metaphysical Essay

D. Hull*

ONE OF THE most persistent and frustrating controversies in biology concerns the level (or levels) at which selection can take place. Richard Dawkins (1976, 1978) has presented the most parsimonious view. According to him, genes are the primary focus of selection. In asexual reproduction, the entire genome might be the unit of selection. In cases in which no crossover occurs between homologous chromosomes, entire chromosomes might function as units of selection. But sexually reproducing organisms and anything which might be considered a group can never function as units of selection. In the vast majority of cases, genes are selected and everything else goes along for the ride.

The current majority view is that genes mutate, organisms are selected, and species evolve (Ayala, 1978; Mayr, 1963, 1978). Any changes in higher taxa are merely consequences of changes occurring at the species level or lower. Because genes are parts of organisms, they are selected but only indirectly by means of the selection of entire organisms. Finally, some authors argue that under special circumstances entities more inclusive than organisms can be selected, entities such as kinship groups, populations and species. Because these higher-level entities have been thought of traditionally as groups, the advocates of this position have been termed 'group selectionists', in one sense of this term (Eldredge and Gould, 1972; Gould and Eldredge, 1977; Stanley, 1975; Van Valen, 1975; see Sepkovski, 1978:224 for additional references).[1]

The empirical issues involved in this controversy, as complex and indecisive as they may be, have at least been dealt with at

* Numerous people have read early versions of this and related papers. I wish to express special thanks to J. Cracraft, R. Dawkins, S. Gould, S. Kimbrough, E. Reed, M. Ridley, S. Salthe, E. Sober, E. Wiley and W. Wimsatt. The research was supported in part by N.S.F. grant Soc 75 035 35.

some length (Lewontin, 1970; Sepkovski, 1978; Wade, 1978). However, another sort of problem has plagued the group selection controversy which has been addressed, if at all, only indirectly. This is so fundamental that it deserves to be called 'metaphysical'. The close connection between metaphysics and the controversy over levels of selection can be seen in the arguments provided by advocates of the two extreme positions. Given our relative size and perceptual acuity, organisms and species appear to be very different sorts of things. Organisms seem to be paradigm individuals, so much so that biologists tend to use the terms 'organism' and 'individual' interchangeably. Populations and species, to the contrary, give every appearance of being groups. Advocates of organism selection argue that our perceptions are veridical. The first thing which gene and species selectionists contend is that regardless of how they might seem, organisms and species are really the same sort of thing. However, they disagree about the sort. For example, Dawkins (1976:36) is forced to argue that, regardless of how they might appear from the human perspective, from the evolutionary point of view organisms are not stable, coherent individuals. Instead they are actually as amorphous and ephemeral as populations and species:

In sexually reproducing species, the individual is too large and too temporary a genetic unit to qualify as a significant unit of natural selection. The group of individuals is an even larger unit. Genetically speaking, individuals and groups are like clouds in the sky or dust-storms in the desert. They are temporary aggregations or federations.

Eldredge and Gould agree that appearances are deceiving, but the illusion is just the opposite to that claimed by Dawkins. Regardless of how they might appear from the human perspective, from the evolutionary point of view, populations and species are not groups. Instead they are as much unified and cohesive wholes as are organisms. For example, in response to a variety of questions about the nature of biological species, Eldredge and Gould (1972:114) conclude:

The answer probably lies in a view of species and individuals as homeostatic system—as amazingly well-buffered to resist change and maintain stability in the face of disturbing influences. . . . If we view a species as a set of subpopulations, all ready and able to differentiate but held in check only by the rein of gene flow, then the stability of species is a tenuous thing indeed. But if that stability is an inherent property both of individual development and the genetic structure of populations, then its power is immeasurably enhanced, for the basic property of homeostatic systems, or steady states, is that they resist change of self-regulation.

The initial reaction to being told that organisms are temporary federations or that species are homeostatic systems is likely to be, 'But that doesn't sound right.' Many of the things which scientists say when they are reworking the foundations of their discipline sound peculiar, as peculiar as subatomic particles being able to move from one place to another without traversing the distance between or space being curved, but that cannot be helped. Inherent in the scientific enterprise is the need to go beyond ordinary usage and common conceptions. Given our relative size and duration, we can see the distance between organisms, their diversity and gradual replacement. However, the cells which comprise an organism are just as diverse and even more rapidly replaced. If we were the size of atoms, organisms would look like clouds of atoms, comprised mainly of empty space. If we were the size of planets, species would take on the appearance of giant amoebae, expanding and contracting over the face of the earth (Williams, 1980). Questions such as these cannot be decided by common conceptions. Instead, whether organisms and species are the same sorts of thing or different must be decided in the context of the interplay between current scientific theories and empirical phenomena.

One reason that the controversy over the levels at which selection takes place has remained so intractable is that some of the issues are basically metaphysical: what sorts of things are organisms in contrast to groups, what general characteristics must an entity have to be selected, can entities which have what it takes to be selected also evolve or are the requisite characteristics mutually exclusive, etc.? Biologists discuss these issues but only indirectly and sporadically. In this paper I attempt to set out explicitly and in detail a metaphysics which is adequate to handle evolutionary phenomena. Secondly, the phrase 'unit of selection' is inherently ambiguous. Sometimes it means those entities which differentially replicate themselves, sometimes those which interact with their environments in ways which are responsible for this replication being differential. Both processes are *necessary* for evolution by natural selection to occur. In most cases, entities at *different* levels of organization perform these two functions. In this paper, I consistently differentiate between these two functions and the entities which perform them, set out the general characteristics which these entities have, and show which problems can be dissolved by making the necessary distinctions. I also distinguish between these two processes—replication and interaction—and a third process which they produce—evolution. I argue that the entities which function in all three processes are the best sort of thing—individuals. Groups play no role whatsoever in the evolutionary process. However, many things which are commonly treated as groups or even classes are actually 'individuals' in the generic sense of this term.

Individuals, classes and lineages

The metaphysical categories which I use in this paper to discuss the evolutionary process are *individual, class* and *lineage*. I place no special weight on these particular terms. Dozens of others would do as well. I have settled on 'individual' and 'class' because these terms are used by Ghiselin (1966, 1969, 1974) in his initial discussion of these issues, and 'lineage' seems to be standard usage in this connection. Terminology to one side, the conceptual distinctions are important. By 'individual' I mean any spatiotemporally localized entity which develops continuously through time, exhibits internal cohesiveness at any one time and is reasonably discrete in both space and time. Individuals are historical entities, individuated in terms of their insertion into history (Hull, 1975). Although they can be in principle absolutely simple, in most cases they themselves are composed of other individuals. Thus most individuals are 'complex particulars' (Suppe, 1974).

The term 'class' is used by philosophers, scientists and the general public in a wide variety of ways. When I use it in this paper, I intend to refer to those things which can have members, regardless of how this membership is determined, just so long as it is *not* determined in ways which limit it in advance to a finite number of entities or to a particular spatiotemporal location. As I am using these terms, Mars is an individual while planet is a class. Mars is a spatiotemporally localized individual. Planets are the class of all relatively large, non-luminous bodies revolving around stars. At any one time there may be no planets or a finite number of planets. If the universe exists for a finite duration, the total number of planets *sub specie aeternitatis* is also finite. However, 'planets' still refers to a class because any entity, anywhere and at any time, which has the requisite characteristics would count as a planet.

All sorts of ways exist for defining classes, fixing referents, etc. I couch my exposition in terms of spatiotemporally unrestricted classes because of the role traditionally played by classes in laws of nature. Classes are a dime a dozen, but the only classes which concern scientists are those which function in scientific laws, that is, natural kinds. On the traditional definition, scientific laws are generalizations (preferably universal in form) which are spatiotemporally unrestricted. The claim that the earth is the third planet out from the sun is true and important, but it cannot count as a law of nature because it refers to particular individuals. The law of universal gravitation is at least a candidate for a genuine law of nature because it refers to any entities which happen to have the appropriate characteristics. Generalizations are also a dime a dozen, but the only generalizations of interest to scientists are those that hold some claim to being laws of nature. Hence, as I am using these terms, 'natural kind' and 'law' are interdefined.

Because the connections between individuals, classes and laws are so central to my exposition, they must be spelled out in greater detail and possible misunderstandings avoided. The distinction between genuine laws of nature and other generalizations which just happen to be true is as central to our understanding of science as it as problematic. Although numerous marks of genuine laws of nature have been proposed, no analysis has as yet proved to be totally satisfying (see, for example, Smart, 1963, 1968). But the intuition remains strong that not all generalizations which turn out to be true are equally important in our understanding of the empirical world. A similar felt difference exists for classes in general and genuine natural kinds. Difficulties in presenting a completely adequate analysis of this felt difference are equally infamous. I happen to think that the source of our intuitions about laws and natural kinds is the same source. The fact that (nearly) all organisms here on earth use the same genetic code is important, but it is not a law of nature. It results from the fact that life most likely had a single origin here on earth. To put the point in just the opposite way, since all organisms here on earth use the same genetic code and we know of no lawful reason for the universality of the genetic code, we conclude that all organisms are descended from common ancestors who first developed the code.

The crucial factor is the relative primacy of similarity and descent. If similarity takes priority to descent, then the entity is a class and at least a candidate for inclusion in a scientific law. For example, all particular samples of gold may have developed originally from hydrogen, but that genesis is irrelevant on current physical theory to something being gold. Gold is a genuine class, a natural kind. If descent takes priority to similarity, then the entity is not a class and hence reference to it must be excluded from any genuine laws of nature. For example, there may be a star somewhere else in the universe with exactly the same characteristics as the sun, save spatio-temporal location. Yet, on no account would this star count as the sun. Hence, 'Sol' does not refer to a class but an individual, an historical entity. Statements about Sol may well be true, important in science, etc. They are not, however, laws of nature.[2]

The final metaphysical category which I need to introduce is that of a *lineage*. Certain individuals come into existence, persist for a while, and then cease to exist. They may consist of other individuals as parts, but these individuals do not 'give rise' to each other. For example, a fleet of ships might be considered an individual. Ships enter the fleet and leave it, but ships typically do not give rise to other ships. However, some individuals form *lineages*, spatiotemporal sequences of entities which causally produce each other. Entities in the sequence are in some sense 'descended' from those earlier in the sequence. Terms like 'descent', 'ancestor' and 'successor' are used in a variety of ways in a variety of contexts. For example, in mathematics 6 is the successor of 5. That does not mean that cardinal numbers form a 'lineage' or that 6 is 'descended' from 5 in the sense relevant to the operation of selection processes.

That we conceptualize lineages as individuals and not classes can be seen by the decisions which we make when similarity and descent do not universally covary. Usually entities related by descent are similar to each other. A is similar to B because A gave rise to B. However, they need not be similar, and even when they are not, they remain part of the same lineage. Human family trees are paradigm examples of lineages. Any baby produced by the union of two parents belongs to their lineage regardless of how peculiar, abnormal or dissimilar this baby might be. Conversely, no matter how similar a person might be to the people in a particular lineage, that person cannot belong to that lineage in the absence of the appropriate descent relations.

Lineages differ from other individuals in a second way. Not only are they made up of individuals which tend to be similar to each other because they are related by descent, but also they are capable of indefinite amounts of change. Most individuals have relatively discrete beginnings and endings in time and are capable of only a finite amount of change in the interim. As much as an organism can change during the course of its ontogenetic development, that development is circumscribed and to some extent programmed by its genetic makeup. However, organisms form lineages which are capable of indefinite change. Whether or not these lineages are coextensive with species is another matter.

In sum, individuals are spatiotemporally localized, internally cohesive entities which develop continuously through time. Usually an individual exists for a finite time and has an upper limit to how much it can change without becoming numerically a new individual. Lineages are those individuals composed of entities which serially give rise to each other in ancestor-descendant sequences. As such, lineages can continue to change indefinitely through time. Classes are the sorts of things which have members, not parts. Classes can be defined in a wide variety of ways. However, those classes which function in spatiotemporally unrestricted laws must themselves be spatiotemporally unrestricted. From a purely philosophical point of view, the distinction between those classes which function in genuine scientific laws and those that do not might seem extraneous. From the point of view of philosophy of science, it is not. Scientists are not interested in all classes or all individuals. One of their chief goals is to discover ways to divide up the world into classes which function in natural regularities. Similarly, the only individuals which are scientifically important are those which are acted upon by natural processes (for further discussion, see Wiley, 1980).

Replicators, interactors and lineages

Dawkins' work on evolutionary theory has elicited comment primarily because of his heavy emphasis on selection at the level of particular genes. He has taken the arguments which organism selectionists have used against group selection and turned them on the organism selectionists themselves. Although I find a certain poetic justice in this manoeuver, I think Dawkins' work is worth commenting on for quite a different reason. Although he is likely to be shocked, if not offended, at being told so, Dawkins (1976, 1978) has made an important contribution to the metaphysics of evolution in his explication of 'replicators'. Like Monsieur Jourdain, who was astonished to discover that he had been speaking prose all his life, Dawkins may well be surprised to discover that he has committed an act of metaphysics. Dawkins' discussion has two important virtues: in it he provides a general analysis of replicators and leaves as a separate issue the question as to which entities in the empirical world happen to have the requisite characteristics. He happens to think that in most instances only single genes possess these characteristics, but nothing in his general analysis precludes other, more inclusive entities from also functioning as replicators. However, Dawkins' analysis has one vice. In it he tends to run two quite distinct functions together into one: replication and the interaction of entities with their environments. In this section, I set out Dawkins' general analysis of replicators, distinguish between replication and interaction, and introduce a term of my own, 'interactor'.

Dawkins interrupts his analysis of replicators to ask:

Why 'replicator selection' rather than 'gene selection'? One reason for preferring replicator selection is that the phrase automatically preadapts our language to cope with non-DNA-based forms of evolution such as may be encountered on other planets, and perhaps also cultural analogues of evolution. . . . The term replicator should be understood to *include* genetic replicators, but not to exclude any entity in the universe which qualifies under the criteria listed (Dawkins, 1978:68).

By using the flexible word *replicator*, we can safely say that adaptation is for the good of the replicator, and leave it open exactly how large a chunk of genetic material we are talking about. One thing we can be sure of is that, except in special circumstances like asexual reproduction, the *individual organism* is not a replicator (Dawkins, 1978:69).

According to Dawkins (1978:68), the qualities of a good replicator may be summed up in a slogan reminiscent of the French Revolution: Longevity, Fecundity, Fidelity. As striking as this slogan is, it can easily be misunderstood. The fidelity which Dawkins is talking about is copying-fidelity, and the relevant longevity is longevity-in-the-form-of-copies (Dawkins, 1976:19, 30). Neither material identity nor extensive material overlap is necessary for copying-fidelity. The genetic material is reduced by half at each replication until a descendant gene may contain little if any of the matter which had been part of the physical makeup of a distant ancestor. What counts in replication is the retention of *structure*. When we are told that an organism receives half its genes from each of its parents, on an average a quarter from each of its grandparents, etc., genes are being individuated on the basis of substance, not structure. In most formulations of the problems posed by the cost of meiosis, once again genes are treated as material bodies. But what really matters in selection processes is, as Dawkins points out, *retention of structure through descent* (see also Cassidy, 1978). Two atoms of gold can be structurally identical to each other without one being a replicate of the other, or both being replicates of some other atom. Descent is missing. Conversely, a complex organic molecule can be broken down into smaller molecules by rupturing its quarternary bonds, and these molecules broken into even smaller molecules, etc., but the resulting molecules would not form replicates because retention of structure is missing.

For selection to take place, spatiotemporal sequences of replicates are necessary. Similar entities alone won't do; neither will spatiotemporal sequences of entities alone. Dawkins' exposition is couched, however, not in terms of *similarity* of structure, but in terms of *identity* of structure. Although nothing much rides on the decision, I find requiring structural identity too strong. For example, physicists consider two atoms to be atoms of the same element even if they are not structurally identical. Isotopes are allowed. Similarly, biochemists consider cytochrome *c* to be a single protein even though extensive variation in its composition is common. Such examples could be multiplied indefinitely.

Even though Dawkins requires structural identity for replicators, he allows for considerable variation in the amount of genetic material which can count as a single replicator. Followng G. C. Williams (1966, 1975), Dawkins (1976:30) defines a gene as 'any portion of the chromosomal material which potentially lasts for enough generations to serve as a unit of natural selection'. The structure of the genetic material can be altered chiefly in two ways—mutation and crossover. 'Now comes the important point. The shorter the genetic unit is, the longer—in generations—it is likely to live. In particular, the less likely it is to be split by any one crossover'. Thus, Dawkins' definition of a gene as a replicator is 'not a rigid all-or-nothing definition, but a kind of fading-out definition, like the definition of "big" or "old"' (Dawkins, 1976:34).[3]

One might be tempted to suggest to Dawkins that he make his notion of a replicator more widely applicable by adding a second dimension of fading out—degree of structural similarity. In general, the modification of a single amino acid rarely makes a molecule a new molecule, any more than the few corrections which Darwin made in the second edition of his *Origin of Species* made it a new book. Ideally, on Dawkins' view, the ultimate replicator is the single nucleotide. It is so small that it is never subdivided by crossover. It is also so small that it lacks an equally important characteristic of replicators—a pattern worth preserving. A replicator must be small enough to retain its structural pattern through numerous replications, yet large enough to have a structural pattern worth preserving. Dawkins' analysis of genes as replicators already includes one gradually changing variable. A second wouldn't hurt. In line with Williams' definition of the gene, one might say that two genes are similar enough to count as the same replicator if they react similarly to similar selection pressures.

Replication by itself is sufficient for evolution of sorts, but not evolution through natural selection. In addition, certain entities must interact causally with their environment in such a way as to bias their distribution in later generations. Originally, as life evolved on this planet, one and the same entities may have performed both of these functions simultaneously, but the characteristics of a good replicator are sufficiently different from those of a good interactor that eventually these functions began to be performed by different entities at different levels of organization. However, in one place Dawkins (1978:67) attributes both functions to one and the same entity—the replicator:

We may define a *replicator* as any entity in the universe which interacts with its world, including other replicators, in such a way that copies of itself are made. A corollary of the definition is that at least some of these copies, in their turn, serve as replicators, so that a replicator is, at least potentially, an ancestor of an indefinitely long line of identical descendant replicators. In practice no replication process is infallible, and defects in a replicator will tend to be passed on to descendants. If a replicator exerts some power over the world, such that its nature influences the survival of itself and its copies, natural selection, and hence progressive evolution, may occur through differential survival.

In this quotation, Dawkins is running two powers together—the power to reproduce one's structure and the power to do so differentially. These powers are sufficiently different to be distinguished terminologically. As Mayr (1978:52) emphasizes, evolution through natural selection is a two-step process, '(I repeat!), a two-step process'. Thus, I think Dawkins' general analysis of replicators needs supplementing with a general analysis of the entities which function in this second step. For want of a better term, I suggest 'interactor':

replicators—entities which pass on their structure directly in replication;

interactors—entities which produce differential replication by means of directly interacting as cohesive wholes with their environments.

A pervasive ambiguity in the literature on levels of selection can be eliminated by consistently distinguishing between replication and interaction. When gene selectionists such as Dawkins argue that genes are *the* unit of selection, they mean to claim at very least that genes are the only entities capable of replication. When organism selectionists such as Mayr argue that organisms are *the* unit of selection, they mean to claim at very least that organisms are an important focus of interaction with the environment. Genes, of course, can also function as interactors. They interact directly with their cellular environment, but they interact only indirectly with more inclusive environments via the interactors of which they are part. The point at issue is whether entities more inclusive than single genes or possibly entire genomes can function as replicators.

Both replicators and interactors exhibit structure; the difference between them concerns the directness of transmission. Genes pass on their structure in about as direct a fashion as can occur in the material world. But entities more inclusive than genes possess structure and can pass it on largely intact. For example, one paramecium can divide into two, each new individual possessing the same structure as the original. In such cases, Dawkins would say that the entire genome is functioning as a replicator because its structure remains intact in the process. The justification which I am suggesting concerns the structure of the organism itself. But a quite similar situation can occur in sexual reproduction. When two organisms mate which are genetically homozygous and quite similar to each other, the resulting offspring are likely to be equally similar, regardless of how much recombination occurs. Once again, Dawkins would say the genomes are functioning as replicators, while I would argue that the organisms themselves might be viewed as replicators, the only difference being in how direct the mechanism of replication happens to be. We part company most noticeably in cases of sexual reproduction between genetically heterogeneous organisms. Dawkins would argue that only those segments of the genetic material which remained undisturbed can count as replicators, while I see no reason not to consider the organisms themselves replicators if the parents and offspring are sufficiently similar to each other.

Genes tend to be the entities which pass on their structure most directly, while they interact with ever more global environments with decreasing directness. Other, more inclusive entities interact directly with their environments but tend to pass on their structure, if at all, more and more indirectly. *Both* processes must be performed successfully if evolution by natural selection is to take place. Reasons for choosing one necessary element over the other as *the* unit of selection are hard to come by. The best I can do is the following. Everyone agrees that both genes and organisms are individuals, and that genes form lineages by replication. Any change in a gene is reflected immediately and directly in successive replicates of that gene. Because the sort of inheritance attributed (inappropriately) to Lamarck does not occur, changes in the phenotype cannot be transmitted directly to the genetic material to be passed on to future generations. Instead, the only influence which changes in the phenotype is which organisms succeed in reproducing themselves and which not. Genes causally produce other genes. They also enter into the causal production of organisms. But the only thing that organisms can do is influence quite indirectly the statistical distribution of genes in future gene pools. In passing from the action of genes to the action of organisms, we proceed from definite gene lineages to amorphous gene pools, from causal connections to relative frequencies. As persuasive as these considerations may (or may not) be, they depend on viewing species as classes rather than as lineages, an interpretation which biologists are beginning to question in increasing numbers.[4] However, before discussing this highly controversial issue, two minor points need mentioning.

Dawkins hopes to reason analogically from selection of genes in biological evolution to the selection of memes in cultural evolution. If both genes and memes are to function as replicators, then Dawkins is going to have to make his notion of a replicator a good deal more general. The structure of memes, like the structure of genes, is what counts, but memetic structure is hardly transmitted directly the way that genetic structure is. Dawkins (1976:206) says that 'memes propagate themselves in the meme pool by leaping from brain to brain via a process which, in the broad sense, can be called imitation'. Maybe so, if mind reading were a prevalent mode of human communication, but as things stand, we must resort to some sort of system of symbols. I express my thoughts in words which, if I am lucky, may lead you to have similar, possibly identical, thoughts. However, the causal transmission of memes in culture is easily as indirect as the causal transmission of the structure of organisms in biological evolution. Either memes cannot function as replicators, or else the notion of a replicator must be expanded somewhat. I prefer the second alternative (Hull, 1981).

Finally, even if Dawkins' general analysis of replicators is accepted, his blanket rejection of sexually reproducing organisms as replicators does not apply as totally as he thinks. If biologists such as Mayr (1963), Carson (1970) and Eldredge and Gould (1972, 1977) are right, speciation among sexually reproducing organisms usually occurs when a very few organisms become isolated from the main body of their species. The effects of such a rapid reduction in population size are numerous and fundamental. For example, in most populations, several different alleles exist at most loci. One pregnant female, to mention the most extreme case, is unlikely to express much of the genetic heterogeneity of her population in her offspring. The ensuing inbreeding characteristic of such small populations is likely to increase homozygosity even further. It may well be true that the genomes of sexually reproducing organisms are 'torn to smithereens' at meiosis in large, genetically heterogeneous populations, but according to the model of speciation by 'genetic revolutions' currently so popular, all that is going on in such large populations is the haphazard fluctuation of allele frequencies. When it really matters, when new species are arising, sexually reproducing organisms converge on functioning as replicators.

Groups as individuals

Another instance of the relevance of metaphysical considerations in the controversy over levels of selection is the claim made by advocates of group selection that species are not 'groups' but individuals, possibly homeostatic systems. In the preceding section I distinguished between replicators and interactors. Although they differ in several important respects, replicators and interactors are both individuals. Hence, anyone who wishes to argue that species can function as units of selection, in either of these two senses, must first argue that they are individuals.

Although homeostatic systems are not the only sort of individual which can function as replicators or as interactors, they are paradigm examples of such systems and as such warrant some discussion. In particular, the similarities and differences between homeostatic systems and selection processes need to be pointed out.

Homeostatic systems consist in a larger system and smaller included subsystem, usually thought of as a regulating device. The two systems differ both with respect to relative size and with respect to rapidity and magnitude of action. Relative to the total system, the changes which occur in the subsystem are minor, rapid and require only a minimal expenditure of energy. They in turn produce more massive, ponderous changes in the system at large. One of the minor effects of these latter changes is to alter the smaller included system, and so on. The causal feedback loop between the two systems involves minimal energy flow. Most of the energy expended in the system is used in the functioning of the larger system.

In homeostatic systems, the feedback loops are so organized that one or more parameters of the larger system are kept within certain limits in the face of considerable (though not unlimited) changes in its environment. One variation on this theme is a system which undergoes progressive, programmed change. Instead of the system being maintained in roughly the same state, it is changed with each action of the feedback loop to a partially predetermined new state, a type of system termed 'homeorhetic' by Waddington (1957). Organisms as they function at any one time are good examples of homeostatic systems. As the temperature external to poikilothermal organisms varies, the temperature of the organism as a whole begins to vary, activating processes which counteract the effects of the environment. Organisms as they undergo ontogenetic development are just as good examples of the progressive variant. The interplay between an organism's environment, its genetic constitution, and the developing organism produces a series of changes in the state of the organism. Although the genetic constitution of an organism does not rigidly programme its development, it constrains it somewhat, sometimes quite narrowly.

This same cybernetic model has been used to characterize

selection processes. For example, C. J. Bajema (1971:2) says:

Natural selection, when viewed from the perspective of cybernetics (see diagram), is the feedback mechanism which favors the production of DNA codes—'programs'—which enables the species to adapt to the environment. It is via natural selection that information about the environment is transmitted to the gene pool of a population. This is accomplished by differential reproduction of different genetypes changing the frequency of genes in populations.

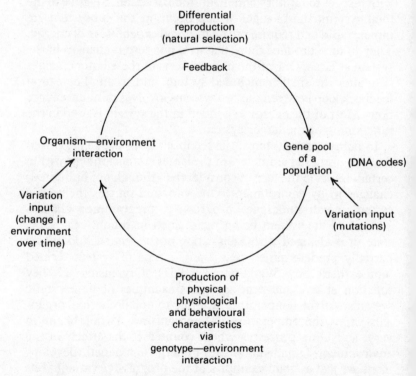

Diagram 1.   A cybernetic model of selection, after Bajema (1971).

In the diagram referred to by Bajema (see Diagram 1), changes in both the genetic makeup of the organisms involved and in the environment affect the organism-environment interaction, resulting in differential reproduction, which in turn changes the gene pool in the next generation. These changes, along with additional mutations and environmental variation, further modify the organism-environment interaction, and so on around the circular diagram. As described, the operation of natural selection does appear to be quite similar to the functioning of a homeostatic (or homeorhetic) system. However, if the highest-level system recognized in biological evolution is the organism, then appearances are deceiving, because no feedback loops are actually becoming established. In both homeostatic and homeorhetic systems, changes in the smaller subsystem produce changes in the larger system, which in turn produce changes in the *original* subsystem, which feedback into the *original* total system, and so on. The states of these systems may change, but as systems they remain numerically the same. In selection processes, they do not.

In Bajema's diagram, genes help produce the organism of which they are part as well as new genes. In the production of new genes, mistakes can be made. If these mistakes occur in somatic cells, the organism itself is affected and feedback loops can become established. However, if they occur in the germ cells, the organism itself is not affected, only its progeny, and its progeny are numerically different systems. Hence, no feedback loops can be established. Wimsatt (1972) has argued that functionally organized systems arise only through selection processes. As I have argued elsewhere (Hull 1980), selection processes give rise to functional systems by themselves *becoming* functional systems. The chief difference between the organization of the two sorts of systems is that, in functional systems, the effects of a single interaction between the larger and smaller included systems feed back into numerically the same systems, while in selection processes they do not. They affect new, distinct systems.

According to gene selectionists, genes are individuals which form lineages. Only genes, or possibly entire genomes, can function as replicators, because only genes can pass on their structure directly in replication. Gene selectionists admit that more inclusive individuals exist, that interactions between these individuals and their environments play a role in the evolutionary process, but for some reason this role need not be mentioned in evolutionary theory itself. Evolutionary theory can be couched entirely in terms of replicators and replication.

Gene lineages, not species, are the things which evolve. According to organism selectionists, both genes and organisms are individuals and both form lineages. Genes certainly function as replicators. Organisms also might function as replicators in certain circumstances, but at the very least they function as interactors, and both replication and interaction must be mentioned in any adequate theory of evolution. On their view, both gene lineages and organism lineages can be said to evolve.

Advocates of species selection go one step further. Not only are genes and organisms significant individuals in the evolutionary process, but also species themselves are properly construed as individuals. If species are monophyletic units, then they have the continuity in space and time required of historical entities. Whether they are also sufficiently well-integrated, cohesive wholes is more problematic. Biologists can be found on both sides of this issue. However, one thing is certain: if species are to function as either replicators or interactors, they *must* be individuals. In order to function as replicators, species must exhibit structural characteristics and be able to pass on these characteristics. Species must somehow 'reproduce' themselves as distinct individuals. One of the major reservations which biologists have to species selection is that they do not see how species can make the necessary copies of themselves to permit selection at the level of species. But even if species cannot function as replicators, they still might be sufficiently cohesive to function as interactors. If so, then a species would survive or become extinct because of characteristics which the species as a whole has, not because of the aggregative effects of the success or failure of individual organisms. In either case, according to the species selectionists, species do not and cannot evolve. A species, once formed, is not capable of extensive change. Instead, species form lineages, and it is these lineages which evolve (Hull, 1981).

Conclusion

The main purpose of this paper has been to set out the general characteristics which replicators and interactors exhibit and the roles which they play in the evolutionary process. A process is a selection process because of the interplay between replication and interaction. The structure of replicators is differentially perpetuated because of the relative success of the interactors of which the replicators are part. In order to perform the functions they do, both replicators and interactors must be discrete individuals which come into existence and cease to exist. In this process they produce lineages which change indefinitely through time. Because lineages are integrated on the basis of descent, they are spatiotemporally localized and not classes of the sort that can function in laws of nature.

This general description is straightforward enough. It gets complicated only when one tries to pin it down to particular levels of biological organization. For example, Dawkins argues that variable amounts of the genetic material can function as replicators, possibly entire chromosomes, on occasion entire genomes, but nothing more inclusive. Species selectionists do not argue that everything which taxonomists call a species can actually function as a replicator or an interactor but that *some* do. For example, they argue that nothing more inclusive than the single organism in cases of asexual reproduction functions in the evolutionary process. Asexual species really are not 'species' or to put it differently, if asexual species count as species, then not all species are individuals.

The main conceptual problem in the dispute over levels of selection is that selection, in both senses of this term, seems to wander over traditional levels of organization. In certain groups, nothing more inclusive than single genes may function as replicators, in others entire genomes, in others possibly organisms. In certain groups, one and the same entity may function as a replicator and as an interactor. For example, Dawkins agrees with Eldredge and Gould about asexual organisms, Dawkins admitting that the entire genome functions as a replicator in strictly asexual reproduction, while Eldredge and Gould argue that the organism in such cases is the most inclusive entity which functions in the evolutionary process. If one wants to formulate widely applicable generalizations about evolution, a good strategy might be to abandon the usual ontology of genes, organisms, kinship groups, populations and the like, and adopt an ontology designed specifically for this purpose—the ontology of replicators, interactors and lineages.

Notes

1 Several different but related issues are commonly discussed under the heading of 'group selection'. The one which has received the greatest attention concerns how 'altruistic' genes can become established in a population. How can a gene which decreases the fitness of the organism which possesses it become established in a population even if it benefits the group to which the organism belongs? One answer leaves the status of groups untouched: by helping organisms which also possess this gene. Another is to argue that certain commonsense groups are really not 'groups' at all but well-organized wholes. For early discussions of these issues, see Wynne-Edwards (1962) and Williams (1966).

2 The knee-jerk response to the claim that genuine laws of nature cannot make uneliminable reference to spatiotemporally localized individuals is to cite Kepler's laws which mention the sun. However, if Kepler's laws had turned out to be true only for the sun and not generalizable to other star systems, they would have gone the way of Bode's law. A scientist calling something a law does not automatically make it one.

3 Dawkins' 'perverse' definition of genes in terms of selection pressures irritates Gunter Stent (1977) because it 'denatures the meaningful and well-established central concept of genetics into a fuzzy and heuristically useless notion'. Memory is short. Mendelian geneticists raised exactly the same objections to the perverse redefinitions of the gene being urged on them a generation ago by such molecular biologists as Stent (Carlson, 1966). Mary Midgley (1979) is even more irate over 'altruism' being turned into a technical term in science. The dangers of equivocation are too great. Such protests over changes in language are almost as effective in redirecting the evolution of language as prayers are in stopping the flow of molten lava.

4 L. J. Cohen (1974) responds to the claims made by Ghiselin (1966, 1969, 1974) and Hull (1974) that species are not classes, by defining species in terms of spatio-temporal relations to spatiotemporal foci. However, if this sort of definition were acceptable, then particular organisms could also be viewed as classes, by defining them in terms of cellular descent from the zygote which gave rise to them. On this view, nearly everything becomes a class. The manoeuvre also accomplishes nothing because the need remains to distinguish spatiotemporally unrestricted classes (like planets and gold) from spatiotemporally restricted 'classes' (like Richard Nixon and *Homo sapiens*). Of course, the relevant distinctions can be made in terms other than those I have used (e.g., Reed, 1979; Sober, 1980, 1981). Conversely, certain philosophers have argued that laws need not refer to natural kinds (Dretske, 1977), nor be spatiotemporally unrestricted (Earman, 1978).

References

F. J. Ayala (1978) 'The Mechanisms of Evolution', *Scientific American*, 239, pp. 56–69.
C. J. Bajema (1971) *Natural Selection in Human Populations*, John Wiley & Sons, New York.
E. A. Carlson (1966) *The Gene: A Critical History*, Saunders, Philadelphia.
H. L. Carson, 'Chromosome Tracers of the Origin of Species', *Science*, 168, pp. 1414–8.
J. Cassidy (1978) 'Philosophical Aspects of the Group Selection Controversy', *Philosophy of Science*, 45, pp. 575–94.

L. J. Cohen (1974) 'Professor Hull and the Evolution of Science', *The British Journal for the Philosophy of Science*, 25, pp. 334–6.

R. Dawkins (1976) *The Selfish Gene*, Oxford University Press, New York and Oxford.

R. Dawkins (1978) 'Replicator Selection and the Extended Phenotype', *Zeitschrift für Tierpsychologie*, 47, pp. 61–76.

F. Dretske, (1977) 'Laws of Nature', *Philosophy of Science*, 44, pp. 248–68.

J. Earman, (1978) 'The Universality of Laws', *Philosophy of Science*, 45, pp. 173–81.

N. Eldredge and S. J. Gould (1972) 'Punctuated Equilibria: An Alternative to Phyletic Gradualism', in *Models of Paleobiology*, T. J. M. Schopf (ed.), Freeman, Cooper & Company, San Francisco.

M. T. Ghiselin (1966) 'On Psychologism in the Logic of Taxonomic Principles', *Systematic Zoology*, 15, pp. 207–15.

M. T. Ghiselin (1969) *The Triumph of the Darwinian Method*, the University of California Press, Berkeley.

M. T. Ghiselin (1974) 'A Radical Solution to the Species Problem', *Systematic Zoology*, 23, pp. 536–44.

S. J. Gould and N. Eldredge (1977) 'Punctuated Equilibria: the Tempo and Mode of Evolution Reconsidered', *Paleobiology*, 3, pp. 115–51.

D. L. Hull (1974) 'Are the "Members" of Biological Species "Similar" to Each Other?', *The British Journal for the Philosophy of Science*, 25, pp. 332–4.

D. L. Hull (1975) 'Central Subjects and Historical Narratives', *History and Theory*, 14, pp. 253–74.

D. L. Hull (1976) 'Are Species Really Individuals?', *Systematic Zoology*, 25, pp. 174–91.

D. L. Hull (1978) 'A Matter of Individuality', *Philosophy of Science*, 45, pp. 335–60.

D. L. Hull (1980) 'Biology and Philosophy', in *Chroniques de Philosophy*, Vol. II, *Philosophy of Science*, G. Fløistad (ed.), Paris, forthcoming.

D. L. Hull (1981) 'Individuality and Selection', *Annual Review of Ecology and Systematics*, forthcoming.

R. C. Lewontin (1970) 'The Units of Selection', *Annual Review of Ecology and Systematics*, 1, pp. 1–18.

E. Mayr (1963) *Animal Species and Evolution*, The Belknap Press, Cambridge, Mass.

E. Mayr, (1978) 'Evolution', *Scientific American*, 239, pp. 46–55.

M. Midgley (1979) 'Gene-Juggling', *Philosophy*, 54, pp. 439–58.

E. Reed (1979) 'The Role of Symmetry in Ghiselin's "Radical Solution to the Species Problem"', *Systematic Zoology*, 28, pp. 71–8.

J. J. Sepkovski, Jr. (1978) 'A Kinetic Model of Phanerozoic Taxonomic Diversity I', *Paleobiology*, 4, pp. 223–51.

J. J. C. Smart (1963) *Philosophy and Scientific Realism*, Routledge & Kegan Paul, London.

J. J. C. Smart (1968) *Between Science and Philosophy*, Random House, New York.

E. Sober (1980) 'Evolution, Population Thinking, Essentialism', *Philosophy of Science*, 47, forthcoming.

E. Sober (1981) 'Significant Units and the Group Selection Controversy', in *PSA 1980*, Vol. 2, P. Asquith and R. Giere (eds), Philosophy of Science Association, East Lansing, Michigan.

S. M. Stanley (1975) 'A Theory of Evolution above the Species Level', *Proceedings of the National Academy of Science*, 72, pp. 646–50.

G. Stent (1977) 'You Can Take Ethics Out of Altruism but You Can't Take the Altruism Out of Ethics', *Hastings Center Report*, 7, pp. 33–6.

F. Suppe (1974) 'Some Philosophical Problems in Biological Speciation and Taxonomy', in *Conceptual Basis of the Classification of Knowledge*, J. A. Wojciechowski (ed.), Verlag Dokumentation, Pullach/München.

L. Van Valen (1975) 'Group Selection, Sex, and Fossils', *Evolution*, 29, pp. 87–94.

44 *Philosophy of Evolution*

C. H. Waddington (1957) *The Strategy of the Gene*, Macmillan, New York.

M. J. Wade (1978) 'A Critical Review of the Models of Group Selection', *The Quarterly Review of Biology*, 53, pp. 101–14.

E. O. Wiley (1980) *Phylogenetics, the Theory and Practice of Phylogenetic Systematics*, John Wiley & Sons, New York.

G. C. Williams (1966) *Adaptation and Natural Selection*, Princeton University Press, Princeton, NJ.

G. C. Williams (1975) *Sex and Evolution*, Princeton University Press, Princeton, NJ.

M. B. Williams (1980) 'Is Biology a Different Kind of Science?', in *Pragmatism and Purpose*, J. G. Slater, F. Wilson, and L. W. Sumner (eds), University of Toronto Press, Toronto.

W. C. Wimsatt (1972) 'Teleology and the Logical Structure of Function Statements', *Studies in History and Philosophy of Science*, 3, pp. 1–80.

V. C. Wynne-Edwards (1962) *Animal Dispersion in Relation to Social Behaviour*, Oliver & Boyd, Edinburgh.

2 Organismic Evolution and Subject-Object Dialectics

P. Beurton

WHEN looking down at the history of living beings, the multiform crowd of plants and animals and the rich complexity of their adaptive devices, it will be difficult to find a language common to all of them. However, a certain unity exists in that they are all examples of a never ending occurrence of uniquely designed organisms which somehow always defy prediction and yet, once having come into being, fall harmoniously into place with their forerunners. This reveals the intriguing paradox of evolution in which new qualities arise which cannot simply be deduced from existing forms (or nothing would be new about them) and which nevertheless arise from just these forms (or there would be no causality in evolution). Hence, we may simply state: evolution is the origin of the new (and this involves dialectical contradiction).

Anybody will grant this to the philosopher. Normally the scientist will straightforwardly proceed to investigate what evolution implies in his particular field of research. A nineteenth century Darwinian would find variation and selection to comprise the major forces of evolution. Advances in population genetics frequently lead the present-day biologist to consider evolution as a change in the gene pool of a population or as differential reproduction, or he may simply say evolution is the process of mutation and selection.

Now is evolution nothing but this? True, if we dissect organic life with respect to its revolutionary content, we will eventually arrive at nothing but its minute genetic variations and, by inference, we will find that the more successful ones have been gradually gathered up by selection. Population thinking seems to eliminate the main objections originally levelled against Darwin; for instance, that heritable variations occur too seldomly to allow for explanation of the diversity of organic life; or that it would surely be an extreme coincidence if all those

45

minute variations supposed to form the beautifully adapted vertebrate eye were found together. In whatever individual a promising variation may occur, selection will spread it throughout the population in no time. Hence, any individual may accumulate the positive variations of every individual. This is supposed to be why organisms evolve only in populations.

This is what makes it so apt to look upon evolution as if it were nothing but differential reproduction, etc. Therefore, evolution is said to be nothing but the increase in ratio of certain genes, and by this increase we learn that these are the more successful ones. Evolution becomes the proliferation of genes. (Of course, one may intervene, it goes without saying that evolution affects the whole organism. I will ignore this for the moment.) If evolution is nothing but the change of genes in populations, organisms will be there to produce genes. The saying, the hen is only the egg's way of making another egg, becomes quite true. The organism's flesh and blood is thinned down to a meaningless world outside of evolution, to a kind of impersonal ether. There is no longer any intriguing paradox of evolution; it has been explained away. This is the reductionist or analytical position. In this paper it will be referred to as the 'only-genes concept'. The objective here is to contribute towards recovering this paradox.

This picture arises partly because I am selecting only one side of it. There are others. One of particular relevance, which is common knowledge in today's synthetic theory, is the concept of organisms as organic wholes. In fact, everybody agrees that organic diversity comprises more than some twenty amino acids or a handful of nucleotides which ultimately we may attach evolution to in genetic analysis. Organisms as compositionist or organized wholes (where diversity is a consequence of organization) cannot be understood merely in terms of the resultant activities of their independent parts or particles, but only in terms of organization brought about by the interrelations established among these parts.

To begin with, the contribution to evolution of any newly selected mutation is dependent not entirely on itself (if we keep in mind that in genetic analysis a mutation ultimately may be reduced to a mere rearrangement among a handful of nucleotides, or even to a single one of them) but rather on such factors as where the particular amino acid, which now will be coded, is lined up in the protein. The properties of the protein itself do not depend simply on the kinds of amino acids which form the peptide; they are brought about by the sequence or arrangement, that is, the relations at work between the amino acids. The properties of the peptide cannot be reduced to little portions of the same properties leading a home-life in the single genetic sub-units or, ultimately, in each single nucleotide. Similarly, it is well known that genetic recombinations serve the principle of finding out over generations in just what setting a particular gene may be of optimal value to the organism, before being picked up, eventually, throughout the population.

We are quite far from understanding in detail how the cooperation among proteins, enzymes and their substrates produce, say, a vertebrate eye or a living animal. However, if our knowledge were more sophisticated, we would see how these same principles of organization extend continuously from the biochemical sub-units right up to the organism's overallness. Just as the proteins come about through organization, and involve not merely the sum of genetic sub-units they contain, the vertebrate eye can only be understood in terms of the working together of lens, retina, circular and meridional muscles for accommodation, iris etc. In turn, the vertebrate eye, itself being part of the whole organism, can only display its visual qualities in an overall organismic context.

Reference is often made to the concept that organic wholes comprise 'more' than the parts they consist of. It is quite obvious that no single portion of, say, the lens is living inside any one mutation or gene. Any mutation's contribution to evolution depends on its participation in organization, that is, whether this particular mutation shares via this or that genetic recombination in the many in-between steps we do not yet completely appreciate in modification of, say, the vertebrate eye or the bird's wing.

The principle of organic wholes, as a well-known phenomenon, needs no further elaboration by examples. But the principle itself and its implications for evolutionary theory demand further attention. It lends itself to recovering the paradox of evolution, the origin of the new. Newness is organization, in a certain manner, of the rather anonymous genetic particles like nucleotides, genes and, similarly, of proteins and morphological structures which give rise to the hitherto nonexistent, the vertebrate eye or the bird's wing. (Of course, evolution doesn't proceed simply from parts to wholes, but from one kind to another kind of organism, say, from fish to land vertebrate or reptile to bird. However, the newness thereby displayed cannot be traced back to individual properties of numerous genes, but only to them in reorganization.)

With these things in mind, we may inquire how evolution is actually explained away when saying that evolution consists simply in changes in the gene pool. It is precisely by no longer allowing for the properties of the genes to be determined by the relations they establish and enter into that the idea of evolution as an affair of numerous individual genes leads to the elimination of the most essential characteristic of evolution: newness by organization. The assumption, that the bird's wing evolves merely in the form of accumulation of certain genes, indeed does imply that these genes possess the qualities of the bird's wing independently of the relations they establish. The process of becoming of the bird's wing, the realization of its newness in organization, is transformed into the condition of being—in the form of minute portions of it living inside its least particles.

As indicated above, this picture arises partly because I am depicting only this side of it. Though such statements of the only-genes concept are quite common, anybody maintaining them, when accused of being reductionist, will immediately concede: 'I don't actually mean evolution to be nothing but genes. Rather, I believe by the accumulation of genes to explain organismic evolution outside there'. And outside there are the living organisms in all their richness, their intricacy, harmony, complexity, orderliness or organic newness. True, it is this straightforward experience of factual evidence of evolution which any evolutionary concept *supposes* to explain. And yet, we may add, when giving this explanation, that is, when turning from outside reality to theoretical analysis, these features vanish. The organism's flesh and blood has evaporated. Though suggesting by this concept to explain what is beyond genes, reality is not actually captured and vanishes by explanation inside the theory. Thus, there remains a tendency to reduce evolution to genes and nothing but genes.

How then can one recover inside theory what is omitted in analysis? After all, a vertebrate eye is a real material quality in its own right. The notion of evolutionary newness produced through organization of genes, etc. is not merely a kind of verbal reverberation or noise of things out there. Any anatomical or morphological structure is full of 'stuffness'. We should, therefore, see that the parts do not simply enter here and there into different relations and thereby exhibit properties which are transitory. If this were the case, we could be content with viewing the properties as actually belonging to the parts and thus, though granting organization some allowance, there would be no 'stuffness' other than the parts. Rather, the properties without these relations are virtually non-existent. And when the parts establish relations which generate these properties, these properties in turn dominate the parts. The evolutionary nature of genes is non-existent outside the whole. It is not contained in genes that animals evolve. These properties as stable properties which dominate the parts form the empirical 'stuffness' of the whole or, philosophically, its newness. Thus, not only things but relations themselves, in determining things, are material.

Clearly, we would have a very poor evolutionary understanding without knowledge of the activities of the plentiful genes in populations. Thus, reduction or analysis in itself is a very sound method in science as long as its limitations are respected. However, these limitations are no longer respected, and reduction becomes reductionist when we rest content with the assumption that this method actually does explain the overall context of evolution.

Evolutionary thinking implies two steps: first, of dissecting the evolutionary context into abstract entities and thereby making distinct what analytical representation of the outside world does not cover; second, of subjecting this gap to theoretical consideration, that is, the generation of newness or the intriguing paradox of evolution should be recovered in the theoretical context. This makes the theory as dialectical as the outside world. However, rather than making a theory of science I will continue by following up the situation in evolutionary biology.

The tendency towards the only-genes concept receives its

distinctness not when talking about genes but rather in the way it is associated with a specific concept of natural selection. The suggestion that the essential manifestations of evolution are identical with its effects on gene ratios, etc. leads, consistently, to a notion of selection as possessing nothing but a preservative function. So we are frequently told that natural selection is a process which works after the fact and nothing but after the fact.

If we agree, however, that organic wholes essentially consist in combination and organization of their least particles, and that, therefore, they present something new which is beyond their particles in isolation, we are also bound to agree that selection, by combining these particles, itself acts creatively. This may not be immediately obvious, particularly as mutations always occur in individuals. Within individuals selection cannot combine mutations. It can do nothing but preserve or eliminate any one individual. To this extent selection does act after the fact. However, thus favouring the preservation of a particular mutation, it is selection which spreads it throughout the population in a short time by these individuals out-reproducing others in relatively few generations.

If one has in mind the principle of organic wholes, it proves quite insufficient to visualize this spreading merely in terms of multiplication of what otherwise would be there in lesser numbers. This may be readily illustrated by assuming that in different parts of the population different mutations may occur. Then selection, by spreading them in the population, will cause them eventually to overlap and to combine in the same individuals. In fact, any spreading of mutation involves some recombination. So it actually becomes selection which combines them and which thereby may have generated an organismic property inherent to no single one of them. *Selection doesn't act only after the fact, but, by creating newness, in itself produces evolutionary facts.*

This model is quite crude, to be sure. However, it may serve as an indication of how selection, by merely preserving certain genes (and eliminating others) affects the composition of future individuals in the population and thereby takes part in their organization through combination. A recurrent example may be quoted:

. . . the combination of genetic units which carries the hereditary information responsible for the formation of the vertebrate eye could have never been produced by a random process like mutation. Not even if we allow the three billion years plus during which life has existed on earth. The complicated anatomy of the eye like the exact functioning of the kidney are the result of a nonrandom process—natural selection.[1]

Clearly we see the gap between selection as merely preserving random mutations, that is, the mere accumulation of random events and the vertebrate eye you can actually see and touch. This gap is readily bridged by the creative element in selection which organizes the genetic variations by combining them. Looking at selection as a creative force is one step on the way to recovering inside theory the link between analytical presentation and the outside world.

Frequently it will be granted that organic wholes are at work in evolution (and lucid descriptions be given of them), and yet selection will be said to act only after the fact by doing nothing but preserving favourable combinations or wholes as presented in individuals. To repeat: as regards individuals, selection can only preserve or eliminate them and thereby indeed acts after the fact. However, this should not let us fail to appreciate that by preserving a particular individual selection also preserves the particular mutation or gene which distinguishes this individual from others. And by handing it down to future individuals with other genetic settings or, more generally, by favouring some mutations and weeding out others from these lines of inheritance, it actually becomes selection which combines them and thus produces evolutionary facts. If one views this creative element of natural selection in the evolution of organic wholes, there will be no difficulty in seeing that any organic whole, on which selection sets to work by preserving it, is in fact already a product, to some extent, of selection's creative element.

There is another way of trying to allow for the newness in evolution without granting selection more than a preservative function (which I consider rather trivial). We are sometimes reminded of the fact that in the early days of Darwinian theory selection was seen primarily as a means of eliminating the unfit. This picture is then contrasted with the rather self-evident fact that selection also retains the positive variants and thus promotes the evolution of new structures. Clearly, in both cases selection is considered merely working like a sieve and, as long as its combining effect on genes is not seen, it is absolutely irrelevant which side of the sieve you look at.

In conclusion, whoever visualizes evolution basically as a shift in the population's gene ratios, that is, as an accumulation of suitable genes, will ascribe to selection nothing but a preservative function. And he who says: 'Organic wholes are more than the resultant activities of their components in isolation', will also have to say, 'There is a creative element in natural selection'. The former will visualize the actual achievement in population thinking as the understanding of how populations provide the number of genes, mutations, etc. essential to evolution. To the latter, population do not act simply as a gene reserve; another essential element to him is understanding how populations provide for evolution's creativity, in which selection shares as an essential element. This concept is on the way to recovering the intriguing paradox of evolution as an element within theoretical reflection.

Selection is the agent by which evolutionary coordination is accomplished between the animal and the outside world. Clearly, the only-genes concept, by granting to selection merely a preservative effect, will give rise to a different interpretation of the evolutionary significance of this environmental relation than the concept of creative selection derived from the nature of organic wholes. To elucidate these differences, I will use mainly the textbook example of how giraffes acquired their necks when reaching for foliage.

The only-genes concept will take it for granted that the evolution of the giraffe's neck consists solely in the preservation, by selection, of those genetic variations which contribute towards its greater length. They convey a selective advantage by allowing the giraffe to reach for foliage in a more efficient manner. Thus, there is some relationship between the organism and its environment. After all, we are talking about a theory of adaptation, that is, of adaptation to something. So, in a sense, the environment is vital. However, if evolution is restricted essentially to the 'stuffness' of accumulated variations, the tree appears to be merely a kind of boundary condition which, by eliminating some genes and favouring others, streamlines what is there. The tree doesn't actually share in the production of newness.

Quite a different picture arises when visualizing evolution as organic wholes at work, which themselves are organized by natural selection. Anybody who says that selection, by combining genetic variation in the population, creates organic wholes is actually saying that the environment, by selecting certain genes and thereby combining them, plays an essential part in creating these wholes. When saying that selection, by weaving back and forth the mutations and combining them in the population, creates an organic whole such as the giraffe's neck, we may actually risk saying that it is, curiously, the tree weaving back and forth these mutations and combining them into a giraffe's neck. It is the environment which, by selecting certain genes and eliminating others, shares in combining them in such a way as may give rise to the giraffe's neck as an overall property, which does not inhere in little portions in single genes.

But individual genes never simply blur away into the overallness of the organism's properties. They remain real individual genes, genetic variations, etc. on which the environment works by preserving them. However, by preserving them, they are, at once, combined and the environment thereby shares in generating the organism's properties not simply inherent to them. The environment, by sharing in the determination of the specific combination of genes in the long run, also shares in the generation, via these genes, of organismic overall properties. Hence, the environment determines the organism's evolutionary properties, so to say, from its inside outwards; it determines them intrinsically. (This is an important point in the paradox of evolution, the generation of newness.) This intrinsic effect of the environment on organic systems is, I believe, what induces us to refer to evolving systems as 'open systems'.

Now this is a relation, with the environment at the one end and the organism at the other. Needless to say, this open systems concept doesn't imply that organisms are passively subjected to environmental demands. However, this needs explanation. In fact, it is up to the organism to establish a particular environmental relation. And only by the organism establishing certain environmental relations do these in turn generate, via preservation and combination of genetic variations, the organismic properties. The would-be-giraffe, by reaching for the foliage, establishes the foliage as an element in its particular niche, which in turn leads, via organization of genetic variations, to the actual evolution of the giraffe's neck.

Here we can see how Lamarck's idea of use and disuse of organs as a major evolutionary factor may be recovered *within* the Darwinian tradition. To put it somewhat dogmatically: functions do produce organs. If one keeps the environment constant, it is the organism's behaviour which leads to its own evolution. The organism itself decides via the environment how its genes will be combined into evolutionary newness. Hence the role of behaviour as a key factor in evolution. The open systems concept necessitates, at this other end, that behaviour be considered an intrinsic factor in the evolution of organic wholes. It is precisely this intrinsic determination of evolving systems through themselves which induces us to speak of evolving systems as 'subjects'. *Evolving systems are subjects to themselves because they command their own evolution.* Thus, newness is produced by subjects.

It is appropriate here to insert a comment on 'subjects'. Normally, when visualizing subjects in human society or in the animal kingdom, we associate with them psychological or conscious factors. Whoever attempts to explain evolution ultimately by subjective considerations (and this we are doing in a way) thus seems to be resorting to a non-materialist concept. Therefore, it needs emphasis that the 'subject' presented here is one of purely material relation. To repeat: evolving systems are organic wholes; thus the environment via selection determines the organism's properties from its inside out; but it must be kept in mind that the organism's make-up (I will avoid at present the term 'behaviour') determines its environmental relations; thus it is primarily the organism which determines its own properties from the inside out. This suffices to make it a subject. There is nothing essentially psychological about this. We can do without the specific kind of behaviour known to animals and man because it is basically the material make-up of the objects (be it a stone or a tree, which have no psychology, or an animal) which governs the establishment, by the object, of certain material relations to its outside world and thus, in the evolutionary context under discussion, turns these objects (if at all) into subjects. Hence we may reintroduce the term 'behaviour' not merely as a psychological property to refer to any kind of relation determined by organic wholes and which affects their evolution intrinsically. (This way of looking at behaviour may, I believe, solve the problem of how plants as non-psychological species are able to evolve, similarly to animals, through behavioural relations towards different adaptive zones.)

However, this doesn't make psychological factors invalid. Psychology enhances evolution by making behaviour versatile. However, a psychological novelty will introduce a new evolutionary line only if the material conditions (that is, the organism's material make-up and environmental factors) have already been set in a way that the psychological factor proves merely as an extension of these conditions. In conclusion, after having seen that the environment shares in the generation of the organism's newness, we have now arrived back at the organism itself, but no longer merely as the object of gene accumulation, but as a subject which itself generates newness.

Before dealing with the matter of teleology as one more problem involved in the intrinsic relation between organism and environment, we will have another look at the only-genes concept. When one considers only the 'stuffness' of genetic variations, the object of evolution, behaviour (psychological or in the broad sense), remains outside evolutionary interest: with the tree in the background, the giraffe can only stand by and wait for the inches to be added to its neck. This kind of thinking will promptly discard as one more version, new or old, of Lamarckian psychology the suggestion that the giraffe's behaviour is a significant factor in evolution. True, I am depicting, once more somewhat dogmatically, just this side of the picture. During the last three decades increasing attention has been paid to the role of behaviour in evolution. Today it is common knowledge that: 'Changes in behaviour, such as a preference for a new habitat, food, or mode of locomotion may set up new selection pressures. Much evidence indicates that most major evolutionary shifts (the origin of higher taxa) began with a behavioural shift'.[2]

However, it may be that this statement needs qualification. It leaves unanswered the question of whether selection pressure (and thereby behaviour) will merely accomplish preservation of advantageous mutations or, in addition, their recombination. In the case of Mayr an answer may be given as follows:'. . . natural selection is strictly an *a posteriori* process which rewards current success. . . . Natural selection rewards past events, that is the production of successful recombinations of genes. . . .'[3] If one grants selection only a preservative effect, behaviour towards the environment can no longer be visualized as actually sharing in the combination of genetic variations and thereby in the production of newness in the organism. Though behaviour is granted some significance in evolution, it is visualized only as guiding or streamlining evolution as something in which it does not actually share. Though regarded as facilitating evolution, it is not seen as an intrinsic factor.

So I had better not quote this paragraph from Mayr, but rather cite another with which I heartily agree: 'It is evident that the genes which harmoniously interact in the gene pool of a population were brought together by the action of natural selection', and '. . . much integration (of the genotype) occurs at a . . . level, with natural selection its agent. . . .'[4] However, I have difficulty in seeing how this statement harmonizes with the one above.

The concept of organisms in evolution acting as their own subjects and thereby producing newness may be supplemented by the case for a materialist teleology. Teleology is generally associated with the future outcome of processes taking an active part in their own realization. Frequently, we are told, there is no such thing and many authors believe that such a disclaimer will make teleology more fashionable. I will try and indicate that, on the contrary, precisely such an element in teleology is indispensable to evolution.

The organism-environment relationship constitutes evolutionary strategies, that is, something to do with the future of evolution, its possibilities or potentials. If we agree on our way of recovering newness as an object of theory, that the organism's functions or environmental relations do not merely produce a streamlining effect but actually share in generating the organism's qualities, we may argue that there are relative ends in evolution at work in the present. The organism's intrinsic relation towards the environment conditions the end-directedness of evolution. The giraffe's forerunners, in stretching their necks towards the foliage of the tree, are potential giraffes because this relation in the present affects recombination of the genes which therefore leads to such an end. Certain cross-opterygians, when trying in Devonian times to reach overland habitable waterpools, employed their fins in a manner which assisted overland locomotion. That is, they used them as potential limbs. We may argue that these organisms were the first potential land vertebrates, to the extent to which this new environmental relation began to affect recombination of the genes in a way which would ultimately lead to actual limbs and land vertebrates.

If we agree that selection is a creative process, conditioned by the organism-environment relation, then we may also agree that selection is working to relative ends. The widespread notion of selection never working towards an end clearly arises from the idea of selection acting only after the fact and thus the environmental relation having no intrinsic effect on evolution. This leads once more to the only-genes concept, and teleology will be granted nothing but the regulation of gene ratios. Thus there are writers who suggest the rational element of teleology in evolution to be essentially an increase in reproductive efficiency. Once more the egg produces the hen for the sake of producing more and more eggs. (One might ask, incidentally, if an elephant has a higher reproductive efficiency than, say, an amoeba.) If we appreciate the materiality of the environmental relation, that is, that it causes effects, we may be able to appreciate both that the future is 'contained' in this relation and that this relation affects present-day evolution. However, this needs further explanation.

The environment never has the last say in evolution because it is left to the organism to select its environment and thereby to determine the conditions of its own selection. Ultimately, it is the organism which determines its own future. This needs emphasis because, according to the theses of functions producing organs, one may quite readily arrive at the opposite proposition that the future totally determines the organism.

There are conditions which make it difficult to imagine how it could be otherwise: if we consider the terrestrial zone and the Devonian fish swimming in the water, we do know that in a way it is this terrestrial zone which will eventually demand and, in this sense, cause the new behaviour of the animal and the new functions of its organs, and thereby determine its future as a land vertebrate. True, even when having the land zone in mind, we can imagine to some extent the organism selecting its future, because it is up to the organism to actually contact this new kind of zone and to develop a new kind of behaviour. However, the 'decision making' of the fish seems to be reduced to giving 'yes' and 'no' answers. Once having passed (say) a positive decision with regard to the new zone, the fish would have no further influence on its future, but everything would be left to the environment. The outside world would dominate the evolving system and this system would no longer be its own subject in evolution.

The fallacy lies in us projecting *the* land zone into conditions where it isn't present. In order to see why, two things have to be kept in mind; first, any environment may be dissected into its component parts. I don't quite know what the Devonian landscape was composed of, but we may imagine shrubs, pebbles, insects, herbs, sand, humus, etc., as well as components which may be considered accessory factors, such as humidity, intensity of light, wind, temperature, etc. This dissectability is of significance because when an organism begins to occupy a new zone, it will never be immediately confronted with all the components of this zone, but rather with them one by one. The organism can be visualized as composed of features which correspond to environmental components, and when the organism moves into a new environment it selects and assembles the components in accordance with the demands of its own features. Second, it is very important to know that the environment, similarly to the organism, is never composed merely of the sum of its component parts. Sand in humus has a completely different function and as an integral part of humus receives completely different properties from sand, say, in a desert or in wind which forms a sandstorm. Humidity accumulating in the earth may produce a swamp which is completely different from its component parts, which may be a barren stretch and the humidity falling from above which we call rain. True, it is difficult to give convincing arguments for this principle, in the way it may be done for organisms, because the environmental components are in quite loose association. Nevertheless, *the* land zone is only given by its components in interaction (as any ecologist would tell us).

These two things tell us that when, during Devonian times of drought, certain crossopterygians were forced overland in search of water and encountered a component between the pools which we may call a land bridge, neither had the fish taken up contact with *the* land zone nor with a single portion of this zone. As the fish in its own evolutionary context in the first place singled out the land bridge in isolation from other components of the land zone, this component will be, with regard to the fish, independent of the properties it exhibits in contact with the land zone. To the fish the land bridge is just one more component which adds to all those other components which together form the adaptive zone of aquatic organisms. Romer's hypothesis is well known: the land bridge aids the fish in finding its way not into terrestrial life but into an unshrunken pool, that is, its sole significance at the time was as a component in the context of the aquatic zone.[5] The new component is robbed of its newness by being absorbed into the existing environment as a component of this environment. Clearly, we see not only that there is no immediate confrontation with the new environment, but also, when the fish comes across such a component, no instantaneous 'decision' is made to begin assembling components *as* belonging to a new environment.

Looked upon objectively, the land bridge as a single component was originally nothing but a component within the context of water life. However, what this component also contributed to simultaneously was the *possibility*[6] of new components being added to the organism's environment, which by their interaction would determine this one component and themselves together as a new environment, which is 'more' than contained in the sum of its components. Thus, in a way, the new environment is recovered. It follows that whether the single component originally served as an introduction of the new zone, is determined by the future. Looking back at things after the event, we know that the events were such that they determined the land bridge objectively as what we may call the first component of the new zone. This is how the future works on the present—the dialectics of teleology: inside the present the future is *nothing but* the present; in the future this present will be recovered as *determined by* the future.

A precondition for adding new components is that they are present, that is, that they lead some form of existence *independently* of the fish. However, another kind of condition for a particular blend of components by which the environment is recovered is the particular combination of features in the organism. This is why the organism dominates the teleological element. (It is the fish treating the future component as a present one.) Provided some environment is made up of interacting components, different organisms, when entering into it, will recover or recreate it in different ways. That is why reptiles and mammals are able to occupy the same zone. The organism never simply enters into preexisting relations when, say, the fish begins occupation of the terrestrial zone; in addition, it *establishes* relations towards components of this zone and thereby reconstructs the zone outside itself as a material relation towards itself, that is, into a zone affecting its own evolution. This may suffice to indicate a way of solving the problem of how it is that the organism essentially determines its own future though the environment predetermines this future.

Our attempt at recovering the paradox of evolution, the orderly origin of newness, as an object of theoretical consideration has led to conclusions which may be summarized as follows: organisms themselves produce their newness, hence they are subjects. This demands that they turn the outside world as environments into their objects. Evolution or the orderly origin of newness is the interaction of subjects and objects.

Notes

1 F. J. Ayala, 'Teleological explanation in evolutionary biology', *Philosophy of Science*, Vol. 37, 1970, pp. 1–15.
2 E. Mayr, 'Evolution and behaviour', *Verhandlungen der deutschen Zoologischen Gesellschaft*, 64, Jahresversammlung 1970, pp. 322–36.
3 E. Mayr, 'Teleological and teleonomic, a new analysis', *Boston Studies in the Philosophy of Science*, Vol. 14, 1974, pp. 91–117.
4 E. Mayr, *Animal and Species and Evolution*, The Belknap Press, Cambridge, Mass., 1963.
5 A. S. Romer, *Man and the Vertebrates*, Vol. 1, Penguin Books, Harmondsworth, Middlesex, Repr. 1962.
6 P. Beurton, 'Einige Bemerkungen zur Mosaikevolution', *Zeitschrift für geologische Wissenschaften*, Vol. 3, 1975, pp. 539–45.

On the nature of evolutionary theory: Commentaries on Hull and Beurton

U. J. Jensen

DURING the years Hull has made great efforts to formulate the ontology implicit in the theory of evolution. His paper is a continuation of these efforts. However, he has here a more ambitious aim: to design an ontology suitable for those 'who want to formulate widely applicable generalizations about evolution'. He pleads for an ontology of 'replicators, interactors and lineages'.

Hull is still presupposing the same kind of broader ontological framework as in his earlier contributions to philosophy of biology: a framework of individuals placed in a hierarchy of part-whole relations. Hull has been inspired by Dawkins replicator-metaphysics. He tries to place the replicator categories within his broader ontological framework.

Taking into account the 'Aristotelian', dual character of Dawkins' replicator-genes, this might seem an impossible task. Therefore, it is not surprising that Hull is really reinterpreting the Dawkinsian metaphysics to adapt it to his own straight-forward individualistic framework.

'Dawkins exposition is couched . . . in terms of identity of structure', Hull points out.[1] Hull finds that too strong. 'In general, the modification of a single amino acid rarely makes a molecule a new molecule, any more than the few corrections which Darwin made in the second edition of his *Origin of Species* made it a new book'.[2]

It is important to notice Hull's choice of examples. He is comparing the replicators to individuals characterized by a specific structure. This is all right concerning the one aspect of the Dawkins replicators. They are *also* individual molecules. But they are something more than that. They are *universal*. It simply makes no sense to try to lighten his strong identity claim. If Dawkins gives it up, he has given up his whole permanent-gene metaphysics. Could he not simply do *that* without having

61

to change his overall view on the theory of evolution? *No, he could not*. His central metaphysical idea is that organisms are transient, ephemeral (and, therefore, do not count in the theory of evolution). The genes are the *eternal*; the individuals are appearances. The genes—as essence or structure—the reality.

Hull will not accept that metaphysics. He cannot, having already created his part-whole ontological edifice. In his paper it becomes clear that he has only adopted the *terminology* of the replicator-metaphysics. However, he does not accept the fundamental Dawkinsian conceptions. To Hull genes are not the only replicators working in the process of evolution. Organisms— once for all eliminated from the evolutionary ontology by Dawkins—can, according to Hull, function as replicators (in such cases where 'the parents and the offsprings are sufficiently similar to each other').[3] But of course individuals descending from each other are not *one*, they do not have the unity and permanency of the Dawkinsian gene-replicators.

According to Hull, 'Everyone agrees that both genes and organisms are individuals'.[4] However, this is too simple, taking the complex structure of our gene-attributions into account. Giving up the antique metaphysics peculiar to Dawkins does not just lead us to a conception of genes as individuals. The Johannsen-Dawkins metaphysics is, as stressed in my paper, a consequence of an ontological misinterpretation of an important function played by our concept of genes (its classificatory function in experimental contexts). Giving up the misinterpretations is of course not giving up the gene-discourse. We have to understand what often goes wrong in our reflections on that discourse. There is always a risk of making new metaphysical reification. I am afraid that that is what Hull is doing in his part-whole ontology.

Talking about genes (in pre-(mechanism) representing contexts) is attributing certain—hereditary—states to organisms (or groups) presupposing specific experimental conditions. We now get still better and better theoretical models representing the mechanism behind the heredity states and regularities. However, our gene-discourse is rooted in the experimental praxis. We are selecting the objects of experimentation from the complex relationship in which they are imbedded; the objects are in a way fixed relative to the evolutionary process so that we can make them objects of controlled experimental investigations. In population genetics we are, in the same way, making time-slices of the evolving species, analyzing the populations which have been fixed by our mathematical and experimental tools. Dawkins is interpreting experimentally fixed gene-states as being *one and the same continuous gene* of a strange ontological hybrid character. Hull does something different from that. He interprets the genes as *individual replicators* forming a lineage (individual). In exactly the same way as populations, according to Hull, form lineages.

What is a lineage? It is an individual which *evolves*. There are some problems in understanding that point. First, lineages change *indefinitely*.[5] So, what is the meaning of saying that lineages evolve? It seems, in principle, impossible to talk about *one* lineage evolving into *another* lineage. Second, does the concept of a replicator not lose all content when conceived of as a lineage (being able to undergo indefinite change)? Third, how is it at all possible to *construct* the *evolving units* (the lineage) by arranging (in similarity-series) abstractions (the replicator-with-structure; the population in the sense of a time-slice)? The evolving lineages are said to be built up of individuals producing each other (and so being related by descendence relations. A replicator with a specific structure may be *similar* to another, but is it sensible saying that one is *producing* another? Only if the replicators are actual particular molecules. But this they cannot be, since the lineages are sequences of structures with multiple molecular instantiations.

A *time-slice* population may be similar to another but there are certainly not descendence relations between the two (as there are between members in one specified population). The part-whole metaphysics of Hull, therefore, seems to be an attempt at doing the impossible: that is, constructing an ontology of *evolution* by putting together *individuals* after first having experimentally fixed them and pulled them out of the web of evolutionary processes.[6]

It is the same tension between *rearranging the abstractions* and the aspiration of *understanding the evolutionary processes* abstracted from which is so manifest in Mayr's whole biological thinking.[7] A tension between a nominalistic conception of populations (being subject to statistical analyses) and a philosophical programme: *populational thinking* within a categorical framework of collective entities, transcending nominalism and essentialism.

It is exactly that tension which—under the name of dialectics —was a research motive in German philosophy after Kant, a philosophy which, alas, has not yet been presented in a framework and a language adapted to the problems of contemporary science.

Beurton merits our gratitude in making that dialectical tension a main topic in his paper. He states his position very clearly: 'reduction or analysis in itself is a very sound method in science as long as its limitations are respected. However, these limitations are no longer respected and reduction becomes reductionist when we rest content with the assumption that this method actually does explain the overall context of evolution outside there'. That position is very close to the position defended by me in my paper.

Beurton, educated in the German biological and philosophical tradition deeply influenced by, among others, Schindewolff (but also by Mayr and Marjorie Grene), expresses his provocative theory in a language in some respect alien to the Anglo-American debate. Beurton's paper is a rejection of 'the only genes' concept—the view that evolution is nothing but the proliferation of genes. Dawkins is not even mentioned in the paper, and for good reasons: Beurton did not know *The Selfish Gene* when he produced his paper. This only shows once more that Dawkins' theory is not a new invention. It is a well-presented and provocative formulation of an idea which for a long time has loomed large in biology.

Beurton opposes the gene-selection view. So far he is in complete agreement with Mayr (and many other evolutionary biologists). He insists that the environment plays an *important* evolutionary role. So do the genes. The organism—with its phenotypic traits—is a result of the interaction between genotype and environment. So the environment plays a role in determining the survival of the organism.

However, this is not at all the whole story told by Beurton. He interprets the biological facts in a specific philosophical way. Selection is not only a sieve; it not only acts 'after the fact'.

Selection acts creatively, selection organizes 'the genetic variations by combining them'[8] (by preserving a particular individual, selection also preserves the particular mutation or gene
which distinguishes this individual from others). By saying this,
Beurton is hardly doing more than pointing out that even the
sieve-function is, in an evolutionary perspective, creative.
Beurton is, however, thinking of something more far-reaching.
Organic wholes are—in some way or another—*organized* by
natural selection. He discusses the old story about the giraffe's
neck: '. . . the environment gives rise to the giraffe's neck as "an
overall property" (by selecting certain genes, eliminating
others)'.[9]

Lamarckian views have been defended sporadically in recent
years.[10] Here we seem to have a bold uncompromising
Lamarckian position. Let us take a look at the problems.
Lewontin sums up 'the modern view of adaptation' in these
words: '. . . the eternal world sets certain "problems" that
organisms need to solve . . . evolution by means of natural
selection is the mechanism for creating these solutions'.[11]

To Lewontin, the adaption is *a gradual process* (the end result
is the state of being adapted). Though he speaks of *the organism*
becoming more and more adapted, it is quite clear that his
adapting subject is collective (a population) (e.g. as a region
becomes drier because of progressive changes in rainfall
patterns, plants may respond by evolving a deeper root system
or a thicker cuticle on the leaves).[12] Furthermore, it is clear that
the adaptive change presupposes that *the gene pool of the plants*
in question contains genetic variation for root length or cuticle
thickness, and that there is enough genetic variation so that the
species can change as fast as the environment.

Apparently Beurton is claiming something more than—or
something different from—that. His speaking of the 'newness'
of the organized whole gives the impression that the organizing
cannot be as gradual an affair as it is to Lewontin. One wonders
if Schindewolff's idea of *Baupläne* coming into existence during
the evolutionary process is lurking in Beurton's creative
wholism.

Beurton usually speaks about *the* organic whole (e.g. *the*
would-be-giraffe). If that is serious, his view would be irrecon-
cilable with the view presented by Lewontin. It might, however,

be just an expression of terminological rashness. At one place he really makes it clear that it is a *collective* ('the giraffe forerunners') which is adapting.[13]

He does not mention at all the important condition of adaptation mentioned by Lewontin: the gene pool of the population must contain a specific genetic variation necessary for the change. However, nothing in his presentation seems to exclude his accepting that condition.

Whatever unclarities there may be in Beurton's argument, he seems to be defending a view close to the crucial point *defended by Lewontin: adaptation is a real phenomenon*.[14] To Lewontin, this means the following:

It is no accident that fish have fins, that seals and whales have flippers and flukes, that penguins have paddles and that even sea snakes have become laterally flattened. The problem of locomotion in an aquatic environment is a real problem that has been solved by many totally unrelated evolutionary lines in much the same way.

To Beurton, the reality of adaptation seems to be interpreted in a somewhat different way. Organisms are acting 'as their own subjects'; 'the organism determines its own future'.[15] Any organism is—to Beurton—an organic *whole*, something over and above the sum of the parts. The parts are organized in a specific way. Beurton's conclusion seems to be, there must be *something* doing the organizing work.

If this is Beurton's view he comes close to the position (which he, however, does not really defend) that there is *one principle of organization*, specific to any organic whole, *governing* the coming-to-be of the organisms. Lewontin, on the other side, certainly does not commit himself to such a view. Taking the materialist attitude presented by Beurton into account, he can hardly swallow all the consequences of that kind of holism. All a biologist needs to believe is that disorganized quasi-wholes are eliminated by their actual environment to explain why those that survive are organized. No extra principle is required.

Notes

1 Hull, this volume, p. 32.
2 *ibid.*, p. 32.

3 *ibid.*, p. 34.
4 *ibid.*, p. 35.
5 *ibid.*, p. 41.
6 Jörgen Ringgård has criticized Hull on this and related points in an unpublished monograph on biological classification (Aarhus, 1979).
7 My paper, this volume, p. 14 ff.
8 Beurton, this volume, p. 50.
9 Beurton, this volume, p. 53.
10 see e.g., though the term 'Lamarckism' is still regarded as a term of abuse.
11 *Scientific American*, September 1978, p. 159.
12 *ibid.*
13 Beurton, this volume, p. 57.
14 *Scientific American, op. cit.*, p. 169.
15 Beurton, this volume, p. 57.

PART II

The Transition from the Biological to the Social

3 The role of stage models within a theory of social evolution, illustrated by the European witch craze

R. Döbert

Abstract: After shortly touching upon the controversy between synchronic and diachronic approaches in the social sciences the following article tries to throw some light on the role of stage-models within a more encompassing theory of socio-cultural evolution. Although evolutionary stage-models do not aim at explaining why and by what mechanisms societies actually evolve at all it can be shown that they must form at least an integral part of any dynamic explanation. In order to demonstrate this point, some of the basic facts concerning the genesis and course of the European witch craze will be discussed.

I. Theoretical considerations

1. *Synchrony-diachrony, evolving and non-evolving subsystems*

Due to the functionalists of the early decades of our century diachronically oriented theorizing became more and more marginal in sociology—at least in the non- or anti-Marxian part of the tradition. Functional theories tried to reconstruct the working of social systems within a radical synchronical perspective: social institutions, beliefs and practices must be understood as arrangements which exist in their concrete form because they thus contribute to the fulfilment of certain basic functions or (partly universal) functional prerequisites, to jobs which must get done in societies. It was even argued that one cannot learn anything by studying a given phenomenon diachronically: if the phenomenon investigated still exists it must—according to this line of reasoning—still fulfil the same function as at the time of its origin. But then we can understand its role within the whole system by studying that system

71

synchronically. If, on the other hand, it has changed its function, it can only have a surface resemblance to the mother institution; closer inspection will reveal that the respective practice has changed to fulfil its present function adequately. So we are not studying the same phenomenon and the new phenomenon can very well be understood without recourse to the forerunner institutions. Of course, this description of the functionalists' position carries it somewhat to extremes but on the whole it does not miss the point. And today we still have to deal with the consequences of the polemics of the early functionalists against diachronical approaches. Although the balance between diachrony and synchrony has shifted some-what in favour of diachronical theories, there is still a sort of bifurcation between the two types of theorizing. Structuralist approaches have their emphasis on the synchronic aspects, historical materialism concentrates on the diachronic aspects, and structural-functional or system-theories reproduce the dichotomy usually by a bifurcation of theorizing within their frames: there is an analysis of the (synchronic) input-output relations between the society and its environment on the one hand, and—for the diachronical and somehow more global questions—one constructs theories of social evolution on the other hand. This bifurcation of theorizing seems to be unsatis-factory. Would it not be much more elegant to reduce the diachronic to the synchronic in such a way, that the course of history is disentanged as a simple series of synchronically explained events? But this strategy would not lead to a theory of social evolution, because the knowledge of the whole series would not add anything to our understanding of the single events. The diachrony is in theories of this type virtually superfluous. This contrasts strongly to what the theories of evolution somehow always have claimed. One of the central tenets of theories of this type holds that the synchronic explanations somehow are supported by diachronical know-ledge. Has one to decide for or against one of these diachronic alternatives? Probably not! The point is that the two types of approaches are more than the result of different analytical perspectives or even misdirected theorizing: they correspond to different types of change in reality.

Consider for instance changes in the pattern of distribution of railway-stations and tracks over a given country! If there are many stations closed now in Germany, this can satisfactorily be explained by recourse to changes in the economy (synchronic explanation). Since such a decision influences the conditions under which later decisions concerning the structure of the railway system are being made, there is still the need for a diachronic explanation, the sort of diachronic explanations, with which historians (usually being opposed to theories of social evolution) are mainly concerned. We are dealing with a series of interconnected decisions. But although there may be meaningful questions to be asked concerning the long run change of railway systems nobody would try to tackle this sort of change in terms of an evolutionary paradigm. This because when we speak of evolutionary changes, we do not have in mind simply change over time, but directed change (toward adaption, differentiation, more complexity and so on). The distribution of railway-stations and tracks over the country is too much dominated by external (for instance economic) variables to have a directed history of its own. Phenomena which are totally dominated by other variables are just one example for a type of historical change which does not lend itself to an evolutionary analysis. There are evidently other areas of social life in which evolutionary theories would be misleading. There seem to be cycles of language-transformation (many-few-many grammatical forms) but there is no evolution of languages in the sense that one could say that the languages of modern societies are more highly developed, better working instruments for communication, than the language of any primitive tribe. In the same way it seems to be inadequate to look for evolutionary trends on the level of elementary human behaviour. Initiating communication, forms of address, ways of maintaining distance, clarifying misunderstandings in talk, turn-taking etc. seem to be well developed in all types of societies. These ingredients of social life belong probably to the constitutive factors of social interaction, they are 'too basic', correspond to problems too fundamental to exist in a 'primitive' form.

There are other areas of social life where an evolutionary paradigm seems to be indispensible: the development of techniques of organization and domination, the legal system, technology and the economy are relevant examples. In all these cases it seems to make sense to say, that *society has learned to solve given problems in a better or more efficient way.*

2. *Former deficiencies of theories of socio-cultural evolution and the costs of their removal*

If the different approaches deal with different phenomena or variables there should be no need for any controversy. But there has been quite a lot of controversy. To the extent that there have been polemical debates, they could result only from misapplications of the theoretical paradigm. And indeed there have been misapplications. Nineteenth-century theorists constructed stage models of the evolution of societies or identified long range evolutionary trends, and in doing so very often believed that they had given an answer to the question 'What happened why in history?'. They furthermore reconstructed the history of mankind very often in terms of a *few* stages, without giving sufficient reasons for the fact that there are just these few stages and why there should be stages at all. Evolution could very well have progressed gradually without any dramatic, stage-like transformations. Even the modern system theoretical paradigm (undercomplex systems fighting against complexity in the environment) does not necessarily imply the concept of a stage-like progression, although it is easy to construct stages by recourse to the concept of 'differentiation'.

By now these theoretical misunderstandings have largely been clarified: we have better stage descriptions today and nobody claims that the construction of evolutionary stage models provides the solution of the problem of evolutionary mechanisms or gives an answer to the question why any system developed at all.

Thus, we seem to have to come to the conclusion that the old controversy between synchronists and diachronists (including the reductionist diachrony) simply vanishes once one realizes that the two models pertain to different variables and that there is no need for any polemics if the competing models are adequately applied and restricted to their proper range of validity.

However, this seemingly simple solution had its price. It implies that the stage models of social evolution renounce the claim to add anything to our understanding of dynamics and leave us with the question: for what purpose do we need them at all? Furthermore, we have to introduce into the theory of social evolution a second element, which fulfils the function of explanation: One has to elaborate a theory of evolutionary mechanisms as the necessary complement to the static stage models and to the (purely descriptive) identification of evolutionary trends. And in doing this one is again confronted with the dichotomy between diachronic approaches (the stage models) and synchronic models (the evolutionary mechanisms), only that one reproduces this bifurcation within the theory of social evolution itself. So we are left with an utterly unsatisfactory state of affairs: in contrast to biology whose theory of evolution consists mainly in the specification of the evolutionary mechanism (mutation, selection and stabilization of traits) and where stage models or the identification of long range trends of evolution never played any essential role, the social sciences concentrate in their effort to construct a theory of social evolution mainly on stage models or on evolutionary trends and have little to say about the mechanisms which are the motor of evolution. This situation is of course unacceptable in the long run, since we want to know how evolutionary trends come about and why there are just these stages of evolution. The answer to these questions must in the last instance be found in the theory of evolutionary mechanisms. Therefore one seems to have to conclude, that the social sciences not only concentrate their effort on a theoretical paradigm which is of little use (the stage models), but that they even proceed in the false logical order: only by specification of evolutionary mechanisms can we gain an understanding of evolutionary trends or stages, the synchronic should give us the key to the diachronic. In this way the bifurcation between synchronic and diachronic approaches, which cannot be the last word, would be overcome.

3. *The role of stage models in the social sciences as contrasted to biology*

But there are—and to show this will be one aim of the rest of the chapter—good reasons for social scientists to proceed in a different manner than biologists and to be preoccupied with the

construction of stage models of social evolution before beginning to specify evolutionary mechanisms in detail. In this
respect the intuitions of former theorists were not totally
misdirected.

3a. *A practical motive.*   Of course there are not only theoretical
motives behind this preoccupation. A practical motive is also at
work. Stage models have a very longstanding tradition. In times
of societal crises or under conditions of anomy, uncertainty or
rapid social change, people very often tried to define their
position in the stream of events by constructing stage models of
the evolution of the world order or just the social order (golden,
silver, iron ages etc.). These stage models had an internal logic
which allowed people at least to think that certain events have
come to an end, that certain events will definitely take place and
perhaps that their own suffering is a necessary precondition for
the better time to come. This practical motive probably is also at
work today—the rapidly growing interest in theories of social
evolution would be made more comprehensive by this practical
motive than by purely theoretical reasons. But this does not tell
the whole story; theoreticians usually follow their practical
motives only if they have sound theoretical arguments for their
proceeding as well.

3b. *Theoretical motives: The organization, transmission and
transformation of meaning, and the stage model.*   On the deepest
level, these theoretical reasons have to do with the differences
between biological and social systems and their different ways of
transmitting the information, which is necessary for the respective systems to survive in their environments. Biological
systems are based upon the genetic code, which is realized by
chemical devices in each individual organism. These chemical
devices are characterized by a small probability of generating
errors in the process of self-reproduction (mutations) which
make new forms of life possible. Once a new form of life has
come into being we find a new form of interrelationship between
organism and environment which has, so to say, destroyed the
mode of being of the forerunner systems: the organism cannot
go back to former modes of functioning. Even mutations seem
to be affected by a device, which excludes regressions. For

instance, there seem to be no cases of warmblooded animals becoming coldblooded again by mutation.

The mechanisms, by which social systems store, transmit and 'mutate' information differ in both respects from their biological analoga: information is here stored and transmitted through a collectively shared socio-cultural tradition, that is through systems of meaning. And mutations are here produced through a very flexible entity, the human mind, which is flexible enough to adopt any form of action or orientation if it fits the given constellation of interests, even if that form of action corresponds to a former level of sociocultural evolution. The very possibility of regressing to a former mode of thinking arises from the medium of information transmission itself. It is an essential characteristic of meaning that the fixation of a given meaning does not destroy other meaningful possibilities. A given meaning is always embedded in a horizon of more and possibly different meanings. And to this horizon belong even former levels of the socio-cultural tradition. Usually we do not think any more in terms of a teleological world view, but we *can* very well understand and think in terms of such an orientation system, under specific conditions we may even 'regress' to such a mode of thinking. We may believe that this way of thinking is wrong, but it is for us not totally inaccessible. This alone would make regressions within socio-cultural evolution much more probable than in biological evolution.

When one furthermore takes into account that in the field of social action the mechanisms of mutation and selection are not totally independent, since people do not produce innovations randomly but oriented to given problems, and that some of these problems seem more effectively manageable by the orientation patterns of former modes of thinking, regressions become even more probable. To give just one example for this abstract argument: magical religion is usually thought to represent a more 'primitive' stage of religious evolution than for instance ethical religion. But for farmer populations a magical religion would be much more functional than an ethical one. What farmers need most is weather magic—a form of religious action which is usually banned once an ethical religion has become dominant. But no ethical religion has succeeded totally in eradicating magical practices—they are too 'functional' for certain sectors of the population. Socio-cultural evolution, which is usually written as the history of increasing betterment, could as well be written as the history of an increasing burden of the costs of evolution. In progressing to new levels of organization and thinking usually losses have been incurred which could not be compensated by the new orientation patterns (all particularistic commitments which have been backed by family-, clan- and different sorts of local gods still exist, but do not find any place in high religions). All things considered, the flexibility of the human mind, the ongoing effectiveness of former patterns of orientation and the functional losses which accompany evolutionary progress, one can only conclude that it must be very surprising when one finds in the history of mankind evolutionary trends at all instead of a continuous moving backward and forward under the pressure of changing functional imperatives. To a certain degree this is exactly what one observes. Indeed, in the history of mankind we do observe not only regressions to an extent which seems to have no parallel in biological evolution, but we also have to acknowledge that newly institutionalized orientation patterns never come to dominate social systems totally: there are always social niches and substructures in which older orientation patterns are still effective (see for instance the religious fundamentalism of our time).

But even the flexible human mind, operating within broad horizons of meaning, has to follow its own laws of functioning, which are laws of rationality. The concept of a stage sequence of development or evolution tries to formulate some of the insights into the growth and organization of knowledge which have been gained by the cognitivistic tradition in the sciences of man (Piaget, Kohlberg). Despite the fact that this theoretical programme has been carried through most successfully within ontogenetic research (cognitive development is best understood; role taking, moral development and ego development are newer focuses of research), its range of validity is not restricted to ontogenesis: problems of the integration and coordination of actions are problems which have to be solved on the social (or societal) level as well. Social institutions, roles, norms, principles are just ways of coordinating interaction: And in all world views (*Weltbilder*) and belief systems people have—more often implicitly than explicitly—constructed images of man, of society, of the world order, and of the ways man can act on the world and interact in the world. Although one should not expect a strict parallelism between ontogenesis and phylogenesis, because social systems work under different functional imperatives than do personality systems, there is enough overlap between the two fields to expect at least formal similarities. So it seems worthwhile to try to find out if the concept of a stage sequence is of any use when one tries to reconstruct the evolution of societies. In working with this model one assumes that certain aspects of the history of mankind can be conceived as a learning process, a process of increasing equilibration, which tends toward the full 'realization of a structure'—a state of affairs in which all kinds of information can be handled without cognitive inconsistencies and in which a given problem can be tackled in a most efficient way. One furthermore assumes that the whole process of evolution has not to be conceived as a gradual progression, but as a discontinuous sequence of organizing principles. This assumption of a stage-like progression is an implication of the striving for consistency of thinking. In this respect the stage constructions are therefore cognate to Max Weber's ideal types. They imply that single components of a belief system or organizational pattern cannot be changed without repercussions on the other components of the system. If, for instance, the individual becomes responsible for his/her religious faith and if it is the individual who has to interact with god on his/her own account, it becomes difficult to restrict the range of validity of a religious belief system to a single tribe—individualism entails universalism. Or if the supernatural powers are conceived as spontaneously acting persons, which can grant and deny their favours, the form of religious action has to be adapted to a new state of affairs: magical enforcements have to be changed to prayer.

The stages are in this model conceived as qualitatively different structured wholes, which follow one another in an invariant sequence since the stages are interrelated in a hierarchical way: later ones presuppose former ones and integrate them into more complex modes of functioning. At the same time the later stages are so to say motivationally superior:

In analyzing the genesis of a structure one recognizes immediately after the full realization of that structure, that there are modifications in the behaviour of the subject, which one can hardly explain in a different way but through the full realization or 'closure' of that structure itself. These are basic facts, which manifest themselves within the consciousness of the subject in a feeling of obligation or of normative necessity and in the comformity to these rules.

(Piaget 1973, p. 225.) This theorem of motivational superiority of later stages has one important implication: Regressions to former stages of evolution—though always possible—become improbable. To put it somewhat differently: we have reason to assume that when a given social 'mutation' has to be categorized as a regression, we immediately expect to find, on closer inspection of the system, that it is at the moment working under strong stress.

3c. *Functions of the stage model within the frame of a theory of socio-cultural evolution*   Now let us suppose that this paradigm is in principle valid. What would be its position within a theory of socio-cultural evolution? Two points seem to be relevant here: first the stage model is the counterpart of those chemical devices which prevent regressive mutations on the biological level. Because of the 'motivational superiority' of later stages regressions are at least partially precluded. And some device to fulfil this function has to be built into the evolutionary mechanism. Otherwise the accumulation of 'learning' would be incomprehensible. But inherent to this counterpart is all the precariousness which is characteristic for the 'cultural code' as opposed to the genetic code. The alternatives and former levels of evolution are not 'destroyed', but are just deemed to be 'worse', 'false', 'outmoded' or somehow contrary to the rules— and this only as long as the system can 'afford' to work according to its own standards of rationality. The second implication concerns the relationship between the stage models and the theory of evolutionary mechanisms. Evidently, if there are really structures whose evolution is subject to a 'logical' sequence of stages in the sense defined, one would have to take into account the stage order of 'social mutation' in analyzing the process of selection of variants: all structurally primitive solutions to a given problem are so to say underprivileged; stable innovations lie on a given level of rationality or on the next level of rationality, even if more primitive solutions would be more functional in the given situation. The true belief or better organizational pattern is preferred, even if its costs are high. This implies that one has to have an adequate structurally defined static stage model in order to come to an adequate dynamic explanation. Under these conditions the preoccupation of social scientists with evolutionary stage models would be a *necessary* first step for the explanation of transitions.

Further, there are good reasons to believe that a theory of socio-cultural evolution will be incomplete as long as one can say no more about evolutionary mechanisms than what is trivial: that people try to find new solutions when old ones do not work any more. The problems into which archaic societies run, and the way they solve these problems (if they find a solution at all), differ from the problems and ways of solving problems which are characteristic of modern societies. We have to spell out these details and differences and that is to say that on the socio-cultural level we have to specify stage-specific mechanisms of 'mutation' and 'selection'. To do this, we have to have at least a vague idea about how to delimit the stages; again the synchronic presupposes the diachronic. This line of reasoning can be strengthened by a more elaborate conceptualization of regressions. What follows can be read as a first attempt to construct a theory of regressions which is tied back to some of the assumptions which form the basis of the stage model.

4. *Accounting for regressions*

4a. *The problem* So far I have tried to hint at some of the reasons which may be responsible for the interest which stage models of social evolution or theories of evolutionary trends have found in the social sciences. In doing this, I had to go back to some of the peculiarities with respect to which the cultural code differs from the genetic code. This led to the idea of the stage model. In one respect the stage model can be read as a more detailed version of the theorem so that on the level of socio-cultural evolution the processes of selection and mutation are intermeshed: later forms of social interaction and orientation are preferred because they are 'better' and the stage models try to reconstruct the aspects in which the later forms are better. Since people try to find better solutions to given problems and tend to favour these solutions once they have found them; the process of mutation is governed by the selective pressure of the 'environment', that is the given problem. One 'invents' only 'mutants' which are 'acceptable' solutions to the problem. Little can be said on regressions within this paradigm: *ceteris paribus* they should not happen. The *ceteris-paribus* clause contains 'stress' and stress is an external factor which has to be explained in terms of other theories. This purely negative way of referring to regressions has again and again led to the argument that this type of theorizing should be dismissed, since it is too loosely connected to the real course of human history, which is full of stagnation and regressive processes.

It would be too defensive to rush over this argument simply by stating that one shouldn't expect a theory to produce results which it is not designed to produce. The most defensive way of reacting to an argument is usually the least satisfactory one. Therefore I will try to show in the following part of the article that even the static theories of social evolution can throw some light on social regressions. Of course one cannot expect to deduce a concrete course of social events from the theory. What one can at best hope to accomplish is to present some additional guidelines for ordering the historical data. In order to do that I will again depart from some peculiarities of socio-cultural evolution as opposed to evolution on the biological level. The aim of this analysis is to identify sources of stress and the forms of channelling that stress.

4b. *The dangers of differentiation*   One difference of central importance consists in the fact, that on the biological level each individual organism inherits and is automatically endowed with the species-specific information. In contrast the socio-cultural tradition is a collectively shared sediment of past experiences, which has to be learned by the individuals during their socialization. This difference of passing significant information from generation to generation opens up a new way of accumulating and transmitting experiences, namely specialization and the monopolizing of knowledge and knowledge production by specialists, a device, which of course speeds up the pace of evolution. New stages of socio-cultural evolution in one respect may be marked by new levels of differentiation of knowledge. But differentiation has to be balanced by integration and therefore, even in highly differentiated social systems, we find orientation patterns which are shared by all. People have to have common ideas of what an action is, how motives and consequences are to be taken into account in reacting to transgressions of norms, under what conditions an action is attributed to an actor, how intended and unintended actions are to be taken into account, how the individual actor is to be related to different sorts of collectivities and perhaps even to different parts of the world order, what types of action are to be allowed vis à vis the different regions of reality etc. ... Religion usually appeals to all members of a society. In trying to reconstruct the history of religious evolution one has, therefore, to deal exactly with the qualitatively different ways of interrelating these components of the action space to (from stage to stage new) structured wholes. And even when the production and transmission of knowledge increasingly becomes monopolized by specialists, their activity and their way of approaching reality has to be legitimized and—in a way—controlled within the frame of the commonly shared world view. People do not have to know the details of legal rules or juridical doctrines, but what they have to share with the lawyers are norms like: 'Self-help is the wrong way of reacting to injustice'! 'Another should not be punished, when I have committed a crime'! 'Sometimes one must even obey bad laws'! And: 'The right way to deal with bad laws is to change them according to established procedures'! People need not be acquainted with the mass of knowledge of the natural sciences but what they have to share with the natural scientists are some meta-assumptions. The disenchantment of the world had to be shared by scientists and by non-scientists—otherwise technical interventions into the course of nature would not be permissible. One cannot disturb the gods! One has to share with scientists the view that theories are not part of a holy tradition, which came down to humanity by revelation, but that they are merely products of human beings, and they can and have to be improved. In the same way non-scientists have to share with scientists a certain sort of elementarism. If we did not believe that variables and systems can be isolated, we could not dare to intervene in nature at all. Thus the segmentation between the activities and the knowledge of the specialists on the one hand and the common stock of knowledge on the other has its limits; there is an interlocking, a sort of control between the two regions of consciousness. But one has to recognize that this common denominator of specialists and everyday knowledge is a rather weak form of integration since it leaves to the specialists much free play to be safe from the harmful consequences of their own experimentation. Differentiation and the monopolizing of knowledge by specialists is one of those precarious evolutionary achievements, which may have their costs. Since the specialists are very often far away from the consequences of their new 'inventions' it may—as happens very often, e.g. with new laws—take quite a lot of time until dysfunctional new arrangements get set right. If higher stages imply more specialization, they imply a higher possibility of unchecked faulty experimentation of experts. And this may be a source of considerable stress.

4c. *Transmission of messages—transmission of codes and its costs*
The next argument may best be approached by a short consideration of the different forms of human learning. There is learning through association, through reinforcement, through imitation and there is finally structural learning. Through the first three modes of learning one learns concrete pieces of behaviour, whereas in structural learning one learns a new strategy for producing all sorts of behaviour. In one respect there is thus an analogy between the first three mechanisms of learning and the genetic endowment of an organism. This can be interpreted as a bundle of concrete messages, which is transformed into a new set of messages through a given mutation. In the same way association, reinforcement and imitation transform a given behavioural repertoire through isolated pieces of information: 'This event goes together with that one!' (association), 'Going that way leads to the goal!' (reinforcement), 'This is a way of behaving as well!' (imitation). These mechanisms operate, like mutations, on the level of messages, not on the level of a code. But exactly in this respect socio-cultural evolution seems to differ from biological evolution. New stages of

evolution seem to be characterized not only by more bits of knowledge about the physical or social world, but also by different ways of processing information and of producing new forms of behaviour under changing circumstances. The world is not interpreted any longer as a field of the actions of gods, but as an interplay of mechanical forces. Legal disputes are no longer decided by ordeal, but by very complicated formal procedures. Thus, structural learning concerns not concrete messages, but codes and rules for arriving at concrete messages.

Learning on the level of codes implies much more adaptive flexibility than learning on the level of messages, since codes can and must be applied and in the process of application one can react to different and changing circumstances. But the right application is nothing which is guaranteed. On the contrary! Right applications must be learned by trial and error, they cannot just be deduced. The institutionalization of new social regulations, especially the transition to a new stage of evolution is usually accompanied by a long phase of experimentation, during which one tries to find out how the new orientation pattern has to be implemented in such a way, that social friction is minimized. The institutionalization of the principle of individualism is perhaps a good example for the problem: all individualistic societies are still searching for a proper balance between the individualism and principles of the collective welfare or social solidarity.

If one adds to this difficulty of finding the right application of given principles the previously mentioned fact that the innovating experts are usually not immediately affected by the consequences of their experimentation, one can expect a considerable amount of social friction during transitional phases. So again socio-cultural evolution proceeds in a much more flexible and adaptive way, but this difference of the medium of evolution has its costs: the evolving societies have to carry the burden of 'mismutations' themselves, it is not left to the eliminated inefficient mutants. This circumstance may partly explain why the internal problems of societies are at least as important for the dynamics of social evolution as the difficulties in coping with the external environment; societies do not primarily undergo crises because they have difficulties in coping with nature but because there are no stable solutions for their internal problems. One of the reasons for this circumstance may lie in the risks the correct application of the new codes involves. The possibility of misapplications of a new code constitutes a source of stress.

4d. *Probability of misapplications*   In the next steps of reasoning it has to be clarified under what conditions misapplications become highly probable, under what conditions they take a regressive direction and which type of symbolic organization will be chosen for the regressive variants.

The problem of a heightened probability of misapplications may perhaps best be approached by a short look at the sociology of Max Weber. He has tried to reconstruct the history of the European societies as a process of increasing rationalization. The difficulty one has in understanding this global trend of European history lies in the fact that—as Weber himself has emphasized—all aspects or components of the action space may be rationalized and that the rationalization of different aspects of this space may lead into totally different directions. But how could something like a global trend toward rationality then assert itself? Would one not have to expect that different processes of rationalization would cancel one another out, stagnation being the result? But there is one way to circumvent this cancelling: the possibility of differentiation. And differentiation has indeed been used by social systems just as by biological systems to increase adaptive capacities. As Weber has clearly recognized, differentiation may in the long run lead to a renewed and now perhaps even more intricate problem of integration of the different aspects of rationality, but it seems that it can keep this problem of integration latent for long periods of time. Regarding functions or action problems differentiation means that one tries to deal with each function separately, tries to find the best strategy for dealing with just one given problem of action: It means on the level of symbol systems that one establishes different regions of meaning, different languages for the various spheres of life. It means on the level of social organization that communities of specialists are set up. These communities try to improve the codes for dealing with their problems and to find the right applications of the codes. As long as they care and have to care only for their special problem they can rationalize the respective subsystem. But they will produce misapplications of their code when they are too much influenced by 'external' forces. Religious belief systems usually had to distort their own logic of functioning when they got too much involved with political power, science degenerates to ideology when external interests intrude, the legal system is paralyzed when it becomes exclusively an instrument of oppression in the hands of the prevailing power structure. To put it in a more general way: systems which are functionally overburdened or which are 'overdetermined' since the interests of too many groups are involved, operate under conditions which lead to a distortion of their own criteria of rationality, that is to misapplications. This statement may be valid for biological systems as well, but for social systems the dangers of malfunctioning seem to be especially strong. The specialists, being under pressure, know which 'mutations' have a chance to survive in the given situation and the structure of symbolic codes allows for enough flexibility to direct their application 'appropriately'.

4e. *Probability of regressive misapplications*   If the probability of misapplications is increased when systems are overdetermined, under what conditions are regressive misapplications favoured?

There is first the general factor of 'stress' and friction in the social system. We find a deterioration of functioning especially when 'stress' is experienced as a menace to the sheer survival of the respective system. More highly developed social arrangements usually imply less immediate goal gratification and rest on more indirect and complicated strategies of handling problems. Wrongs cannot immediately be righted by the victims, the king cannot rectify an unjust law by a simple decision, salvation cannot be gained by participation in a ritual, etc. Under stress the temptation grows to regress to more immediate forms of goal gratification and to abandon the complicated procedures, which have evolved during the course of social evolution. The factor of stress constitutes the most important source of regressions. Secondly, the possibility is to be taken into account that the balance of power between various groups which adhere to orientation patterns of different evolutionary levels, changes. Above I briefly indicated that the institutionalization of more highly developed patterns of orientation and interaction never reaches all groups of a society. Former modes of orientation very often survive among minorities (in principle the same type of analysis can be applied to progressive movements). If some of these minorities happen to gain more and more influence, the dominant more highly developed system has to find some form of compromise. Regressive adaptations may be the result of this pressure to compromise. The concessions which missionaries have to make when they try to inculcate their beliefs into the consciousness of a population which adheres to a more archaic religion, is a case in point. Finally, one has to consider the costs of evolution. If it is true that in the course of evolution normative or cognitive codes increasingly lose the capacity to fulfil certain functions, then the following hypothesis has some plausibility: if a constellation of social forces happens to emerge in which the fulfilment of a neglected function becomes very urgent, a strong tendency toward regressive adaptations will result. The situation will be aggravated when at the same time the functional successor of an older action pattern is called into doubt or abolished. To give an instance, let us consider the control and manipulation of the weather. Weather magic works best, since it forces nature to obey one's will. To gods who are conceptualized as persons being able to grant or deny favours, one can only pray and hope that the prayer is heard. This is bad enough, and when the weather does not change for a long time according to one's will there is a strong temptation to fall back on weather magic. Apparently this temptation grows when the conceptualization of gods changes in such a way, that prayers for such concrete favours as good weather are deemed improper.

4f. *The form of regressive adaptations: Substantial and formal rationality* In concluding the more abstract part of this chapter I will try to work out one implication of the stage model (or of a theory of increasing rationalization) for the mould into which regressive inventions are cast or—perhaps more precisely —behind which they hide their regressive character.

As indicated above, the whole process of rationalization has many aspects. One way of grouping these various aspects of rationalization is to distinguish between formal and substantial innovations. A new code usually involves a new content, that is a conception of what type of entities are constitutive for reality, what sort of interrelations connect these entities, which regions of reality have to be discerned from one another and to be dealt with by different models, what types of action are allowed or prescribed, what sort of motives are characteristic for human beings, etc. In sum, new codes entail a new description of the world order and of the problems with which human societies have to deal. A given statement or arrangement is *materially rational* when it conforms to the basic assumptions of the respective world-views.

But at the same time we find a new way of organizing and interrelating the statements or actions which are basic or derivative components of the new code. Max Weber has dealt with these facets of the whole process of rationalization under keywords like systematization and formal rationalization. Systematization refers mainly to the growing capacity to handle abstract terms and deductive relationships and to eliminate inconsistencies between the various regions of thinking and between the many statements within one region. In the same way formal rationality does not refer to the content of actions but to the way they are produced: highly rational actions are reproducible, calculable, and independent of the individual actor.

What do these two components of rationality effect? The fulfilment of social function depends mainly on substantial rationality. The right sentences must be generated within a belief system and the right actions have to be at hand to solve a given problem of action. There has to be the promise of a better life to come to console people and to reconcile them to the misery of this life. How this promise is derived from more basic assumptions and connected with other statements is of secondary importance for the fulfilment of the function. Functions depend on the right content, that is material rationality. But human actors have not only the interest to solve given action problems, they are also motivated by certain meta-interests: results have to be obtained in a dependable, continuous, and efficient way. These meta-motives are satisfied by formal rationality. At the same time formal rationality may be used as a sort of substitutional 'stage-marker'. When one cannot know exactly whether one is acting or thinking rightly, one can reassure oneself and others of the adequacy of one's actions at least by proceeding in the right manner. Quote the right authorities, build up complicated deductions, use some elegant mathematical formulae and everybody will be convinced that what you are doing or thinking must be right or true.

Now let us suppose that at a given time a problem of action or orientation which can be handled only in a rough-and-ready way becomes so urgent again, that a regressive content must be reanimated. Because of the hierarchical ordering of the stages or the levels of rationality, this loss of substantial rationality will not be accompanied by a loss of formal rationality. A regression to a former level of formal rationality would not help. On the contrary, the best solution seems to be to use the most refined techniques of formal rationality to conceal the substantial regression. By using these sophisticated techniques of argumentation or organization of the later stage one can give the impression that what one is doing or thinking must be right and adequate. In sum: regressions to former stages of evolution do not affect the formal side of rationality: There is no identical reproduction of an older pattern of orientation, but the old content is brought into the new form, is processed according to the most sophisticated techniques of the present time. In as much as higher levels of formal rationality grant more efficiency, this redressing of the old orientation pattern may have serious consequences. What may have been functional as long as it was handled in terms of insufficient techniques of organization or argumentation may get totally out of control and become utterly dysfunctional, since it now reaches dimensions which overburden the social system. In applying this to the European witch craze we come to a central substantial argument of this chapter. The extent and the panicky outbursts of the European witchhunting cannot be explained without taking into account the fact that here an old orientation pattern has been reorganized on new levels of formal rationality.

II. Some aspects of the European witch craze

In a short chapter it is impossible to touch upon all aspects of the European witch craze, or to give a satisfactory account of this dark chapter of European history. What follows cannot be more than an outline. The argumentation will start from one basic difference between witchcraft practices in primitive societies and the European witch craze: in primitive societies the witchcraft syndrome usually operates in a controlled way and fulfils important functions for the societies. In contrast, European witch-hunting got totally out of control and threatened to paralyze the social order. This suggests the following proceeding: first, the working of witchcraft practices in a primitive society (the Azande) will be depicted to provide an understanding of the controlled functioning of this set of beliefs and institutional arrangements. This may serve as a background to facilitate identification of those pecularities of the European witch craze which contributed to its dysfunctional implications. Second, it has to be shown which constellation of socio-cultural forces brought about this dysfunctional cluster of characteristics. If we succeed in demonstrating that the dysfunctionality of the European witch craze is at least partly the result of factors discussed above (regressive pull, problems of application, stress, etc.), a strong point has been made for our main hypothesis that the static stage theories may be a necessary ingredient of social dynamics.

1. *Witchcraft practices among the Azande (E. Evans-Pritchard)*

Unlike semiotics sociology is not concerned with all aspects of belief systems or with all the structural relationships which may exist among their components. Sociologists are usually interested only in those aspects of a given belief system which make a difference on the level of social action. The most immediate consequence of the belief in witchcraft on the level of social interaction is the constitution of a special type of action which is defined by that belief: one can bewitch other persons. One way to analyze witchcraft systems would be to analyze the consequences of bewitching and the social context of the witch. But the witch usually had to operate secretly and thus his/her activity was often socially incapsulated. Therefore, the putative victim of the witch is, for the sociologist, of much more interest: he or she could raise a charge against another person and insist on the punishment, or even trigger a larger witch-hunting.

Since the bewitched's action could historically be much more consequential, it is appropriate to start from the (putative) victims of witchcraft and analyze those belief systems. On the most elementary level, we have to deal with the bewitched, the charge of witchcraft and the defendant. Questions which we pose with respect to 'bewitched' individuals are, for instance: what triggers the charge; what motives are responsible for the charge; what motives are ascribed to the witch by the bewitched; what sort of reactions by the defendant are expected; how are third parties expected to react; why does the 'bewitched' person choose exactly this strategy of attack? With respect to the charge, we may want to know whether it is specific (one particular act) or diffuse (concerns the whole person); whether it may easily spread to other persons; whether the crime is deemed to be more or less serious. With respect to the imaginary witch, it may be important to know if there are specific personality traits, or other characteristics which work as criteria for identifying a witch (young or old, male or female, 'bad character'). Certain qualities of the relationship between the witch and the bewitched are also relevant. Is a witch known or unknown; does he or she belong to the ingroup or outgroup; is he or she an equal, a superior or a subordinate; is the relationship between witch and bewitched well defined or not; is it conflictual and competitive? We also want to know which counteractions are open to the defendant and how he can get rid of the charge. Knowing all this it should—on the next level of analysis—be easy to identify the functions which the whole witchcraft system fulfils for persons immediately involved and for the wider social system.

Questions like these are, of course, always posed when we analyze action systems, however, they have to be put into focus here. Since it is one of the central features of the European witch craze that during its predominance witch-hunting got totally out of control, it will be plausible to use this aspect of 'control' as the central focus for organizing the components of the Azande's witchcraft practices. The hypothesis is: the *different aspects of the belief system and the institutional practices of the Azande can be conceived as a careful system of checks and balances,* in which certain elements generate possibilities for accusations of witch-craft and others function as barriers against an intolerable spread of accusations. In presenting the facts I shall implicitly use the above list of questions and indicate by a plus or minus if we are dealing with a barrier to (−) or with an 'amplifier' of (+) a possible witch panic.

Witchcraft among the Azande is not based on learned practices, but on an inherited trait (+: whole clans could become suspect). In witches' bodies one can find a witchcraft substance, which seems to consist of the small intestines in a certain phase of digestion (−: improbable state). It falls from father to sons, from mother to daughters (−: suspicion does not transgress the line between the sexes). The 'soul' of this substance is sent out by the witch to victims or leaves the witchcraft substance during sleep (−: no voluntary act and, therefore, only a minor delict; +: a person may be a witch without knowing it) and 'eats' the 'soul' of an organ of an enemy who then falls ill. The soul of the organ is not eaten up at once, but piece by piece over a period of time (−: only lingering illnesses). But the suspicion of witchcraft arises not only in the case of illness: the Azande tend to explain every instance of misfortune by recourse to the concept of witchcraft (+: numerous occasions). At the same time, witchcraft explanations are not applied to certain types of action or event: breaches of taboo lead to 'sanctions' which are not mediated by witchcraft; where legal procedures exist, these are used; stupidity or laziness are not denied; breaches of the moral code cannot be explained or excused by recourse to witchcraft. In sum, the concept of responsibility is upheld (−).

Furthermore, those who inherited the capacity to bewitch others are not expected to use their capacity always: the witchcraft substance can remain 'cool', inactive (−). The witchcraft substance of children is still too weak; it has to grow and the children have to be trained by experienced masters of witchcraft before they can utilize their capacity (−: barrier against irresponsible fantasies of children).

Since the witchcraft substance is a concrete material entity within the individual, witchcraft does not assume the proportions of a generalized entity (the principle of evil) which would exist outside the individual (−: the danger is punctual). At the same time the Azande do not have a theoretical interest in witches; one tries to find out whether someone has bewitched another in a concrete situation, not whether someone *is* a witch, that is the centre of many possibly dangerous acts (–: low level of generalization).

When a suspicion arises that witchcraft is at work, the victim has to focus his suspicion on certain persons. There are some general rules for doing this. Males can be accused by females and males (+); females can be accused only by females (–: a male charging a female with witchcraft would be charged with adultery); there are no accusations within kingroups (–: because of inheritance of witchcraft one would be immediately involved); the nobility or the king are never involved; influential commoners are rarely accused since one has to fear their vengeance. The standard suspect is an equal neighbour, with whom one has had some quarrel or who has had reason to quarrel with oneself. Although witchcraft is deemed to be inherited, only the closest relatives of defendants or former witches are suspected to be witches too. Thus there is no faction building; by and large the matter is dealt with between two persons (–: one has to be cautious since one has to live together with one's neighbour, and third parties will try to keep out of the affair).

Furthermore, to suspect someone of witchcraft is not to accuse someone of witchcraft. The suspect has to be identified definitely as a witch. Further barriers are incorporated into this process of identification. There are only certain occasions which lead to accusations: the sudden death of a relative must be pursued; bad luck which cannot be changed does not lead to identification of a witch; misfortune which can be changed (illness) leads to identification. Suspected witches are identified by casting oracles or by consulting medicine men. The oracles are, in a way, based on a random number generator (–), which can be manipulated (+) in such a way that people with bad character or quarrelsome neighbours can be selected. The oracles of the prince(ss) are consulted only when a close relative has died. The names of those who are convicted by the princely oracles are kept secret (–: social incapsulation, exclusion of third parties). When medicine men are consulted they have to proceed in a very careful way in order to avoid the revenge of suspects (–). They usually identify as witches only those persons held in low esteem by public opinion, a social system too badly organized to carry out successful action (–). Even if someone has been convicted of witchcraft, his situation is not desperate: there are standardized routines of justification and putting things in order. One can exhume a close relative and demonstrate that the corpse does not contain any witchcraft substance. One can say that the witchcraft substance has become active against one's own will. In any case, one has to undergo a standardized ritual which guarantees that the power of witchcraft ends. Thus the whole episode comes to a definite end (−).

There is no functional overdetermination of the institution of witchcraft. The witchcraft beliefs merely allow the individual to explain coincidences of events for which we have no explanation. By moralizing the natural order in terms of the actions of witches, primitive societies can give accounts of chance events in such a way that the individual can do something about his/her trouble. At the same time he/she contributes to the maintenance of the moral order: the accusation of 'bad characters' emphasizes the validity of the shared value system. But because the wider social system becomes involved only as diffusely structured 'public opinion', the individual always has to be careful in bringing charges against his neighbours.

If one takes together all the information about the witchcraft beliefs and practices of the Azande, one may perhaps say that this institutional arrangement could be functional for Azande society, because the generative components of the whole belief system (bewitching is a way of inervening in the course of nature and in principle everyone could be a witch) are institutionalized in such a way that the institution does not get out of control. In the following passages, it has to be shown which socioeconomic and cultural factors led to a transformation of the popular European witchcraft institution in a direction which made it increasingly difficult to hold this institutional practice in check. Further, it will be shown that these transformations are at least partly the result of medieval European society being a more highly developed society and at the same time a rapidly changing society which had to find new institutional arrangements by trial and *error* (misapplications).

2. *The transformation of popular European witchcraft beliefs*

An analysis of the social consequences of a given belief system has to proceed on two levels: on the one hand, one has to spell out the semantic content of that belief system and assess how this may influence concrete actions; on the other hand, one has to investigate how this belief system is embedded in the social structure or how it is institutionalized. Both aspects are only analytically independent. The most important difference between the Azande and late medieval witchcraft beliefs is institutional: the interpretation and application of the cultural tradition was not any longer diffusely spread among the whole population but lay in the hands of a powerful, hierarchically structured organization, the Church, which was one of the centres of contemporary rationality. During the scholastic era, theological experts had trained and refined their capacity of formal operational thinking. Deductive reasoning was highly developed and the need for a coherent worldview called for an increasing systematization of thinking. But although the Church had been the dominant cultural force during the Middle Ages, it had never gained an exclusive monopoly over the consciousness of the population. Popular religious and magical practices had never been totally eradicated, because the Christian belief was not fully adequate, functional equivalent of the older layers of religious consciousness. Furthermore, the Church itself practised its own semi-magical rites and did not wholeheartedly try to prevent Christian ceremonies from being redefined in magic. Nor had the Church ever denied the reality of witchcraft, because the Bible contains references to acts of bewitching.

The Church seems to have dealt with witchcraft during most of the Middle Ages simply by 'selective awareness' or by what Evans-Pritchard has called 'secondary adaptive mechanisms'. Witchcraft was not a matter of serious concern for the Church; one could not acquire a theological reputation by writing on witchcraft. The Church did not intervene seriously in these popular practices, but confined itself to an occasional application of Christian countermagic. Thus, under the surface of official doctrines, many fragments of the older belief system survived (as Thomas has shown). These fragments seemed to have been used in much the same way as witchcraft beliefs among the Azande. People were mainly preoccupied with concrete acts of bewitching (maleficia) which apparently caused some damage to persons or livestock; friction and tensions among neighbours apparently guided the identification of the imaginary witch in the same way as among the Azande. Similarly, third parties seem not to have been involved, except in the form of the diffusely structured local public.

There are many factors which led to a reanimation of these relics of an older belief system in the late Middle Ages. But before going into detail on the processes which led to a functional overburdening (involvement of state and church agencies) of this self-contained mechanism of local social control, it has to be clarified how the old witchcraft practices were transformed when they were incorporated into the official doctrine of the Church, and in what respects these transformations can be called genuine regressions.

Whereas popular magic was mainly concerned with counteracting isolated acts of bewitching, without theorizing about the working of magical practices, the clerical intellectuals gradually developed encompassing demonologies, that is, systematic, formal-rational accounts of the way in which witchcraft worked. In these 'theories', several (in former times) isolated components of popular consciousness and of the experiences of the Church with sectarian movements were fused. According to the new theories, the witches could reach their goals only through apostasis from God and by making a deal with the Devil. In this pact, the Devil promised to help the witches to commit their crimes; in exchange for his services the witches had to become members of a Devil's sect. The members of this sect met at remote places where they celebrated black masses during which all sorts of sexual crime were committed. The witches reached these places by riding through the air on broom-sticks—a 'humanized' version of the popular belief in the night-flights of Diana and her followers. Most witches were women, since women, because of their wicked nature, easily gave in to the temptations of the Devil.

By this systematization and rationalization, the traditional witchcraft syndrome became a more serious danger for the social order—if not for the world order—than in its older form. By translating the language of concrete actions of popular witchcraft belief into the language of generalized intentions and action principles of the time, it could no longer suffice to counteract concrete and isolated acts of bewitching, because these were just symbols or indicators of generalized entities: on the one hand, of the principle of evil as such (the Devil), on the other hand, of the general malice of the witches and their willingness to destroy the whole social order. The danger seemed to be enhanced by the fact that the witches did not act as isolated individuals but as members of an organization: the sect of witches. Thus extraordinary actions seemed to be necessitated: the witches had to be destroyed physically instead of applying countermagic against isolated acts of bewitching. This tendency was enhanced by the gradual destruction of the belief in the effectiveness of Christian countermagic (Thomas). This, in turn, was probably an implication of the gradual emergence of the concept of a self-contained natural order which functions by and large according to its own laws. The time of miracle working had passed, according to Church doctrine. But the idea that interventions into the course of natural events had been possible only during a certain phase in the history of mankind, was not transferred to the beliefs about witchcraft. The concept of a natural order was too vague, bare of content, and at the same time still too directly intermeshed with the concrete practical interests of humanity to render explanations for, or to be at least compatible with, the seemingly unorderly aspects of nature. The more the concept of a self-contained natural order prevailed, the more pressing became the problem to account for the seemingly unorderly aspects of the universe. Since these aspects could not be accounted for within the concept of nature, they were excluded from it: they resulted from witchcraft and from the actions of the Devil. Thus the rational need for a well ordered and controllable universe led to the exclusion of all irregularities from it. Again this 'rationalization' enhanced the possible danger of bewitching, since misfortune which led to witchcraft accusations was no longer an integral and 'normal' part of the one world, but an indicator of the forces of a counterworld which tried to overthrow the world order.

This outline of late medieval witchcraft beliefs stressed the elements of rationalization (generalization of the action frame of reference, concept of a self-contained natural order) which were implied in the transformation of popular witchcraft beliefs and as a consequence of which the putative dangers of witchcraft grew out of proportion Thus we seem to be dealing primarily with the initial phases of a new stage of the process of rationalization, during which misapplications of newly formed concepts are to be expected. This impression is enhanced when one looks at the way in which the newly formed belief system was supported by formal deductive argumentation. All references to witchcraft in the authoritative texts were compiled and all counterarguments were systematically refuted. In this way, doubts which had always existed and which existed even at the height of the European witch craze were eliminated. It seemed absolutely certain that the newly written treatises contained nothing but the truth. But I think there are good reasons to believe that we are not dealing with a case of a 'normal' misapplication of newly formed concepts, but with one of a regressive misapplication, in which a given level of formal rationality is used just to conceal the regression. The two most obvious regressions concern the concept of responsibility and that of the natural as opposed to the social order.

To begin with *the concept of responsibility*: as we have seen in describing the belief system of the Azande, this included the idea that one could bewitch others without willing or knowing. In these cases, conflict between the two involved parties was not very intense, and the problem was solved by undergoing a standard ritual in which no emotions were aroused. It was a minor affair, because the imaginary witch was not fully responsible for what had happened. Thus the concept of responsibility of acting was upheld. The European intellectuals took a totally different stance. They paralyzed this central component of the everyday action frame of reference. Institoris and Sprenger write in their 'Malleus Maleficarum' for instance: 'Experience has often shown us and from the confessions of all those which we have burned it has become clear that they themselves were not willing to commit the acts of bewitching; and they did not say this in the hope to come free, because the truth of their confessions was proved by the beatings they got from the demons when they did not obey at once . . .' (Quotation from Becker, *et al.*, p. 352). Thus being forced to act in a certain way was not any longer accepted as an excuse for that action. The reason for this transformation of the concept of action was of course—as the reactions of modern states to terrorism still show today—the supposed danger of the witches. In view of this danger one apparently could not afford to proceed according to the usual rules and accept the excuses, which were accepted in other cases as a matter of course. The witches had to be burned, irrespective of whether this had been a voluntary act or not—and this is a very clearcut case of regression.

Things are more complicated in the case of *the concept of a self-contained natural order*, because, as we have seen, there were rational motives at work too: in one respect the belief in witchcraft was one way of striving for a more precise definition and delimitation of the natural order. But if there were rational motives at work, these were just accessories, because the result of the new constructions was in effect a total remoralization of nature. All obnoxious natural events could be attributed to the actions of malicious witches. Even those elements of popular belief which had been rated as superstitious in former times were now included in the official belief system: nightflights of human beings were now deemed to be possible in the same way as certain forms of weather-magic (the causation of hailstorms, etc.). The regressive character of the late medieval witch craze is further evidenced by the fact that the proponents of the witchcraft belief never succeeded totally in eradicating the doubts of opponents, although they tried to refute the counter-arguments point by point and with the most sophisticated techniques of argumentation of the time. To succeed, they had to use force. One should also notice that the sceptics did not have to argue at all before witch hunters gained predominance. They simply stated their disbelief. This is typical for the relationship between different levels of religious consciousness. Older forms of belief are not and usually cannot be strictly refuted, but they are rated simply as outmoded and wither up. Those who want to keep them alive have the burden of proof, and once the balance of power between sceptics and proponents shifts again, the regressive belief simply vanishes without being refuted in detail. This happened at the end of the witch craze.

The form in which the sceptics cast their doubts is also noteworthy. When Protestants and Catholics argued about the tenets of the right faith, or when Platonists and Aristotelians argued about the right philosophy, polemics may have become very sharp and much hatred may have been involved, but the opponents did not deny one another's capacity to tell the truth. The philosophical or theological systems were dealt with as being right or wrong, not as indicators for mental health or madness. What was wrong was not thereby a delusion, but simply erroneous. This was different with respect to the witchcraft syndrome from the very beginning. Critics wondered whether the belief as such had to be rated as a delusion, and whether people who confessed to be witches had not to be regarded as mentally insane—more in need of medical help than of punishment. This assessment became common towards the end of the witchcraft period. To classify a given belief system as delusive is to say more than that it is false. It is to say, that the belief is false and at the same time that the mistake one makes is a false type of mistake—one which is not permitted. This double condemnation is not typical for the relationship of competing theories of a given stage (within-stage-relationship); one can often observe it when theories or belief systems of different stages are confronted with one another.

It seems safe to conclude that the late medieval witch craze constituted a genuine regression. Elements of an older level of religious consciousness were taken up by the cultural élites of the time, were formally rationalized and in their rationalized form implanted in the consciousness of the masses. Penitential preachers and many editions of devil's books disseminated the new belief and embroidered the dangers inherent in the new witch sect. But if this belief system really constituted a regression, the more surprising are its success and the uncontrolled dysfunctional consequences it eventually generated. To explain this, one has to examine the social base of this superstition. The clerical intellectuals had constructed a seemingly convincing account of all misfortunes in the world. But this 'theory' or general language in terms of which disasters could be formulated had to fulfil additional functions, and had to be used in a specific way to produce its horrible consequences.

3. *The social base of the witch craze*

As we have seen above, among the Azande, witchcraft accusations were by and large a matter concerning only the witch, the bewitched and a diffusely structured public. In the late Middle Ages the social context of witchcraft differed radically from this. Now we have to deal with the population as the reservoir of possible witches and bewitched victims, with the Church monopolizing all matters of spiritual well-being and of right belief and, finally, with state agencies, especially the legal system.

3a. *The situation of the population* The clerical and legal agencies concerned with the prosecution of witches could operate only when the population cooperated, that is, when the popular belief in witchcraft led to denunciations and accusations of witches. The prosecution machinery needed an input. Even if that input had remained constant, the new involvement of state and clerical agencies would probably have led to an intensification of witch-hunting. But—as is evidenced by England, where continental ideas about witchcraft were not adopted and where the legal apparatus operated more as a barrier than as an amplifier of the witch craze (Thomas, Macfarlane)—there was an intensification of concern about witchcraft even on the popular level. This popular witch tradition was very similar to that of the Azande: one was mainly concerned with concrete maleficia, accusations were occasioned by misfortune, and conflicts among neighbours channelled the process of selection of the imaginary witches. Thus an intensification of concern about bewitching on the popular level may result from two sources: there may be more occasions for suspicion to arise (more misfortune) and/or the social structure may generate more and new types of social conflict. Without having exact data, I think it is safe to say at least the following about the comparative amount of misfortune: the period we are dealing with was one of transition. Feudal institutions had disintegrated or were eroding; at the same time, early forms of capitalism were beginning to emerge. Economic development was extremely uneven: unseen riches had been accumulated at the same time as an immense proportion of the population had to live without any regular source of income, close to starvation, without housing and—connected with this—without any rights in the institutional order. Feuding, robbery and continuous

warfare made life extremely uncertain. Additionally, a considerable part of the population was concentrated in towns which
were riddled by plagues because of bad sanitary conditions. Big
fires could destroy the fortunes of thousands of people within
one night. To the evils of a relatively stable society (like that of
the Azande) were added the evils of a society in transition,
afflicted with problems resulting not only from nature and the
'ultimate conditions of human existence' (illness and death), but
also with those of a much more complicated society in
transition. It is no wonder that people tried to improve their
lives by spiritual or symbolic means. They could, of course, pray
to God for help. But God could deny or grant, and his help was
therefore uncertain; additionally, the religious impulses of the
Reformation were directed towards an increasing spiritualization of religion, with the consequence that it became increasingly suspect to pray for such concrete things as relief from
misery. One must conclude that there existed a strong regressive
pull to fall back on magical practices. And people practised
white and black magic and knew that others did so.

If we take it for granted that there was a strong regressive pull
to use magical practices, and that there was widespread
suspicion that witchcraft was practised, it still has to be clarified
into which social channels the craze was directed. The direction
scapegoating takes may very well be an important factor in
determining whether the witchcraft syndrome gets out of
control or not. As we have seen among the Azande, the fact that
everyone can fall under suspicion may very well act as a barrier
against an uncontrolled increase of witchcraft accusations,
because one has to be cautious. (Indirectly, this hypothesis is
corroborated by European evidence: in the panicky outbursts of
the witch craze, eventually members of all social groups and
categories were accused and burned. But this breakdown of
minority stereotyping seems to have brought an end to witch-
hunting: the experience was bitter enough to need no further
lesson.)

To give an account of the social distribution of witchcraft
practices and witchcraft accusations is difficult because of lack
of precise data and because of the working of the witch-hunting
machinery which tended to blur social distinctions. Therefore,
the following remarks must be a little speculative. The manifest

function of witchcraft accusations is to help people in coping
with misfortunes of all sorts. Taking into account that the
hardships of life increase the more one descends the social
ladder, one would expect that witchcraft accusations were
especially frequent among people of the lowest ranks of society
(within-rank-accusations). One would also assume that to these
within-rank-accusations were added—following the line of least
resistance—across-rank-accusations from above. But these expectations are not borne out. The low, but not the lowest, ranks
were primarily involved. The reasons for this 'deviation' are
manifold (inability to pay legal charges, sentences for 'normal'
criminal offences). But the main reason may very well conform
to our theoretical expectations. Anthropological studies of
witchcraft indicate that a witchcraft accusation is a strategy of
mystical attack which is used primarily by status superiors vis-
à-vis inferiors or by equals against one another in diffusely
structured and competitive role relationships. Beggars, vagrants
and people without housing definitely did not belong to the
community. Their status was not 'diffusely structured', and
their role relationship to 'respectable' members of communities
was not at all competitive: they were simply too weak to compete
at all. Furthermore, the rate of mobility among these lowest
ranks of feudal society was high; one had to migrate to survive.
This mobility prevented witchcraft accusations, because these
were the end product of a longer process in which a suspicion
arose, was condensed to a rumour and, finally, crystallized in a
publicly validated accusation. Thus stable residence and closer
acquaintance were preconditions for witchcraft accusations—
preconditions which were not fulfilled in the case of the lowest
ranks of society. If one disregards these groups (and the effects
of the highly organized, official witch-hunting machineries), the
hypotheses resulting from anthropological studies of witchcraft
are useful guidelines for a reconstruction of the causes of the
European witch craze. We know that conflicts among neighbours played an essential role in the process of initiating a witch
accusation, in the same way as they did among the Azande. But
why were these conflicts intensified during this period, and how
were they socially channelled? Some of the following factors
seem to be relevant: *the emergence of a new economic ethic, the
breakdown of neighbourhood solidarity, the emergence of a new*

family structure and deteriorating economic opportunities for women. To begin with the last point: during the European witch craze the system of guilds had long passed its climax. Diminished economic opportunities had led to increasing 'closure' of the guilds. For journeymen it became more and more difficult to become members of the guilds, and women were in many towns excluded from them altogether. Since more men than women fell victim to wars and epidemics, widows very often formed a large proportion of the population. Often these women met with difficulties and would have needed the helping hands of their neighbours. But the ethic of neighbourhood solidarity was declining and public welfare did not yet work as a substitute (Macfarlane). People began to prefer to accumulate money and to invest it profitably. The poor, among whom women were overrepresented, became a burden and were denied any help. But the obligation to give neighbourly help was still valid, and those breaking the bonds of solidarity projected their bad consciences on their poorer fellows. Witchcraft accusations were the result. This antifeminist constellation was aggravated by a transformation of European family structure. Age at first marriage rose to 25-30 for men and 23-27 for women. At the same time the proportion of people remaining single rose to 20 per cent 'This shift toward later marriage would lay a social basis for trends toward crystalization of the nuclear family as well as emphasis on marriage by choice (and not by arrangement)' (Midelfort, p. 184). The economic and especially the social consequences of this shift seem to have been enormous. To quote Midelfort again: '. . . theoretically, legally, and perhaps emotionally the patriarchal family was considered the basis of society. In the light of these concepts, the growing number of unmarried women would have appeared as a seditious element in society, especially after the death of their fathers removed them from patriarchal control altogether' (Midelfort, pp. 184-5). The ambiguous and ill-defined roles of a large porportion of women may have generated a lot of uneasiness. But the fact that many of these women were not willing to carry their burden without protest and strove toward emancipation may have been beyond the limit. This definitely provoked attack in the form of witchcraft accusations: what could previously be dismissed as 'alien' was now defined as 'immoral' (Lewis). The old ugly women became the prototype of the stereotype of the witch. Since old ugly women were a minority within society, witchcraft accusations became a safe strategy of mystical attack which the majority could use freely. The concentration of witchcraft accusations on a minority group thus opened the way to an increase of such accusations. Thus, paradoxically, the seeming delimitation (in the semantic dimension) of possible witchcraft accusations had exactly the opposite effect (on the pragmatic level): one factor which had held the system in check in former times (and, as we have seen, among the Azande) had been removed.

In summary, late medieval or early modern times were times of transition when life was full of suffering and uncertainties. Because of the spiritualization of the belief system, religion more and more lost its capacity to aid people in coping with the risks of life. A new stage of rationalization of consciousness was accompanied by a functional loss. This combination of increasing misery and loss of the function to cope with this misery generated a strong regressive pull to fall back to the level of magical thinking. Women were especially susceptible as victims of witchcraft accusations because of their marginal economic position and their ambiguous social position. By concentrating witchcraft attacks on a minority group, the witch craze could reach formerly unknown dimensions.

3b. *The situation of the Church*   It is always difficult for a large organization to withstand a regressive pull which is strongly backed by the majority of its followers or clients. The medieval Church did not resist the regressive pull from below: on the contrary, it took an active lead in witchhunting. On the one side, it systematized and generalized the conceptions of witchcraft and thereby overdramatized the dangers inherent in bewitching; on the other hand—and this is probably the most important factor accounting for the tremendous growth of the witchcraft syndrome—by its very intervention it changed the social context of witchcraft accusations and witchhunting in a decisive way. Two points seem to be relevant in this respect: the Church was, first, the most powerful single institution in the late medieval or early modern period. When the Church sided with the accusers in a witchcraft episode, the balance of power between the accuser and the victim of an accusation was definitely overthrown. One may have had a chance to defend oneself against one's neighbours, but one definitely had no chance to defend oneself or take revenge against the Church. Once one was suspected of being a witch, one was definitely lost, and those accusing others could be safe from revenge. Thus a further element which had kept the witchcraft syndrome among the Azande in check had been removed. It was made too safe to accuse others—a circumstance which may have been aggravated by the transformation of social and family structure. We know that courts acted more cautiously when they knew that an accused had lots of friends or relatives in the vicinity. The more the network of social bonds was atomized, the more family relationships were reduced to the nuclear family, the easier it was to attack others.

The second institutional factor which has to be taken into account is the organizational power of the Church. The more Church officials convinced themselves of the danger of the witch sect, the more urgent the need for setting up a special organization to fight against witches. Thus the Inquisition, which was the instrument of the Church to oppose sectarian movements, acquired additional responsibility, professional witchhunters were licensed or the responsibility was shifted to the worldly courts. Thus an additional factor came into play. Organizations set up for the prosecution of deviant behaviour have a given capacity and they tend to function in such a way that the capacity is effectively employed. This means that the intensity of prosecution is at least partly a function of the capacity of the prosecuting agency; if there are not enough victims, the criteria for victimization are changed accordingly (Erikson). The organizational potential of the Roman Catholic Church—being the heir of Roman rationality—was high, having no parallel in a more primitive society like that of the Azande.

The same considerations applied to the role the worldly courts and emerging nation states played in the European witch craze. Once a worldly court became concerned with witchhunting it produced its rate of witchcraft accusations and the individual had no chance to resist. But before going into the role played by the legal system, some additional remarks about the situation of the Church seem appropriate. The Church had always believed in the possibility of witchcraft; to explain the European witch craze it is, therefore, not enough to look at the transformation of witchcraft beliefs effected by the Church. The Church could have done that before. We have to ask what constellation of situational factors and functional imperatives led the Church to an elaboration of its witchcraft beliefs. Enough has been said about this topic that I shall give here just a sketchy outline.

Toward the end of the Middle Ages, the Church had managed to become one of the mightiest worldy powers, but at the same time its spiritual legitimacy declined: its appearance was too worldly to be a credible representation of God on earth. It was a channel of social mobility and attracted many of the uprooted who were religiously unqualified. Even criminals joined its ranks because they were safe from prosecution once they were members. The financial resources of the Church were always insufficient and, therefore, the Church added its burden of taxes to those of the worldly states. It was also a powerful legal agency because it was the only institution having enough trained staff. And these clerical lawyers not only protected the interests of the Church more than those of the population; they also proceeded according to the rules of Roman law which was very often in conflict with local customs. This period also saw the birth of the modern nation states and the crystallization of national consciousness. The more this process proceeded, the greater the tension between the supra-national Church and mass consciousness became. The gulf between the appearance of the Church and popular expectations may have widened because of a shift in the social composition of believers. The towns had freed themselves from the grip of the feudal nobility and the feudal Church had to transform itself into the religion of townspeople. And townspeople tend, as Max Weber has shown, toward an ethical religion. For these moralizing believers, a new form of cure of souls had to be invented: penitential preachers moved from town to town and stirred up the sentiments of the masses. Sensational stories about the Devil and the new witch sect were thrilling highlights for these preachers and they belonged, therefore, to the main proponents of the new witch craze.

Dissatisfaction with the Church gave rise to a series of

heretical movements, culminating in the Reformation. The reaction of the Church was twofold: on the one hand, it set up the Inquisition as an instrument of oppression; on the other hand, there were tendencies to reform the Church itself. The monastic orders had the main responsibility for reasserting the holiness of the Church. And since asceticism is always deemed to be an indicator of other-worldliness, one insisted increasingly on the strict celibacy of clergy and monks. This in turn led to a strong antifeminism within Church teachings: women being the main temptation to barely repressed monkish greediness had to be deprecated. Furthermore, women had played a prominent role in most heretical movements, because the sects did not discriminate against women. Deviant movements usually grant a more prominent role to the weak because they find it more difficult to gain a following. Even within the monastic orders of the Church, strivings towards the emancipation of women were considerable. This, of course, made women the more prone to become the victims of stereotyping and mystical attacks. The more the worldly position of the Church was endangered and the more its cultural monopoly was destroyed, the more pressing became the urge to exhort a sort of terror, which could be directed against everyone. Where (as in Germany) the power balance between Catholics and Protestants constantly shifted, where the position of the Churches was especially ill-defined, witchhunting seems to have reached its climax. When in 1555 a religious peace was declared in which the contracting parties agreed not to prosecute people because of their beliefs, witch-hunting became an apt instrument of concealed religious prosecution, which was used by Catholics and Protestants alike.

The theoretical implications of this analysis of the situation of the Churches are twofold: first, it can be seen that the witchcraft syndrome fulfilled for the religious system too many functions to expect witchhunting to be ended easily by the religious authorities. Second, an important theoretical point: institutions can concentrate on the fulfilment of their main function as long as their existence is not endangered. As soon as the mere survival of an institution becomes questionable, the fulfilment of its main function is postponed. All efforts are concentrated on securing the sheer existence of the institution and there is no willingness to waste time on considerations about the legitimacy of given means. If regressions serve the end of survival, they will occur in this situation. That the religious authorities perceived their situation as such an emergency is indirectly evidenced by the use they made of the legal system. The Church courts proceeded according to the motto 'with mercy and severity'. Where the position of the churches was most precarious, the prosecution of witches was handed over to the worldly authorities in order to get rid of the imperative of mercy. Mercy was— as the next section will show—the last thing to be granted by the worldly courts.

3c. *The role of the legal system*   When one speaks about the legal system and the European witch craze, one single factor of utmost importance comes immediately to mind: torture. And a comparison of the figures for continental states which allowed the use of torture and England, where it was forbidden, immediately shows that torture was indeed the one factor without which the incredible amount of witch-burning on the Continent cannot be explained. Under torture, witches confessed their 'misdeeds' and denounced other persons as witches. These, in turn, were tortured and denounced further persons—a chain without end. Where the Azande used a chance procedure (the chicken oracle) which gave the suspected a good chance to get away, in Europe a 'multiplier', which could not be stopped, formed the kernel of the process of conviction. But although torture is a factor of utmost importance for the explanation of the panicky outbursts, it would be oversimplifying to reduce the analysis of the heights of the European witch craze to torture as such. There were regions where, despite the use of torture, witchhunting was relatively limited. It should also be noticed that the European witch craze had long passed its climax before torture was finally abolished in European legal systems. It was well known that torture could be abused, and the codification of the criminal law from 1532, the Constitutio Criminalis Carolina, aimed, among other things, at a prohibition of misuses of torture. To concentrate simply on torture would, therefore, be misleading. What one has to analyze is the way torture was embedded in the legal system. And one cannot gain an understanding of the working of this system unless one recognizes that our period covers exactly the time during which

Roman law was adopted, and during which the legal apparatus was made to serve the purposes of the central state authorities. This involved not only cognitive problems but also organizational ones. Lawyers had to be trained, and financial resources to pay them had to be mobilized. The old institutional structures could not be used for the new purposes. For these reasons, one may expect during this period all the problems of transitional phases during which new institutional practices are tested. If there is trial, there is error; that is, misapplications of the newly established rules are to be expected. As hypothesized above, misapplications will occur especially when the system operates under stress. This seems to have been the case and therefore, the following account will be the history of a series of interlocking misapplications. Whether these were of a regressive nature is difficult to decide. One would answer this question in the affirmative if one took, for instance, the 'Carolina' or the most refined legal knowledge of the time as a yardstick. One knew that torture excessively applied could lead to false confessions, that children were bad witnesses and that the accused should be aided by defence counsel. In the witch processes, one did not stick to this knowledge and, therefore, one is tempted to classify them as legal regressions. On the other hand, the 'Carolina' did not represent a set of commonly accepted and well tested legal practices, but was still to be realized and carried through on all levels of the legal system. If one finds in this phase of the process of institutionalization that especially the lower levels of a hierarchically structured system did not work according to its leading principles and produced lots of faulty decisions, one cannot speak of 'regressive misapplications'. One is dealing with 'normal misapplications' which are an implication of the fact that a new *code* (and not a set of concrete 'messages' or behavioural instructions) is established or a new evolutionary stage is emerging. The fact that during the European witch craze the top agencies of the legal system did much better than those at the bottom supports the hypothesis of normal misapplications! But there are regressive features too, the most important being the short-circuiting of action under stress. The rules constituting the organizing principles of 'higher' interactional structures usually do not allow the direct gratification of impulses, but demand that one sticks to complicated procedures and even accepts 'faulty' decisions. During the height of the witch craze, the 'goal' of action totally dominated the decision process. Fear had to be overcome and this was done irrespective of legal procedures. The suspected witches had to be burned at any price. In this respect, the legal system *regressed* during the early modern period.

The analysis of misapplications has to proceed in two directions: One has to analyze the cognitive-structural dimension, on the one hand, and the dynamic-motivational dimension, on the other hand. To begin with the cognitive-structural aspect: the transition from the Germanic legal practices to Roman law implied that the old trial of indictment ('Anklage-prozess'), which was part of the legal tradition of selfhelp, was replaced by the inquisitorial trial, which was an implication of the emerging concept of a public order which had to be safeguarded by the state. One consequence of this transition was the growing importance of circumstantial evidence. According to the old practices, an accuser had to prove himself that his charge was well founded. If circumstantial evidence was not unequivocal, he could substantiate his matter by producing oath assistants ('Eideshelfer'). The accused could defend himself by taking an oath of innocence ('Reinigungseid'). This practice very often produced materially irrational results, and the transition to Roman law was, in this respect, progress. But the procedures of the criminal trial according to Roman law were apparently difficult to handle, since one had, for instance, still to learn how to combine logic and circumstantial evidence. This difficulty partly explains the prominent role which torture played in late medieval trials. To illustrate an ill-directed use of a certain type of circumstantial evidence let me quote again from Midelfort (p. 103):

In this list we obtain an incredible view of the witchhunting mind at work, rigorous, methodical, logical. For example, if she were innocent, how could she have *known* that a demon had taken her place beside her husband, while she was out at the nocturnal sabbath? Or again, if she claimed to be guiltless, how could she explain *knowing* that an associate's lover-devil was named little feather (fedterlein)? It did not occur to her examiners, that she might not have 'known' these facts but simply have invented them. Surely part of the *révolution mentale* separating that age from this, was a growth in the sense of the impossible. But just as important a part was a redefinition of the term *knowledge*. Torture, as we saw earlier, rested on the hope of uncovering facts that an innocent person simply could not know. We see here, what that could mean in practice.

But that the consequences of this type of reasoning were unacceptable, and that the reasoning was false, could not become conscious because this kind of thinking represented the highest level of formal rationality.

The situation of the defendants was worsened by a set of institutional factors which have to do with the social distribution of legal knowledge. This, in turn, is just one manifestation of a process in which systems of indirect social intercourse and hierarchically structured organizations are laid upon the basis of the primary social relationships. One implication of this process was that the law faculties which constituted the top of the legal hierarchy were far removed from the consequences of their scientific discourse. Already contemporaries complained that the law faculties produced elaborate books on the right gradation of torture for different crimes, without taking account of how torture was handled in practice. But most law faculties were, in comparison to the lower ranks of the legal order, lenient when consulted in a witch trial. They constituted the top of the legal hierarchy, they knew not only the laws and procedures, but they also had at least a certain sense of the meaning and function of laws and procedural rules. But—and this is typical of periods when new social practices are institutionalized—what worked at the top of the hierarchy did not work among its lower ranks. Many lawyers and judges were too badly trained and had to proceed according to 'trial handbooks' which only contained concrete prescriptions for managing the trial. The laymen jurors knew virtually nothing about Roman law, and very often did not understand what was going on at all. No wonder that the lower courts were especially rigorous witchhunters.

If we add to this picture the constellation of interests involved in the witch trials, it becomes difficult to see how witchhunting should *not* have become uncontrollable. Despite the serious shortcomings of the older legal tradition of selfhelp, its administration guaranteed one decisive advantage: it was administered by the people themselves and therefore, the main manifest function of a legal system was never totally overridden. Legal systems are designed to regulate conflict situations and breaches of social codes in such a way that every individual involved gets his or her 'due' share. Although the working of the older legal tradition apparently generated many 'false' judgements, these mistakes were not systematically related to the fact that the legal system was dominated by another imperative than the protection of the rights of individuals. This changed with the emergence of centralized nation states and with the concomitant adoption of Roman law. The state tried to assert its authority against the competing feudal powers and against the self-directed activities of its subjects. A 'public order' had to be established and a 'public peace' had to be carried through. But public order and public peace were constantly endangered by feuding, robbery and breaches of the law. In this situation, the legal system became an instrument for asserting state power. Its main function was no longer to protect the rights of individuals but to uphold the position of the central agencies. If it was deemed necessary for the fulfilment of this newly emerging function to sacrifice the rights of individuals for the benefit of state interests, this was done. For the administration of criminal law, this shift of function had the consequence that the courts proceeded with increasing severity and rigour. There was no room for mercy. Not only were the central state authorities involved. The plague of robbery and feuding had made trade routes insecure. Therefore, the towns wholeheartedly supported the increasing severity of the courts. The 'law and order thinking' was most marked with respect to crimes in which the state order was directly attacked, that is, the *crimina excepta*. Among these were treason, *lèse majesté*, counterfeiting, assault upon the king *and bewitching*. To illustrate this point, let me again quote from Midelfort (p. 118):

In addition to this remarkable logic, he argued that witchcraft was a crimen exceptum, freed from the normal legal restrictions and precautions. In fact, God punished men for weak toleration of such crimes. Witches, therefore must never be let go. In cases of doubt, defendants may be put to the judgment of God. The real crime, he insisted, was lenience; *judges were responsible for the commonwealth, and not merely for individuals.* It might be best for individuals (respectu nominati) to apply Kager's rule, but it would certainly not be best for the state (respectu reipublicae et boni publici).

Thus the balance between individual and society had changed strongly to the advantage of the state. The experience of the peasant wars was still fresh, and it is no surprise that state authorities were overanxious and defended their interests sternly. This was easy enough because the judges of the new inquisitorial trials had to fulfil different functions at the same time: they were prosecutors and judges (functional overdetermination). A regressive misapplication of legal rules was the result.

A final point needs to be mentioned here: financial interests. The further the adoption of Roman law proceeded, the more professionally trained lawyers and lower official staff penetrated the legal system. These personnel had to be paid, and the official agencies were unable to raise the considerable amount of money needed. Legal charges and confiscations of property of convicted defendants were ways to raise funds. Thus corruption could contribute to an increase in witchhunting. Even where confiscations were handled according to strict regulations, a considerable amount of money was involved (the court costs amounted in Mergentheim to 9559 Gulden in 1631). Even if contemporaries exaggerated, they certainly had a point when they complained about 'the greed of jurists for the profits of witchtrials' (Midelfort, p. 178). Financial interests thus generated additional third-party-interests and contributed to the uncontrolled outbreaks of witchhunting.

Summarizing, one may say that the situation of possible victims of witchcraft accusations deteriorated due to the involvement of state agencies. But to the mere fact of state involvement was added the quality of functioning of the legal system. The adoption of Roman law, that is, the institutionalization of a new legal 'code' which entailed a far-reaching differentiation of the legal system within the whole social process and, at the same time, a higher level of internal differentiation, was accompanied by a series of difficulties which may be subsumed under the concept of 'normal mis-

applications' (cognitive difficulties in applying the new principles, lack of adequately trained staff, differentiation of
decision and consequences of a decision). These normal misapplications were supplemented with regressive tendencies. The
real or imaginary menace of the state led to a shift of function of
the legal system (from just treatment of individuals to assertion
of state power) which, in turn, generated the temptation to
override legal procedures and to resort to 'direct action'.
Without this legal regression, hundreds or thousands of witches
may have been burned, with it hundred-thousands of victims
were involved.

4. *Concluding remarks*

After protracted discussion of the constellation of factors by
which the European witch craze was determined, it may be
useful to look back, to synthesize what has been presented in an
analytical perspective and to pick up the threads of our initial
theoretical considerations.

The above account of the causes of the European witch craze
was governed by the idea of a 'logical' sequence of evolutionary
stages of action and belief systems. The idea of evolutionary
stages was explicated by the idea of transformations of a cultural
code, that is, of a set of rules and basic assumptions about the
physical and social reality which governed the production of
'concrete messages' (single actions and beliefs). Code-shifts
imply misapplications. The learning of a new cultural code does
not take place in one step. On the contrary, one has to expect
that during a trial and error phase misapplications of the new
code will be frequent and that these misapplications will only
gradually be eliminated. Therefore, the above outline of the
causes of the European witch craze can in one respect be read as
the history of a set of interconnected misapplications. The
causes for misapplications are usually twofold: on the one hand,
one has to identify the cognitive difficulties which the actors had
in applying the code; on the other hand, one has to look for the
situational pressures to which the actors are exposed, and for
configurations of interests to which a given misapplication may
fit. As far as this type of analysis carries (and convinces the
reader), a first argument for the necessity of stage models within

the social sciences has been produced. If we have to reconstruct socio-cultural evolution in a series of shifts from one code to another, we have to build into the historical process a certain amount of discontinuity. Codes do not shift as fast as concrete opinions, and even if a new code or organizing principle is not adopted and realized in one step, it becomes obvious to delimit a period of history by recourse to the domination of a given code.

But our main interest was not in 'normal misapplications'. A stronger argument for the necessity of stage models could be made if our expectations concerning regressive misapplications were supported by the historical evidence. Although the historical research, upon which this outline of the causes of the European witch craze is based, has not been guided by some version of a theory of socio-cultural evolution and is in this respect unbiased, it has been possible to identify some supportive evidence for the regression hypothesis. Critics of the witchcraft belief did not rank it with normal scientific errors but debased it as superstition or even evidence of mental illness. The proponents had to concentrate all instruments of formal-rational argumentation in order to obscure the regressive character of their delusion. But this alone did not suffice. Contrary to the medieval tradition of a free theological dispute, sceptics were—typically in a situation in which there is no chance of getting the upper hand by better arguments—threatened with physical extermination. Further, it could be demonstrated that a strong 'regressive pull' was generated by the coincidence of increasing misery of the population, on the one side, and, on the other, decreasing capability of the Church to aid people when they suffered from misfortune. It could also be shown that the Church, as well as state authorities, experienced considerable 'stress' and was fighting for survival. Thus all elements of the situation apparently complement one another in a constellation which is typical of a 'compulsive' and regressive course of events. But the question can still be posed whether the stage model is really indispensable for gaining an understanding of a phenomenon like the European witch craze. Did we not present all the relevant causal factors in terms of the well-known framework of the theory of social action? Anti-evolutionary-minded historians have, after all, written excellent accounts of this historical phenomenon and Evans-Pritchard's pioneer work, which was not at all formulated in terms of a theory of social evolution, has proved to be a fruitful guideline for historians. Nor would anyone suggest that witchcraft among the Azande has anything to do with regressions. This line of argument must seem more convincing the more one concentrates on the common characteristics of European and, for instance, Azande witchcraft beliefs. Indeed, in both cases misfortune is explained by the actions of malicious members of the ingroup and fulfils the additional function of maintaining a given moral code. In constructing a typology of witchcraft systems, one is, therefore, tempted—as Mary Douglas suggests —to subsume Azande and late medieval witchcraft practices under the same type. Of course this is possible but whether it is a wise theoretical strategy is at least questionable.

My doubt is motivated by the following: in giving my outline of the factors contributing to the European witch craze, I analyzed the transformation of the belief system, the situation of the population, the role of the Church and of state agencies. In each case, I tried to show that the mere involvement of the respective subsystems, and the fact that in these subsystems tendencies toward 'normal' or 'regressive' misapplications were at work, contributed to the destruction of the careful balance between 'amplifiers' and 'barriers' which was characteristic of the witchcraft system of the Azande. In each case, a 'contribution' of this sort could be found, the result being that witchhunting got totally out of control. This finding suggests the following hypothesis: the late medieval/early modern European witchcraft syndrome was functionally overburdened or overdetermined and, therefore, got out of control. But if it had not been overdetermined, it would not have been possible to carry it through and maintain it, because it contained too many regressive features. Overdetermination, especially by institutions which operate under stress, generates institutions which are unbalanced and in the long run intolerable for the social system. To state it somewhat differently: regressions have to be overdetermined and overdetermination implies long-range dysfunctionality of social institutions. A stage model of sociocultural evolution allows us easily to identify regressive transformations as regressive and thereby channels our research activities and expectations adequately: stage adequate phenomena will be stable and determined by just a few factors whereas phenomenologically similar regressive phenomena will be multidetermined and, in the long run, unstable. Phenomena which are to be dealt with in such a different way have to be conceptualized as different. Stage models conceptualize them as different.

Notes

Because of the length of this chapter, I have made only few references to the literature within the text. But some hints are necessary. A useful summary of the biological theorizing on evolution is to be found in W. Stegmüller, *Hauptströmungen der Gegenwartsphilosophie*, Bd. II, Stuttgart, 1975. Implicitly, S. Toulmin's account of the development of scientific ideas in his *Kritik der killektiven Vernunft*, Frankfurt, 1978, has served me as a countermodel which helped to clarify my own ideas. A summary of the cognitive-structural approach can be found in J. Piaget, *Erkenntnistheorie der Wissenschaften vom Menschen*, Frankfurt/Berlin/Vienna, 1973. Of all the literature on witchcraft, I enjoyed most H. C. Erik Midelfort, *Witch Hunting in Southwestern Germany*, Stanford, 1972; A. Macfarlane, *Witchcraft in Tudor and Stuart England*, London, 1970; K. Thomas, *Religion and the Decline of Magic*, Penguin Books, 1973, and, of course, E. E. Evans-Pritchard, *Hexerei, Orakel und Magie bei den Zande*, Frankfurt, 1978. The following were also indispensible: M. Douglas (ed.), *Witchcraft, Confessions and Accusations*, Tavistock, 1970; I. M. Lewis, *Ecstatic Religion*, Penguin Books, 1971; C. Honegger (ed.), *Die Hexen der Neuzeit*, Frankfurt, 1978; G. Becker *et al.*, *Aus der Zeit der Verzweiflung*, Frankfurt, 1977; K. T. Erikson, *Die widerspenstigen Puritaner*, Stuttgart, 1978; H. R. Trevor-Roper, *Religion, Reformation und sozialer Umbruch*, Frankfurt/Berlin/Vienna, 1967; R. Kieckhefer, *European Witchtrials*, Berkeley, Los Angeles, 1976; E. W. Monter, *Witchcraft in France and Switzerland*, Ithaca/London, 1976. Older works by J. Hansen, Soldan-Heppe, and Diefenbach (references in Midelfort) were also useful.

During the summer term, 1980, I held a seminar at the Free University of Berlin on the European witch craze. I have to thank Richard von Dülmen, University of Munich, for his generous advice in planning the seminar. Looking back, I fear that I profited from the participants of the seminar more than they from me. Through their pertinacity, I was urged to look more closely at the situation of women in the late Middle Ages and to recognize that a line-of-least-resistance hypothesis was oversimplifying. I have to thank especially Susanne Keunecke, Anja Lucke, Ilka Monheimius, Vera Ruhland, Petra Schömer and Julia Sieferle for their initiative and their 'material' contributions in the form of unexpected papers. Finally, I have to thank Suzanne Libich for eliminating the worst aberrations of my 'German English'. On those which are left I insisted.

4 From Moralization to Class Society or from Class Society to Moralization: Philosophical Comments on Klaus Eder's Hypothesis

P. Ruben

KLAUS EDER'S book giving a genetic explanation of mankind's social evolution raises the question from a new angle.[1] New is the inclusion of the biological synthetic theory of evolution into the range of empirical social sciences. The scientific implications of such a step are undoubtedly far-reaching. In principle, it may suggest prospects for a universal evolutionary understanding applying to both human and non-human nature. There is no doubt, I believe, that a combination of the explanatory principles of the synthetic theory with the specific findings of the social sciences will render scientific progress possible. In this sense, Eder's concept is most certainly a contribution relevant to any further serious investigation into the evolutionary laws of human sociability.

Having this in mind, there are yet serious objections to be made to Eder's concept, particularly to his philosophical prerequisites on the basis of which he links biological evolutionary theory and sociology. I will limit myself to three main remarks.

1. Historical Materialism and the 'Theory of Socio-Cultural Evolution'

The historical prerequisites for Eder's concept are not only Darwinism and Spencerism, but also historical materialism, of which Eder says that it has 'remained rather a "theoretical program"'[2] than that it has become an analytical, mature teaching on the evolution of human society. This parallelization of the concepts of two empirical sciences with a philosophical

120

concept suggests a theoretical competition which, in fact, does not exist: philosophical and empirical investigations differ in quality; they do not compete, although clearly they enter into a certain relationship with each other.

All empirical analysis, whether it concerns non-human or human nature, deals with objects you can actually see and touch and which in principle are experimentally manipulatable. They serve as a means for representing the properties and relations of interest. The interest of philosophical investigation, however, is no longer the object as representation of a property, but rather *the relationship of such a representation to the reality of this representation*. In Marxist philosophy, this relation has been described by Engels as the 'great basic question of all philosophy'.[3] Hence, empirical analysis, by beginning with representation of objects, conditions philosophical investigation. The latter is accomplished by realizing and inquiring into the difference between the representations as mediated by consciousness and reality as independent of consciousness.

Needless to say, philosophy as a special science can accomplish such an understanding theoretically only through the use of *concepts* of objective reality, of consciousness, etc. Thus the confrontation between representation and reality that really takes place in practice can be 'thought' philosophically only by going beyond empirical cognition and visualizing 'reality', 'consciousness', etc. Theoretical understanding of the difference between the representation (mediated by consciousness) of a thing and this reality of the same thing independent of consciousness preconditions determination of both, the representation and reality through conciousness which by this act is becoming philosophical! Philosophy is awareness of the relation between objective reality and consciousness. Awareness of consciousness *and* of reality outside of our consciousness is what the basic question of philosophy consists of. Being a philosophical idealist or materialist depends on the dominance presumed to exist in this relation.

If one accepts the difference indicated between the empirical sciences and non-empirical philosophy, then it is clear that one cannot expect philosophical solutions from an empirical science just as little as one can expect empirical solutions from philosophy. He who rejects a philosophy because it does not solve his empirical problems simply shows that he has not grasped the difference between philosophy and the empirical science. And he who burdens philosophy with empirical problems shows that he does not yet have the empirical instruments to solve his problem adequately, that is, empirically.

Historical materialism is a constituent part of Marxist-Leninist philosophy. Its basic questions originate as soon as social scientific (economic, sociological, socio-psychological, political, etc.) ideas, that is, social scientific representations, are formed about human behaviour. Then it is necessary to confront these representations of consciousness with the real human beings, to 'think' this confrontation with reality. This type of thinking preconditions the *concept* of the real human being, that is, it is an act of theoretical determination by which historical materialism actually receives its special character when compared to dialectical materialism. However, such a special philosophy of man is not peculiar to historical materialism. Rather, it is characteristic for every philosophy. For example, when Hegel in his *Enzyklopädie* accepts the conditional: 'If it is correct (and it probably is), that the *human being* is distinguished from the *animal* through thinking, then everything human is such and is alone such because it is caused by thinking',[4] then he has accepted an elementary concept of man, namely the identity of being human and being caused through thinking. This view is clearly the fundamental idealist position as it presents itself to historical materialism.

And it is precisely here that my criticism of Eder's concept would set in. The problem is that his theoretical premises are based expressly on a *philosophical* image of man. In line with the Neo-Kantian differentiation between 'nature' and 'culture', culture is laid down as being the species-character of human societies (Eder says 'social systems'): 'Culture is that which distinguishes human forms of socialization from biological sociality. Cultural universals are what constitute the social systems.'[5] How does Eder define the 'cultural universals'? He determines them by 'deduction' from 'the specific properties of lingually-organized processes of learning and lingually-organized systems',[6] in other words, he claims the faculty of *speech* to be a specific feature of the human species: 'phonological differentiation, syntactic organization of sounds (morphemes) and the association of the meanings with symbolic representatives is the key ability of the human species'.[7] While Hegel assures us that thinking is what distinguishes the human being from other natural species, Eder suggests that it is speech.

If one accepts the position of Marx and Engels: 'The "mind" is from the outset afflicted with the curse of being "burdened" with matter, which here makes its appearance in the form of agitated layers of air, sounds, in short, of language',[8] then one will agree that Eder's viewpoint is not so different from that of Hegel. By the way, Hegel certainly did not suggest the existence of speechless thinking, but quite to the contrary, he expressly presumed the sensible certainty of language in order to substantiate that 'true reality' lies in thinking alone.[9] So when Eder presumes the faculty of speech to be the particular human potential, then he is idealistically presuming the domination of consciousness over the objective reality of human existence. And this is the philosophical characteristic of his theory of social evolution. It is undoubtedly that this characteristic results from taking over Habermas's separation of 'instrumental action' and 'interaction'[10] and will concern us later.

So we may sum up critically: it is not that Eder includes historical materialism as a given prerequisite for his theory on social evolution, but that, in fact, Eder's concept has a direct idealist philosophical basis.

What image does historical materialism give of the human being?

Since we are dealing with the Germans who are devoid of premises, we must begin by stating the first premise of all human existence and, therefore, of all history, the premise, namely, that men must be in a position to live in order to be able to 'make history'. But life involves before everything else eating and drinking, housing, clothing and various other things. The first historical act is thus the production of the means to satisfy these needs, the production of material life itself. . . . Therefore in any conception of history one has first of all to observe this fundamental fact in all its significance and all its implications and to accord it its due importance. It is well known that the Germans have never done this, and they have never, therefore, had an *earthly* basis for history and consequently never a historian.[11]

The fact that they produce their real lives themselves makes the biological humans humane humans! So, what distinguishes human beings from other natural beings—at least when accepting historical materialism—is that (1) they appropriate a part of their natural environment, that is, they realize property relations, (2) they turn the appropriated objects into objects of use, that is, they realize *concrete labour*, and (3) they appropriate the *products*.

The essential difference between the philosophy of Eder's concept of social evolution and historical materialism is obviously that Eder, like the enlighteners, seeks and finds a special 'natural condition' for human beings: the faculty of speech; while historical materialism, without ignoring the natural prerequisites for human evolution, states that the qualitative change in the evolution of a special biological species is given as soon as these use *objectivated* organs—tools—to work on appropriated parts of nature for the physical reproduction of actually existing populations. Labour as species, activity mediated through tools, is the essence of the human being as historical materialism depicts him. Cognition, the production of knowledge in this process, is to be understood as an element of the universal.[12] In other words, the faculty of speech and, in association with this, the perceptive faculty, is a necessary, but insufficient condition of human evolution.

In addition, it must be strongly emphasized that labour is a behavioural response of *collective* subjects. Hence, the sociality accomplished in biological evolution is a genetic precondition for the transition to human evolution. So, under historical-materialist prerequisites, the issue can never be to explain some kind of 'social synthesis' or 'socialization' as such. There is no human evolution without sociality as a *prerequisite*. The actual point in question is that of the specific determination of sociality in this or that mode of production. It is not the existence of the species that can be explained on the basis of atomized individuals (dialectically, an absurd undertaking), but the evolution of both the species and the individual must be explained through the evolution of property and of labour!

It is superfluous to note that the premise of a collective subject for labour also makes thinking, cognition, a collective performance (as every native language shows).

2. *Mode of Production or 'Social Organization'*

The empirical relevance of historical materialism appears in the concept of the *mode* of production which is a historically determined *mode* of production. That is, production is perceptibly presented in that distinguishable modes of producing are presented. Marx comments: 'In broad outlines, Asiatic, ancient, feudal, and modern bourgeois modes of production can be designated as progressive epochs in the economic formation of society.'[13] This distinction, of course, by no means shows which are the specific characteristics for each mode of production. It is the task of empirical social analysis to find this out, and to do so it will need to employ all the relevant social sciences. Let us leave aside such considerations.

What interests us with a view to Eder's concept is the semi-Lamarckist interpretation of the dialectical unity conceptually expressed in the mode of production, of productive forces and production relations. Eder appears to hold the opinion that historical materialism sees this dialectical process as one of more or less spontaneous innovations in production techniques which enforce an adaptation of the production relations. I would not deny that during the course of the theoretical emancipation of the working class, there have been ideologists who have proclaimed such a—one may say—mechanistic interpretation of the language of dialectics. This is exactly what it is: the indicated Lamarckist interpretation presumes the term 'productive forces' to be the term of some particular physical quality; the term 'production relations' is treated in the same way. Then claims are made in terms of the usual idea of causality that change in the productive forces must be followed by change in the production relations. Thus, the mode of production as a *functional* connection becomes the premise in which the productive forces play the role of an independent physical quality, while the production relations take on the role of a dependent physical quality. Of course, one can think like this. However, this has nothing to do with dialectics!

And it is precisely this version of the unity between the productive forces and the production relations that Eder holds to be 'historical materialism', which he then counters: 'While the description of this context will serve to explain behavioural adaptations, it is unsuitable for deriving revolutionary structural changes.'[14] Here we would agree with him when countering the opponent he poses; but this opponent is not actual historical materialism! Historical materialism defines the productive forces to be socially materialized faculties of physical and mental labour in a living and objectivated form, while the production relations are those which people develop towards the means and objects of their production and also among themselves, during production. So neither are the productive forces purely things (technical means), nor do production relations refer to relations between people only. The productive forces are, in fact, the individual and collective as well as the subjective and objective labour faculties of the production conditions. And because production has a collective subject and is always work on a part of the natural environment, those faculties for labour become real productive forces only through and within production relations! Therefore, both factors are analytically *inseparable*. Thus a functional interpretation of the mode of production is out of the question from a Marxist viewpoint, because it is inevitably linked with an objectivation of the productive forces and the production relations in opposition to one another. In reality, one cannot even perceive any productive force in isolation from its production relations.

So with what does Eder replace the mechanistic deprivation of the mode of production concept? In order to derive evolutionary structural changes, he says, 'we must go back to the phenomenon of consciousness, to orientation systems of social action'.[15] This unmistakably implies that for Eder the elements of a social system are exclusively human individuals whose sociality appears in communication. And this implies in particular that people's ownership of the objective conditions of labour in this sense is essentially *not* a social relation. It follows that social revolutions as qualitative changes of property relations are irrelevant to Eder's 'theory of socio-cultural evolution', and that every revolution (evolutionary structural change) appears solely as a 'revolution in thinking'. Such a conclusion must be drawn from every social theory which starts from the premise that a social system is nothing but a structured set of human individuals.

In contrast to this, historical materialism and the materialist view of human history to which it gives philosophical substantiation states that social systems are the structured set of human individuals and their tools and labour objects. Otherwise one cannot seriously consider property relations as the dominating production relations. (Unless one presumes property to be originally a relation between people, and thus slavery to be that production relation which sets in when production becomes an expression of *humanized* life!)

If one concedes that concrete labour is the unity in motion of its subjective (human) and objective (non-human) conditions, then one must also concede that the bearers of the subjective conditions must be the proprietors of the objective, if labour is to come about. From this follows that every system of human society has as its premise a set of bearers composed of two subsets: (1) the set of relevant human individuals, (2) the set of relevant means and objects of production. If the objective conditions of production are owned by only a fraction of the subset, we speak of 'special' or 'private property'; if all the human individuals own these conditions, we speak of 'communal property'. Historically, communal property (tribal property) was the first production relationships. And every theory on societal evolution must explain how private property emerged from the condition of communal property, and it must anticipate how the communal property of the truly developed human species can emerge from the condition of private property.

Clearly, such a task cannot be solved where a theory *a priori* presumes the irrelevancy of property conditions for 'socio-cultural evolution', and thus imputes human beings devoid of property as the natural condition of human beings. Indeed, the question arises, how it is possible for theoreticians to accept such a premise, although it is obvious that the faculty of speech cannot satisfy hunger! Eder intelligently understands the significance of this question, so we will not go into it further, but continue to another problem connected with it.

As the theory of socio-cultural evolution reduces the social system to a population of human individuals, it is quite clear that the social system cannot have an *economic* foundation. In particular, it is incapable of grasping the fact of the analytical division of the total product in necessary and surplus product. It presumes the condition of a neolithic household-economy of self-sufficient agricultural communities in which allegedly no surplus product is visible. An empirical fact *appears* to substantiate this, namely, that the archaic communities, in spite of certain technical potential, did not produce a surplus which could have served other communities as a means of consumption. R. L. Carneiro notes:

For example, all Amazon Indians basically did agriculture; but at times when they still lived in a primitive state, they did not produce a surplus. That they were technically able to produce such a surplus is shown by the fact that a number of tribes, stimulated by the European settlers' demand for food, planted manioc for purposes of trade in quantities considerably above their own needs. So the means for creating a food surplus were certainly there; what was lacking was the social mechanisms necessary to induce the use of these means.[16]

This idea of the non-existence of a surplus product when such social mechanisms are lacking arises purely from the misinterpretation of the appearance of things. This becomes clear if one remembers that every human population is analytically divided into the subgroups of those in actuality capable of work and those in actuality incapable of work. The product which ensures the physical reproduction of those able to work is called 'necessary labour'. That product which ensures the reproduction of those not able to work is called 'surplus product'. Every social system is faced with the analytical problem of dividing the total product into necessary and surplus product. And the regulations created for distribution of these products provide the norms for 'justice' in each system. So the existence of a surplus of labour beyond necessary labour is given *a priori* in every system of labour, and one can say that sociality, in contrast to individuality, is perceivable exactly in this surplus product. In this sense, the evolution of sociality, in so far as it differs from individuality, is essentially the evolution of the surplus product. It is the struggle for the surplus product that constituted sociality!

If one now observes that no 'surplus' is produced in certain social systems, this means simply that the surplus product does not go beyond a certain quantitative limit. So it is not the existence of a surplus which is questionable, but the quantitative determination of the surplus product. Thus, a social mechanism that is especially a mechanism of political domination (so important to Eder) does not serve as a genetical precondition for bringing about the surplus product, but as a means for its quantitative expansion. So it is not politics (and to speak with Herr Eugen Dühring, not the man with the sword) that creates economy, but the economic basis provides the possibilities for constituting politics.

To sum up: if a social system is suggested to be constituted by cultural universals, as Eder does, labour is *a priori* reduced to the technical realization of ideas (this was Lukacs' notion).[17] From this follows that the product of labour is not to be visualized as the economic objectivation of society, and thus it is indicated that surplus labour sets in only through communicative structural changes. If, to take the contrary case, a social system is visualized as a unity of its subjective and objective production conditions mediated through property, it becomes clear that the production of ideas is an element in labour and the labour product with its natural division into necessary and surplus labour is a reflection of that condition which social development has reached. To speak with K. H. Tjaden:

The basis of historical materialist theory of society presumes . . . the factual and continuing condition for societal life of human beings, which therefore cannot be isolated from the evolution of those conditions in that it is seen as a socio-cultural evolution having no preconditions or taking place independently. Societal evolution is the evolution of those systems of social activity which are based on the natural evolutionary distinction between human and non-human nature and cause the problematic exchange between these two natural elements.[18]

Put more concisely: social evolution is set going when the biological species of *Homo sapiens* living in real populations appropriates a piece of non-human nature and turns it into objective conditions of production. It is this activity through which human society is constituted and distinguishes itself from animal sociality—and this as a definite mode of production. Thus, nature gains a double existence: first, as raw material and

tool *within* the social system and, second, as environment of that
same system.

3. *On the Social Position of the Political*

The last comment to be made here concerns Eder's central
thesis on the moralization of law as a genetic precondition for
the emergence of class societies.

The process of learning, which has led to the political constitution of
society, can be described as the moralisation of . . . social relations of
inter-action. The society is moralised when the emerging structures of
domination have legitimate authority. Whoever lays down the law is
then not merely *umpire*, but *judge*: this is the step taken in learning
which made it possible for the high cultures and the early high-cultural
class societies following them to arise.[19]

Eder attempts to explain the genesis of political power
through the internal conditions of the system: 'Subjugation, etc.
in primary state formation' are out of the question as 'mechanisms of selection'.[20] While this may sound good as regards the
self-sufficiency of evolving systems, in my opinion it is an
illusory programme. Eder himself shows up the illusion when
he deals with how states actually formed in empirical history:

Vedic culture in India, Homerian Greece, the new Babylonian empire
and the Assyrian empire, the China of Chou and also the Inka and
Aztec empires . . . are the result of integration of nomadic barbarian peoples into already existing high culture. It was only these
high cultures which were in a position . . . to become politically
stable . . .[21]

Here, Eder himself describes the encounter between bar-
barians and neolithic agriculture to be the genetic condition for
realization of political stability. And how can one speak of the
realization of politics or political domination without presuming
political stability? However, if that encounter is the condition
for political stability, what is left of the concept of a purely
internal genesis of politics?

From the Marxist viewpoint, the state is clearly an instrument in the hands of the ruling class, so the genesis of the state is

also the political consequence of the genesis of class domination which consists firstly and above all in the economic fact of the appropriation of another's surplus labour (while it is quantitatively extended). And how this happens is best demonstrated by Carneiro through the example of the Inca state.[22] The question here is, indeed, one of *subjugation* of one community by another, it is the situation described so well by Hegel in his *Phänomenologie* with the fiction of two struggling individuals resulting in the establishment of a master-slave relationship. That victory as well as defeat in such a struggle are the result of purely social conditions, also in the sense of a socio-cultural evolution of struggling communities, need not be disputed. Eder's mistake is not to presume such an evolution, but to identify with it the evolution of mankind.

We will leave aside the problem of an empirical legitimation of Eder's thesis and investigate only its philiosophical basis. To understand this, one must appreciate that Eder's transition from umpire to judge is a classical problem of reflection which appears in a different form in the question of the transition of a particular type of commodity to money. Eder knows very well that the ruler has the meaning of a *representative*: 'The ruler need not necessarily himself be the judge or instructor of judges; he "represents" the institutional framework within which a traditionally substantiated and codified law can be pronounced.'[23] So, the ruler-judge is a representative, a means of reflection of that which those he represents have in common. But what is the common interest of those represented by the ruler-judge directed at? Of what intentionality is their political behaviour which is represented by him individually? The answer is simple: the appropriation of another's surplus product needs to be ensured instrumentally. Therefore, only in the process of delimitation from the non-represented are one (or more) individuals defined as representatives among those thus being represented. In other words, the ruler-judge described by Eder is the *representative of the dominators* and not of the *subjugated*. Eder attempts to 'derive' the ruler-judge from the processes of learning visualized as the objectivation of political behaviour within a single community. He tries to suggest that— how much German ideology is contained here!—the state is the product of 'moralization of law' rather than of class antagonisms. However, he cannot prove it factually. The nomadic barbarian tribes, by penetrating into the 'ecological niches' of neolithic agriculture thwart his purposes. They bring forth *struggle* as the prerequisite for the birth of politics and thus the ruler-judge. Thus they demonstrate that the emergence of domination at once conditions the emergence of subjugation. And the suggestion that the representative of the dominators be at the same time the representative of the subjugated, leads to logical indigestion.

Let us examine the problem of reflection through the well-known example of how the internal contradiction of commodity becomes objectivated in the polar opposites of commodity and money: it is clear that money, as a special type of commodity, acts as the representative of the value of all other commodities. Thus it occupies the same position as does the ruler-judge towards the subjugated. Both represent figures in a certain system; they represent determinations of reflection. Marx notes at this point: 'Such reflective determinations form a very curious class. For instance, one man is king only because the other men behave as his subjects. They, on the contrary, imagine they are subjects because he is king.'[24] Of course, money represents substantialized social labour power while the ruler-judge represents the realized political power of the exploiting class.

Now, it is important to note that money not only represents as value the products of labour which may replace it, but at the same time it excludes those which cannot replace it as unsaleable or non-commodities. Once money has arisen within the general system of mutual exchangability of products between independent producers and owners, then—according to the Marxist theory of the evolution of the form of value[25]—this exchange for money now determines that a product of labour becomes a commodity. Whatever is offered as a commodity without being realized as a commodity by really being bought, now leads an existence as a non-commodity. Therefore, money, the representative of value, is not alone the means for presenting the abstract *unity* of realizable commodities, but at the same time the means of actual delimitation of unrealizable products from commodities!

And we must direct attention to this delimiting function of the representative, in order to correct the assumption that a representative figure or means of reflection is such simply because it represents the class of objects which may replace it. In addition, the representative, just because it represents a *class*, of necessity has objects outside of itself, which in relation to the represented class, in set-theoretical terms, can function readily as representatives of the corresponding *empty* class, i.e. they substantialize the *nothing* against the *being* of that class. In other words, the representative is not only the *polar* extreme in opposition to the represented, it is also the *real* extreme against those objects excluded from representation.[26] And no species property is really determined if it is not determined in the sense of a real extreme against another species.

If we now, with Eder, accept the representational function of the ruler-judge, in which we see this reflective means of the political power of the ruling class, then, according to the dialectical theory of reflection, we must also accept that the existence of the ruler-judge is conditioned by the existence of those persons who are excluded from power, that is, by the existence of the subjugated who are members of the exploited class—under pre-capitalism usually the members of the former defeated community. If these now realize political power, then under no circumstances within the 'institutional framework' represented by the given ruler-judge (or any other political authority), but only under the condition of creating political and individual as well as social innovations which opens up a real possibility of a new institutional framework. An exploited class which is incapable of such innovations is, historically, not a potential bearer of evolutionary structural changes.

So what can we now say philosophically about Eder's 'moralization of law' as the presumed precondition for political power? As Eder does not assume social systems as basically economically determined systems of labour, but as forms of appearance of cultural universals, the struggle for the surplus product must necessarily remain hidden from his theoretical sight. Thus he cannot explain the genesis of politics with the collision of various communities, but must turn to the cognitive revolution which is explained internally within *one* community in accordance with the principles of synthetic theory. Consequently, according to Eder it is not politics that determines morals (of class society, as goes without saying), but morals that determine politics. At least from a materialist viewpoint, this is quite unacceptable.

And incidentally, it is also unacceptable from the standpoint of synthetic theory. For, according to the concept of the synthetic theory, the internal fluctuations around the species norm are generally an expression of lethal mutations, and the selection advantage for certain mutations is not determined without the environment of that particular system. So while Eder employs the synthetic theory, he does not sufficiently take into account its strict prerequisite, i.e. to be a theory of *open* systems.

It seems to me, in connection with the social scientific employment of the synthetic theory, that one more factor is vital: as social systems are modes of production, they imply the *property* relation among the bearers of the subjective working conditions and the means and objects of labour. Thus they have a fundamentally different relationship to external nature than organic systems. For the latter, nature is 'environment'; for the former, however, 'divide and rule' is the constitutive factor in relation to external nature. Social systems, when a part of nature, constitute themselves by being appropriated and thus become an *internal* condition of the system which is further cultivated, while the environment to this system constitutes the rest of nature. This so-called 'second nature' is nothing but the appropriated cultivated nature. And precisely property is not a structural part of organic systems. Therefore, the existence of property in human systems throws up the question of how to give the synthetic theory a new development; property does not allow for application of this theory to social development without new elementary considerations.

This problem can be tackled only if one grasps the actual cultivation idealistically, purely as the realization of cults, as the use of constructive rules which are, in fact, used for concrete labour. As all real labour expesses itself in determinable forms, it is possible—metaphysically—to interpret labour as the realization of ideal forms, in other words, to interpret prosaic cultivation as being the expression of the holy cult. However, here it is forgotten that objectivation of the forms of labour, their fixation in rules of action, is the inductive work of cognition which, in actuality, cannot take place without the prerequisite of a concrete unity between the subjective and objective conditions of labour. Hunting rituals gain their socially orientating power because they set in as a form of mental digestion of hunts that have already taken place! The cult provides a social bond because the social bond has already been experienced in practical cultivation.

Therefore, we insist on dialectically deriving, in the sense of the theory of evolution of forms of value, the 'socio-cultural evolution in the construction rules of the societal world'[27] out of the actual reality of *a priori social* labour. If we do not accept this challenge we limit ourselves to mere enlightenment and are thus forced to distinguish the subject of social evolution through a specific difference (be this thinking or language) and must then of necessity reduce evolution to development as a kind of unfolding. In face of the real struggle existing for the surplus product, such a position is left with nothing but a wavering between the hope for a quantitative accumulation of reason and the scepticism on whether this will take place. If one, in contrast to this, considers the revelant 'construction rules of the societal world' as a result of objectivation of forms of labour that really have unfolded within a mode of production, one then gains the necessary philosophical ataraxy, and in view of history so far, this is a state of mind that should not be despised.

Notes

1 Klaus Eder, *Die Entstehung staatlich organisierter Gesellschaften: Ein Beitrag zu einer Theorie sozialer Evolution*, Frankfurt am Main, Suhrkamp Verlag, 1976.

2 K. Eder (ed.), *Einleitung zu: Seminar: Die Entstehung von Klassengesellschaften*, Frankfurt am Main, Suhrkamp Verlag, 1973, p. 7.

3 F. Engels, 'Ludwig Feuerbach und der Ausgang der klassischen deutschen Philosophie' ('Ludwig Feuerbach and the End of German Classical Philosophy'), *Marx-Engels Selected Works*, Progress Publishers, Moscow, 1970, p. 593.

4 G. W. F. Hegel, 'Enzyklopädie der philosophischen Wissenschaften', in *Hegel, Werke, Bd. 8*, E. Modenhauer and K. M. Michel (eds), Frankfurt am Main, Suhrkamp Verlag, 1970, pp. 41-2.

5 K. Eder, *Die Entstehung . . .*, *op. cit.*, p. 124.

6 *ibid.*, p. 125.

7 *ibid.*, pp. 126-7.

8 K. Marx/F. Engels, *The German Ideology*, Progress Publishers, Moscow, 1976, p. 49.

9 Hegel comments, 'Als ein Allgemeines *sprechen* wir auch das Sinnliche *aus*; was wir sagen, ist: *Dieses*, d.h. da *allgemeine Diese*, oder: *es ist*, d.h. das *Sein überhaupt*. Wir stellen uns dabei freilich nicht das allgemeine Diese oder das Sein überhaupt *vor*,

136 *Philosophy of Evolution*

aber wir *sprechen* das Allgemeine *aus*; oder wir sprechen schlechthin nicht, wie wir es in dieser sinnlichen Gewißheit *meinen*. Die Sprache aber ist, wie wir sehen, das Wahrhaftere; . . .' (in *Phänomenologie des Geistes*; J. Hoffmeister (ed.); Berlin, Akademie-Verlag, 1964, p. 82). The point here is Hegel's phrase 'Wie wir sehen' (as we see): What we should *see*, i.e. perceive by our senses is the form of sentence 'this is p' in the elementary sentence 'this is red', 'this is beautiful', etc. See also P. Ruben, 'Von der "Wissenschaft der Logik" und dem Verhältnis der Dialektik zur Logik' in *Seminar: Dialektik in der Philosophie Hegels*, R.-P. Horstmann (ed.), Frankfurt am Main, Suhrkamp Verlag, 1978, pp. 70–100.

10 J. Habermas, *Erkenntnis und Interesse*. Mit einem neuen Nachwort, Frankfurt am Main, Suhrkamp Verlag, 1973, pp. 71 ff.

11 K. Marx/F. Engels, *The German Ideology*, *op. cit.*, pp. 47–8.

12 See also P. Ruben, 'Wissenschaft als allgemeine Arbeit', in Ders., *Dialektik und Arbeit der Philosophie*, Cologne, Pahl-Rugenstein Verlag, 1978, pp. 9–51.

13 Marx-Engels Selected Works, Preface to the Critique of Political Economy, *op. cit.*, p. 182.

14 K. Eder, *Die Entstehung . . .*, *op. cit.*, p. 49.

15 *ibid.*

16 R. L. Carneiro, 'Eine Theorie zur Entstehung des Staates', in *Seminar: Die Entstehung von Klassengesellschaften*, pp. 155–6.

17 'Through labour', says Lukacs, 'a teleological setting is realised within material being as the origination of new objectivation' (in *Ontologie—Arbeit*, Neuwied u. Darmstadt, Luchterhand, 1973, p. 13). Thus, labour is thought as Telos realization and the birth of Telos unexplainable, Eder gives only a pseudo-explanation at this point by grasping the individual Telos as a variation in a Telos pool—with the prerequisite of analogization of the biological gene-pool with the 'pattern of interpretation' of the ideologie of the social system. Even if this analogization is certainly possible, it is based on the prerequisite of the existence of the ideas pool. At the most this is Cartesian thinking—and not the explanation for the origins of the ideas pool, which is exactly which is needed.

18 K. H. Tjaden, 'Naturevolution, Gesellschaftsformation, Weltgeschichte. Überlegungen zu einer gesellschaftswissenschaftlichen Entwicklungstheorie', *Das Argument*, 19, 1977, p. 101.

19 K. Eder, *Die Entstehung . . .*, *op. cit.*, p. 70.

20 *ibid.*, p. 83.

21 *ibid.*, p. 105.

22 Carneiro, *op. cit.*, pp. 164–6.

23 Eder, *op. cit.*, p. 87.

24 K. Marx, *Das Kapital*, Band 1, Berlin, Dietz Verlag, 1953, pp. 62–3, Anmerkung (unauthorized translation).

25 On this, see K. Marx, 'Die Wertform', in Marx/Engels, *Kleine ökonomische Schriften*, Berlin, Dietz Verlag, 1955, pp. 262–88.

26 *Polar* extremes are objects in opposition within the *same* species (e.g. men and women in the human race); *real* extremes are objects in opposition in different species. On this, see K. Marx, 'Kritik des Hegelschen Staatsrechts', *Marx-Engels Werke*, Band 1, Berlin, 1957, pp. 290–4.

27 Eder, *op. cit.*, p. 68.

5 Natural History and Psychology: Perspectives and Problems

P. Keiler

Introduction

THE demand that a psychologist should specify the relationship between biology and the human and social sciences, in order to define the position of his own discipline, confronts him with the difficult task of having to engage in a discussion of scientific method on two apparently quite separate fronts at the same time. In the first place, there are—even today—very few psychologists who can lay claim to an adequate biological view of the processes of nature, that is, one based on evolutionary theory. Second, the recent emergence of human ethology as a discipline of its own within biology confronts psychology with a science which has gradually tried to appropriate part of the terrain which even popular consciousness has regarded as essentially the province of psychology. In doing this, human ethology has not simply acted as a competitor with psychology in the realm of 'pure science', as could be seen, for example, in the relationship between traditional developmental psychology and the behavioural biology of the child (cf. Hassenstein, 1973); it has also, at least since the publication of Konrad Lorenz's much quoted treatise on the natural history of aggression, acquired increasingly ideological relevance (cf. Lorenz, 1963).

Two things appear to be necessary: on the one hand, psychology must be made to include more biological knowledge and material; on the other hand, the limited scope of that very biological discipline closest to psychology needs to be demonstrated. This may seem to pose a paradox, but in fact the task is relatively unambiguous and determinate. In short, it involves the application to both disciplines of a wider historical understanding of man than that which is provided by the biological theory of evolution.

In what follows, an attempt will be made to give a short outline of the perspectives and problems which arise from

137

viewing psychology as a branch of natural history, and the framework adopted will be that of historical and dialectical materialism. Questions concerning the object of study and method will be framed in terms of the single discipline of *psychology*. Human ethology is, nevertheless, equally affected by our investigations, in as much as the establishment of the limitations of an *exclusively* biological interpretation of human development also provides positive guidelines for a biological discipline from which psychology can—far more than has been the case up to now—expect help towards the solution of *its own* problems, most particularly those of a practical nature.

General aspects of an historical approach in psychology

The idea that in constructing a psychology of man, one must be guided by the principle of an historical approach was formulated as early as 1927 by the Soviet psychologist, Vygotsky. His views provided a critical refutation of notions reducing human psychology to its biological aspects. Contrasting these notions, he developed a theory of the cultural-historical genesis of human consciousness. In this theory, the transformation of the natural mechanisms of psychical processes is traced back to the individual's appropriation of the products of human culture in the course of his ontogenetic intercourse with other human beings. Thus the appropriation of social and socially-formed modes of interaction with the environment becomes the fundamental mechanism of the development of the human psyche. Vygotsky's views later excited a good deal of controversy within Soviet psychology (although it was not until the 1960s that Vygotsky's views attracted any attention in the West), but this was essentially because Vygotsky was unable to formulate a unitary model of the socio-historical nature of the human psyche which would simultaneously take into account its bio-physiological and its cultural-historical aspects. At first glance, the only way of overcoming this difficulty seemed to be the acceptance of two alternative methods of approach to the object of study. This, however, would have meant the abandonment of the original goal of constructing a unitary psychology.

Thus, if one was to start by investigating the most complex, and specifically human problems, such as the question of the socio-historical specificity of the various dimensions of personality, the higher emotions or the dynamic of an individual's value-system, one was more or less compelled to operate with purely descriptive—ultimately phenomenological—concepts right from the start. Such concepts, however, could only be related to such notions as were needed to explain the mechanisms of elementary processes on the bio-physiological level at the price of interpreting them in an arbitrary and thus at once mechanistic and idealistic manner.

On the other hand, there are clearly advantages in a method which, as it were, approaches pyschological problems 'from below': one starts by stressing analytic or genetic (that is, phylogenetic) elementary mechanisms, including, for example, such simple relationships and processes as the conditioned reflex. To confront an investigator engaged in such a project with the demand that his work should not lose sight of the fact that man is a social being, is to set him an impossible task. The fundamental concepts which he is using are derived from a system of relationships which is in principle different from the system man-society. Attempts to see such concepts as merely more complicated when applied to human beings, and to 'extend' them by attaching the feature 'activity' to the concept of adaptation, for example; or to supplement the concept of the environment with features such as 'society', 'class' or—once again—'activity' (in the sense of intentional, educational effects upon the individual) are not able to provide a fundamental solution to the problem (cf. Leontiev, 1973, p. 273).

The assertion of two alternative historical methods of approach to the human psyche thus in no way leads to the creation of a unified psychology. Rather, it reproduces (although under quite different theoretical premises) the subject-object-dualism characteristic of traditional psychology, the necessary consequence of which was the growth of at least two different and mutually exclusive forms of 'psychology'.

It appears that the problem of mediation of both the biological and the social in the historical determination of the human psyche can only be solved if, from the very beginning, the scientific analysis of psychological phenomena is derived from Marx's definition of man as simultaneously a 'natural' and a 'social' being. That is to say, the relation of man to his surrounding environment must always be seen as a dual relationship: on the one hand, as a natural relation, and on the other, as a social relation (cf. *Marx-Engels-Werke*, Vol. 3, pp. 29 ff).

Against this background, we may formulate the first and primary task of an historical analysis of the human psyche in the following terms: the identification of the fundamental 'unit' of the life-process which, on the one hand, can be found at all levels of phylogenetic development, and, on the other hand, appears under the particular conditions of socio-historical development as a simultaneously natural and social relation. Leontiev, at one time a colleague of Vygotsky's, identifies this fundamental 'unit' with the *activity* of organisms, seen as an active relationship with their surrounding reality. The multiplicity of activities which find their expression in the various life-relationships which exist between the organism and its surrounding reality are seen as essentially determined by the objects of these activities. More explicitly, Leontiev's claim that every activity of an organism is directed towards this or that *object* (such that an objectless activity is conceptually impossible), differentiates his concept of activity clearly from the unspecific concept of behaviour as employed by the behaviourists (cf. Keiler, 1977, p. 124, n. 5).

The specifically human form of activity is *labour*, a process in which both man and nature participate, and in which man of his own accord starts, regulates and controls the material reactions between himself and nature. He opposes himself to nature as one of her own forces, setting in motion arms and legs, head and hands, the natural forces of his own body, in order to appropriate nature's productions in a form adapted to his own wants (*Marx-Engels-Werke*, Vol. 23, p. 192). On the other hand, in production, man does not just act upon nature, he interacts with his fellow men. They produce only when they interact in a particular manner, and exchange the products of their activities with one another. In order to produce, they enter into certain relationships and relations with one another, and it is only within these social relationships and relations that they act upon nature or that production takes place (*Marx-Engels-Werke*, Vol. 6, p. 407).

Although the particular functionality of the psyche as regards human activity manifests itself in the control exercised over the course of the activity, and in the anticipation of the outcome of the activity, one cannot, therefore, assume that the particular form in which it manifests itself is in any way identical with the *general nature of the psyche*. If one starts from the premise that the psyche is not simply some sort of accompaniment to life, but rather one of the particular forms under which life manifests itself and which inevitably comes into being as life develops (cf. Leontiev, 1973, p. 42), then the necessity of the psyche's arising at all and of its development must be deduced logico-historically from the conditions for the higher development of life itself.

Logico-historical analysis and the 'three-steps' method

The formulation of this approach allows us, at the same time, to solve the problem of the logical ordering of various aspects of the historical method in the investigation of the human psyche. On the one hand, scientific examination of human subjectivity presupposes the internal unity of analyses in terms of natural, social and individual history; while, on the other hand, in the real process of research or in a discursive context there is no way in which this unity can be expressed as simultaneity; it has to be concretized in several deductive steps whose ordering cor-responds to the logico-historical structure of the object.

The most comprehensive context in which human subjec-tivity must be viewed appears to be man's phylogenetic development: a process taking place over millions of years. This expresses itself in a variety of forms as the biological precondi-tion for every stage of socio-historical development within the course of the individual's development (that is, the onto-genesis).

In the second step of the deductive process it must be borne in mind that the natural-historical process of evolution—the product of which is man as 'organism'—undergoes a change within an historical period of transition which is difficult to specify precisely (paleoanthropology suggests a period of some eight million years for this process), so that it is qualitatively transformed and becomes specifically the socio-historical de-velopment of mankind.

Whereas evolution in natural history takes place exclusively

142 *Philosophy of Evolution*

as a process of changes in hereditary structures under conditions of mutation and selection which are peculiar to the species, the bearer of socio-historical development must be seen to be objectified human labour. It is above all labour which, via its objectification, makes possible the preservation, transmission and cumulative utilization of social experience (cf. Holzkamp, 1973, p. 52). Here, the opposition between biology and society is not to be seen as realizing itself in an abstract exclusivity: surely, on the one hand, the conditions of life and the modes of living of mankind change radically and increasingly quickly, whilst the morphological characteristics of the species 'man' (*Homo sapiens*) remain relatively constant and morphological changes do not exceed the bounds of variants. On the other hand, the relative standstill in human morphogenesis from the time of Cro Magnon man obviously does not mean that the laws of biological variability and of inheritance are no longer at work in the case of human beings. They only remain ineffective as regards natural selection in the struggle for existence; for example, the chances for survival of an infant with a hereditary defect are not directly determined by biological mechanisms of selection but are determined in general by a wide variety of social factors (among others, by the level of development of medicine). The essential expression of the 'unity in opposition' which characterizes the biological and social factors in human development is the fact that the 'nature of mankind' in ontogenesis never reveals itself in a pure form, but always in an already socialized one. Thus, theoretical reconstruction of the history of the *individual* will not lead to an appropriate determination of the relationship between the biological pre-conditions of human personality and the social factors which shape it. This can only be achieved by recourse to the transition from natural-historical development to social-historical de-velopment of a mankind as a species-being. Here, the central question is what the properties are which man has acquired in the course of evolution which have made sociability part of his nature. But this does not mean that the realization of his biological possibilities by the individual in his personal develop-ment, via his appropriation of social experience, is to be seen as a simple repetition of the transition within the history of the species from natural history to the history of mankind (in the

form of a 'fundamental bio-socio-genetic law', for example).
However, the area of transition from animal to man offers to
anthropogenetic research an example of the developmental
process which reaches beyond the limits of pure biological
development. Here, it is possible to elaborate scientific categories which, in the analysis of the development of the
individual, may reveal the biological preconditions which, as
biological properties of the individual, make the process of
his socialization possible (cf. Holzkamp and Schurig, 1973,
p. xxxix).

In the third step of the deductive process, historically
oriented psychological research necessarily encounters the
question concerning the mediation between individual historical development of the human being and social-historical
development. For, on the level established in the second step of
the deductive process, it is only possible to comprehend the
special nature of the human psyche as 'consciousness', as
opposed to the various forms of animal psyche, in terms of its
general and abstract characteristics. The consciousness of a
specific human being manifests over and above this, however, a
concrete historical form of his psyche, the concrete particu-
larities of which are dependent on the social conditions of life,
and which change and develop according to economic relations
(cf. Leontiev, 1973, pp. 214 ff).

Once the individual consciousness has been established as an
historical fact, it can be characterized as structured by the
historical particularity of the social structure pertaining to the
respective social epoch. In other words, it is only through
analyses which concretize the specific forms of subjectivity of
particular human beings (seen as the result of the individual
appropriation of socio-historical experience) that factors can be
set off which are not simply features of human sociability in
general but specific characteristics of human sociability under
the life-conditions of, for instance, a particular form of class
society or of socialist society (cf. Holzkamp, 1973, p. 52).

If the necessity of this third step in the deductive process is
ignored, such that one does not take into account the necessity of
relating psychological research to the concrete human being in
his historically determined social relations, psychology loses its
concreteness and becomes a science of the mental life of abstract

human beings, of man as such (cf. Leontiev, 1973, p. 245). In fact, such an abstract level, which would ignore the properties of the structure of consciousness specific to a particular form of society and exclude them from psychological investigation, would constitute an advance in relation to the reductive notion of 'man as organism' (cf. Holzkamp, 1972) which characterizes many subareas of bourgeois psychology. On the other hand (for example, in the psychological analysis of the individual historical process of appropriation under the life-conditions of bourgeois society), it would necessarily be the case that no feature of the personality that could be seen to result from the appropriation of structural factors of bourgeois class reality in their historical specificity would find expression either in the form of theoretical assumptions or as empirical findings (cf. Holzkamp and Schurig, 1973, p. xlviii).

There is another (and equally common) methodological error which is much more serious than the confusion of general human and concrete social conditions within the analysis of the human personality. It consists in the attempt of stating characteristic structural features of bourgeois society not only as constants of *social* historical development but also as '*natural* constants', by claiming, within the context of an apparently scientific *animal*-experiment, to break through the framework not only of bourgeois society but also of social relations in general.

This is the case in the well-known investigations of Wolfe and his collaborators in the 1930s. Chimpanzees were made to learn material means-and-ends relationships of considerable complexity, especially devised for the experiment, involving metal discs, a piece of apparatus called a 'vender', and food. The results of these experiments have repeatedly been interpreted as showing that even such specifically 'intellectual' modes of behaviour as exchange or the use of money are, as it were, timeless, and that commercial relations such as 'credit' and prostitution are fundamentally natural (cf. particularly Nissen and Crawford, 1936, and Fischel, 1967).

From such highly artificial experiments one neither learns anything about the real intellectual possibilities which are characteristic of that level of psychical development which the anthropoid apes represent, nor does one learn anything about the material conditions for the development of labour in general, or about commodity production as the necessary precondition for regulated exchange relationships in particular. What we find here, on the other hand, is that certain general features of the anthropoids' repertoire of behaviour are forced from outside into a specific mould closely associated with the conceptions of developed commodity society. A circular interpretation is then invoked, implying that this part of the behavioural repertoire of the anthropoid apes can be seen as anticipating socially regulated exchange relationships at the animal level.

The essential factor in such an obfuscation is that the animal-man comparison is not used to obtain a more accurate determination of the various similarities and differences between different levels of psychical development, but rather to legitimate the *denial* of a genuine development at all.

In the *popular notion* the evolution of mental structures, even more than phylogenetic affinities in body-structure or in physiological processes, appears to be suitable for making human beings the standard to which theories concerning the *direction* of evolution can be related, thereby simplifying the comprehensive developmental context to a linear continuum in which the respective subject is seen as the focal point of various lines of development. But this is precisely why a *scientific* theory of psychophylogenesis must *not* be identical with the permanent projection of the investigator's level of development back onto the evolutionary process. On the contrary, a factor of considerable significance in ensuring the objectivity of a natural-historical description of the *development* of the psyche is the degree to which the investigator is able to detach his subjective notions from the development of the object of his research. In fact, the most commonly adopted procedure of basing conceptions of psychophylogenetic development on a permanent animal-human comparison is quite simply just a psychologizing anticipation of the actual course of development, in which all the animal behavioural adaptations which have no direct bearing upon current human behaviour are left out of account (Schurig, 1975, p. 37).

Leontiev's logico-historical reconstruction of psychophylogenesis and its methodical implications

A paradigm for an analysis within the field of natural history which is oriented towards objective historical criteria is provided by Leontiev's work on *sensibility* as the elementary form of psychical phenomena. He distinguishes between sensibility and mere *irritability*, which can be observed even in uni-cellular organisms and which constitutes a relatively unspecific basic precondition of any active reflection of the environment. Sensibility, in contrast, *orients* the organism *towards its environment* and provides an integrated reflection of the properties of its environment. The transition to sensibility as a form of reflection with higher adaptive value takes place, on the one hand, through the organism's entering into relations with its environment in increasingly complicated and diverse ways, on the other hand, through the differentiation of organic functions such that some organs become specialized sense-organs with narrowly specified areas of functioning (cf. Leontiev, 1973, p. 38). In this overall context, the significance of the psyche is established by the fact that it places the organism in relationship to environmental influences, which themselves are of no immediate biological implications, but rather *signal* influences which are biologically important to the organism (cf. *op. cit.*, pp. 36 ff). The real internal coherence of irritability and sensibility derives from their common natural-historical origins: specific changes of state or of the metabolism resulting from internal or external factors. In that, the laws governing the elementary level of reflection are by no means suspended or superceded in a quasi-mechanical manner by laws of a higher order, but are dialectically subsumed under the laws of higher and more specific processes. Here, the *opposition* between irritability and sensibility originates not only from the specific function of orientation of sensations but also from the fact that, based upon arousal as a material process, a transition to a qualitatively new form of reflection takes place in which the psyche makes its appearance in reality as the *ideational*.

Since the organism's function of orientation is not a directly observable variable in its ideational aspect, but solely something which can be inferred from the manifest activities of the organism with regard to the object of activity and the biological effect of that activity, psychological interpretation of the mutual relationship between the organism and its environment is necessarily subject to the danger of arbitrariness or of anthropomorphism. A necessary methodical corrective to this has existed since 1894, when Lloyd Morgan formulated his 'principle of parsimony' which has been important for establishing comparative psychology, animal psychology, and ethology on a scientific basis. According to this principle, it is impermissible to interpret an action as the outcome of the exercise of a higher psychical 'faculty' if it can be interpreted as the outcome of the exercise of one which stands lower in the psychological scale. We have to ask ourselves in each particular case, what level of development of the orientation function should be assumed *as a minimum* in order to render explicable the activity in question (Holzkamp, 1973, p. 65). Thus, from a formal point of view, the animal psyche appears as a 'logical remnant' in the context of the comprehensive (as opposed to reductive) theoretical reconstruction of the developed life-relations of the organism; without it, such a reconstruction is not a viable possibility.

Of course, the manifestations of sensibility change not only quantitatively but also qualitatively in the course of the higher development of organic life. The primitive sensibility of the lower animals differs fundamentally from that encountered in the higher animals and man. For instance, the development of intraception and proprioception compels us to approach the definition of sensibility at higher levels of psychophylogenesis in a fundamentally different manner. Nevertheless, the 'mediating' nature of sensibility remains the essential feature of the psyche in general, whatever the level of development or phenomenal form which it adopts. In *this* respect, human sensibility is no exception. The fact that in man it manifests itself as consciousness, expresses what is characteristically human, but this does not alter the fundamental relationships which define its general nature (cf. Leontiev, 1973, pp. 46, 48). Based on the knowledge that psychical processes are qualitatively differentiated in the course of biological evolution, although the psyche retains its essential nature, it is possible not only to reconstruct the *development* of the psyche in animals but also to discover a *general characteristic* of the animal psyche on the basis of the historical analysis of empirical material (cf. *op. cit.*, pp. 155–97). In the context of Leontiev's reconstruction of psychophylogenesis, his conceptual subdividing the process into three phases ('the elementary sensory psychical stage', 'the perceptive psychical stage', and 'the intellectual stage') is far less important than the principle which allows one to develop objective criteria for making a qualitative distinction between the various phenomenal manifestations of the psyche in terms of the *evolutionary progress* which they represent. In this, the conceptual framework used to investigate particular natural historical levels of the development of the psyche cannot be seen as independent of the perspective which the object of investigation forces one to adopt, that is, the selective accentuation of complex organism-environment relations in the form of 'motivation', 'perception' or 'learning'. The fact that, starting from the same fundamental principles, one may develop contrasting conceptual schemes according to the various aspects of the objects of research—as can be seen in the publications of various members of the Psychological Institute of the Free University, West Berlin—is not a sign of conflict. Rather, the different conceptual schemes complement one another and lead to increased precision.

Conceptual variations may be expected to increase as the problems being studied become more and more specialized, since the progressive exclusion of areas which do not explicitly fall within the scope of the object of research necessarily leads to a (until now somewhat uncontrolled) multiplication of specific modes of approach to particular areas. Thus, for example, Lorenz (1961), Thorpe (1963) and Hassenstein (1969), in trying to devise a natural-historical systemization of the various forms of animal learning, arrive at classifications which, in part, vary widely from one to another, although each of them is backed up by empirical evidence. And this is the case, in spite of the fact that they all adopt as a primary and essential criterion the principle that there is a *natural taxonomy* which allows the various species of animals to be arranged according to the degree of their phylogenetic proximity, and that this taxonomy should be used to specify the natural-historical system in which the particular categories of learning can arranged (cf. Keiler and Schurig, 1978).

There is more than one line in psychophylogenesis: the significance of the dolphin investigations

Given the present level of our knowledge, the logical systematization of psychophylogenesis as a field of research possesses less the status of a specialized scientific theory than that of a general *methodical* conception. It is not surprising that the discovery of new empirical facts can not only alter the whole direction of research within a particular specialist area of study but also that these discoveries will initiate considerable reorientation in the study of psychophylogenesis as a whole.

This may be illustrated by an example which bears directly upon an essential problem within human psychology: the problem of the natural-historical preconditions of human consciousness.

Leontiev terms the level of phylogenesis which represents the upper limit of psychical development in animals the 'intellectual stage'. It is characterized, above all, by the remarkable talent for abstraction and problem-solving behaviour (learning through insight) observed in anthropoid apes (cf. *op. cit.* pp. 180 ff). In particular, chimpanzees are not only able to transfer without further trial a solution that they have already discovered to another set of conditions which resemble the original problem-situation with regard to the *perceived* relationships among the objects involved, they are also able to combine several isolated operations into a single unified activity. The paradigm for such situations, the mastering of which involves the combination of isolated operations just mentioned into a single unified activity, is derived from a much-quoted experimental setting devised by Wolfgang Köhler: the bait, a piece of food, is placed outside the cage, beyond the animal's reach. Also outside the cage, beyond the animal's grasp, is a long stick. The only thing the animal can reach with its hands is a shorter stick, by means of which it can touch and move the longer stick, but not the food. To get the food, the animal must use the short stick to pull the long stick within its reach, and must then use the long stick to reach the food (cf. Köhler, 1963, p. 125). The activity exhibited in such an experimental situation can, therefore, be divided into a '*pre-*

paratory phase' and an *'executive* phase', whereby the preparatory phase is in itself incomprehensible in biological terms, and only has a function in the context of the objective relation between the means employed and the proper goal of the activity (cf. Leontiev, 1973, pp. 186 ff). In this, there does not exist an indissoluble linkage between the preparatory phase and the executive phase; they are related via the objective possibilities of achieving the goal of the activity. If, for example, an ape that has already used the stick successfully as a 'tool' in the experimental procedure described above then perceives the stick in a situation in which its use is not required, such as where it has to obtain the goal by a roundabout way, then it will not attempt to use the stick at all.

The achievements of anthropoid apes in two-or-more-phase tasks are evidence, on the psychical plane, of a high level of ability to reflect objective relations between *things*, that is, material situations. In point of fact, the ability to grasp constant material properties and relations demands a far higher degree of analysis of isolated conditions, of generalization and of synthesis than can be found in the context of the simple perceptual organization which characterizes the activity of organisms at the next lowest level of psychophylogenesis. The fact that anthropoid apes not only pay attention to the constant material properties of objects and their relations but can also, in changed situations, rapidly find a novel form of activity to enable them to attain their goals, suggests that these abilities represent some kind of proto-form of the gnostical approach to the world which is characteristic of human consciousness.

What then could be more natural than that the conditions of life and the abilities of anthropoid apes should be the primary interest of those investigating the psychophylogenetic proto-forms of human thought in the abilities for abstraction shown in animal behaviour? This is more especially so in view of the undisputed fact of their evolutionary proximity to man. The problem inherent in this position, however, is that it excludes the principle, ennunciated above, that psychophylogenesis should not be seen simply as a linear process of higher development, but rather as a process in which, under the influence of various different evolutionary factors, differing competing lines of development may have emerged. Further, there are certain factors which are indubitably necessary for the genesis of human consciousness which seem to be entirely absent in anthropoid evolution. Quite apart from the astonishing capacities of community-building insects, there is also the fascinating problem posed by the cognitive abilities of *dolphins*, members of the whale group of mammals, which are based on a wide repertoire of innate behavioural patterns.

The ability of dolphins to respond to training is unique in the animal world. Of particular interest is their ability to achieve exact motor coordination between several individuals in activities involving swimming or leaping out of the water. This deftness in the motor area means that, unlike primates, dolphins are able to learn complicated ball games. However, the assessment of their higher cognitive abilities is not only based on the complexity of the rules of the games that they are able to learn, but also upon the exceptional speed of the learning process, in which a single reinforcement is often enough to produce the desired behaviour. In general, there is an immediate and direct relationship between the high level of psychic development in dolphins and two factors.

First, there is a high degree of organization in their social behaviour. In this regard, as, for example, in the capacity to organize many individuals into a system which operates as a whole—the basis of the way in which they get their food—dolphins are far in advance of primates (cf. the many experimental attempts to investigate primates' ability to behave cooperatively in order to attain a common goal; these date back as far as Köhler). It seems here that organization in complex social groups makes the learning of abstract notions of goals and purposes, for instance, in the form of the rules of a game, considerably easier.

The second factor is the extraordinary range of acoustic signals which dolphins employ. It is probable that these are not only employed to convey information about sources of food or the presence of enemies, but also to maintain social cohesion.

The primary significance of the dolphin investigations for human psychology lies in the view which it opens up of the diversity of mechanisms by means of which a higher development of the psyche may be achieved. It draws attention to a causal structure which is fundamentally different from the conditions of the area of animal-man transition, and provides necessary stricture on the view that the precondition for the higher development of the psyche is provided solely by the ability to manipulate objects—an ability manifested in the anthropoid apes' ability to use and construct 'tools' and in man's establishment of labour relations later leading to the genesis of specific human language and conceptual thought.

Consequently, the view that labour is not only the primary foundation of human existence but also the fundamental condition for the emergence of human consciousness does not lose its status as the primary explanatory model of the conditions of the transition from animal to man and for the development of consciousness. But its formulation must be qualified by taking into account a set of subsidiary factors which constitute the main agents of the emergence of higher psychical development within phylogenetic lines quite separate from that which is represented by the anthropoid apes (cf. Schurig, 1976).

This fact—that it seems that life in a complex social group and the existence of a highly developed communication system provide, in the case of the dolphins, selection factors which are in an adequate foundation for an exceptionally high level of psychical development—also has consequences for the logical systemization of the process of psychophylogenesis. It leads, in particular, to a sharper formulation of Leontiev's concept of the 'intellectual stage'. In this formulation, this stage is character-ized by a specific inherent contradiction. On the one hand, animal activity at this level contains a particular preparatory phase which objectively anticipates the possibility of higher forms of activity (such as the activities of individuals under conditions of the division of labour which, although without meaning in themselves, are significant within the context of a *collective* labour process). On the other hand, it is only relations between *things* which are reflected in the animal's psyche (cf. *op. cit.*, p. 190). But when we take into account the social behaviour of dolphins (the maintenance of which, because of its com-plexity, requires the reflection of the relationship of the animals *one to another* as a *social* situation rather than just one concerning *things*), does it, in its essential aspect, not represent *de facto* precisely that higher form of activity which then, as *cooperative or complementary behaviour*, becomes the determining factor for the emergence of consciousness in the evolution of the hominids? The fact, however, that the transition from animal psyche to human consciousness is not completed in the case of the dolphins is, on the other hand, to be explained by the circumstance that there is no active, instrumentally mediated, appropriation of material reality within the social behaviour of dolphins parallel to the use and preparation of external aids for the completion of operations such as is found in the phylogenetic line of the apes, and which can be seen as an anticipation of human productive (that is, mediated by tools) activity at the animal level. However complex the social life of dolphins may be, the relationships that arise within it are not coordinated by 'the activity of production', they are not determined by it and do not depend upon it.

It is precisely the specifically human characteristic of production—that it is an active appropriation of nature which is realized by the individual, but which is nevertheless always oriented towards the activity of other members of the social group of which the individual is a part—which marks a nodal point in the development of the psyche, since it is here that the laws of an exclusively *biologically* determined process of evolution are integrated within the laws of a process of a higher order. This higher-order process then becomes the object of sciences in which categories other than biological—*economic*, for example—take over the function of providing a theoretical and integrative conceptual framework.

References

W. Fischel, *Vom Leben zum Erleben: Eine psychologische Untersuchung über Leistungen und Ziele der Tiere und Menschen*, Barth, Munich, 1967.

B. Hassenstein, *Die Verhaltensbiologie*, Herder, Freiburg, 1969.

B. Hassenstein, *Verhaltensbiologie des Kindes*, Piper, Munich/Zürich, 1973.

K. Holzkamp, 'Verborgene anthropologische Voraussetzungen der allgemeinen Psychologie', in K. Holzkamp, *Kritische Psychologie: Vorbereitende Arbeiten*, Fischer, Frankfurt, 1972.

K. Holzkamp, *Sinnliche Erkenntnis: Historischer Ursprung und gesellschaftliche Funktion der Wahrnehmung*, Fischer, Frankfurt, 1973.

K. Holzkamp and V. Schurig, 'Zur Einführung in A. N. Leontjews "Probleme der Entwicklung des Psychischen"', in A. N. Leontjew, *Probleme der Entwicklung des Psychischen*, Fischer, Frankfurt, 1973.

P. Keiler, 'Wissenschaftstheoretische und methodische Probleme einer Phylogenie des Psychischen', in K. A. Schneewind (ed.), *Wissenschaftstheoretische Grundlagen der Psychologie*, Ernst Reinhardt, Munich/Basel, 1977.

P. Keiler and V. Schurig, 'Einige Grundlagenprobleme der Naturgeschichte des Lernens', *Z.f.Psychol.*, 186, Heft 1 (Teil I), Heft 2 (Teil II), 1978. Nachdruck in *Forum Kritische Psychologie*, 3, Argument-Sonderband 28, 1978, pp. 91–150.

W. Köhler, *Intelligenzprüfungen an Menschenaffen*, Springer, Berlin, (West), 1963.

A. N. Leontiev, *Probleme der Entwicklung des Psychischen*, Fischer, Frankfurt, 1973.

K. Lorenz, 'Phylogenetische Anpassung und adaptive Modifikation', *Zeitschrift für Tierpsychologie*, 18, 1961, pp. 139–87.

K. Lorenz, *Das sogenannte Böse: Zur Naturgeschichte der Aggression*, Borotha-Schoeler, Vienna, 1963.

K. Marx, 'Lohnarbeit und Kapital', *Marx Engels Werke*, Bd. 6, Dietz, Berlin (DDR), 1970 a, pp. 397–423.

K. Marx, 'Das Kapital: Kritik der politischen Ökonomie', Band 1, *Marx Engels Werke*, Bd. 23, Dietz, Berlin (DDR), 1970 b.

K. Marx and F. Engels, 'Die deutsche Ideologie', *Marx Engels Werke*, Bd. 3, Dietz, Berlin (DDR), 1973.

H. W. Nissen and M. P. Crawford, 'A preliminary study of food-sharing behavior in young chimpanzees', *Journal of Comparative Psychology*, 22, 1936, pp. 383–419.

V. Schurig, *Naturgeschichte des Psychischen*, Band 1, Psychogenese und elementare Formen der Tierkommunikation, Campus, Frankfurt, 1975.

V. Schurig, *Die Entstehung des Bewusstseins*, Campus, Frankfurt, 1976.

W. H. Thorpe, *Learning and instinct in animals*, Methuen, London, 1963.

On the problem of self-consciousness and the origins of the expressive order: Commentaries on Döbert, Ruben and Keiler

R. Harré

THESE three chapters comprise two discussions. Döbert is largely concerned with the analytical conditions under which history can plausibly be made the subject of evolutionary forms of explanation. Ruben and Keiler address one particular problem of historical explanation—the emergence of what is peculiarly human from the natural history of man. Both, though neither explicitly formulate this point, are writing with the presumption that biological explanations must cease to have priority as historical explanations once some characteristic innovation in human affairs has come about.

Unlike several contributors to this volume, Döbert continues to identify 'evolved' with 'advanced'. It is on this basis that he precludes expressive social practices, such as forms of address, from the subject matter of social change theory, on the ground that whatever society we consider, these practices must be part of its constitutive activities. So changes in these practices could not be seen as advances. Changes in other, economic-structural features, on the other hand, can be seen (on the basis of an analogy with Piaget's views) as strivings for higher consistencies and so on, that is, as progressive.

I must confess considerable doubts about this assumption about the concept of evolution, if I have correctly attributed it to Döbert. Of course, one can fix concepts as one likes, provided one is consistent in their use. But in this case I think Döbert has fixed the concept so as to exclude some of the most interesting matters to which the *form* of an evolutionary explanation could be given, that is, an explanation in terms of mutations (poor copyings) and selection (inhibition or not of spread). If we give

155

up the idea that novel social expressive practices are better than their precedessors (though quite what that could mean I am not sure), we can examine the conditions under which new practices are tried out and see under what conditions they spread, reconstructing society as they go. (Bhaskar makes this point about the constructive role of innovations; see the commentary on Part III.)

However, despite this reservation, it seems to me that Döbert has offered a substantial theory of social mutation. If the diachronic-synchonic antithesis is resolved by introducing staging into historical analysis, students of social change can concentrate on transitions. I think that Döbert should be understand as offering primarily a theory of maladaptive practices, against which adaptiveness could perhaps be defined indirectly. I see his important point about the differences between information transmission in the biological and the cultural context as closely analogous to one of my reservations concerning the too ready adoption of the biological analogy. Döbert calls the reproduction of an ancient practice, through the use of a cultural code, a regression. But since, in the biological case, the information that represents ancient forms of adaptation (or maladaptation) perishes with the genes that encoded it, there can be no regression in the way that regression is so typical of human affairs. But Döbert adds a further form of maladaptation, misapplication. The highly differentiated and complex forms that social activities take in our kind of society, admits of the everpresent possibility that a practice may be misapplied, and though adaptive in general be maladaptive in some highly distinctive region. I have not fully grasped Döbert's implicit notion of adaptation that seems to be working in this argument, but if we couple this with his identification of 'evolved' with 'advanced' and that with some form of Piagetian staging, we come close to an account of adaptiveness in terms of the possibility of use of some form of rationality.

The papers by Ruben and Keiler address, I believe, a single topic: at what point and by what mark should we identify the emergence from their natural state of men as truly human. Both authors give the same answer, derived from a specific interpretation of Marx, that it is when labour, understood as the appropriation of some part of nature, appears. Ruben argues in this way for the purpose of rejecting the thesis proposed by Eder and many others, that it is with the emergence of language that men can properly be said to appear, while Keiler is concerned to use the argument more generally as speculative paleoanthropology.

Both authors seem to me to fail rather seriously to take account of the totality of conditions required to identify the emergence of true humanity. And both make the same mistake. It can be summed up in the assertion made by Keiler that 'the specifically human form of activity is labour'. Now I should have had no objection to that claim if it had been preceded by 'a' rather than 'the'. It seems to me that anthropology and history show that there is another specific activity of just as much moment which must share the explanatory role in any account of the origin of men: that form of activity we could call the search for honour and dignity. Ironically, it is a tacit premise in much of the reasoning that Ruben and Keiler either use or subscribe to. Without tacit reference to the second, the identification of distortions of the former, say in Marxist theory of capitalism, would have no moral quality nor could they serve as the source of a political programme. Expropriation of labour must be construable as a form of moral humiliation before there is the basis for a political critique. In similar vein, one can see Ruben's quotation of Hegel's vision of the master-slave relation as the result of 'struggle' as a mere sentimentality, since without a well-defined distinction between the practical and the expressive order, we should have to countenance the fact that slavish persons seek for and even create their own masters, as a counterargument to the use Ruben makes of the notion of 'struggle'. Again, it is at least as compatible with history and anthropology to say that the possibility of the appropriation of the labour of another is provided for by a preexisting theory in the expressive order, assigning different social worth to different categories of persons, defined independently of the social elaboration of the labour relation. Ruben's reply to this form of argument, or one something like it, strikes me as entirely speculative. He says, 'The cult provides a social bond, because the social bond has already been experienced in practical cultivation'. Modern theories of hunter-gatherer cultures would not support such an idea. Women gather but men hunt.

Do they hunt to get food? The answer seems to be that they do not. The contribution to the total food supply from this activity is derisory. But its contribution to the social-expressive order of honour is central to the social lives of many such cultures. Here the expressive order provides for the possibility of hunting as an activity, and not the other way round.

What is really at issue here? I think there is a very deep difference between Ruben and Keiler on the one side and myself, and that it concerns their assumption of *consciousness* as the mark of human psychology, derived from the social organization and practical imperative of labour. But animal studies suggest that this is just the mental attribute that there is the most reason for thinking is shared by us with many other higher animals. It is *self*-consciousness that is the mark of men. Now there is no possible way that the labour theory of human origins could explain the origins of self-consciousness. It can appear only in the expressive order when a creature who can form an idea of itself clearly has advantages in the sexual selection tables over one whose self-presentations are not subject to the kind of control that this ability implies. According to Keiler, quoting Leontiev, 'sensibility [is] orienting the organism to its environment', and is the key psychological attribute. But a little reflection suggests that for a creature to be truly human there must be a mode of sensibility in which an organism orients towards *itself*.

In conclusion: while I think that Keiler and Ruben have made a qualified case for the siting of the moment of human emergence in the labour relation, that is at best a partial condition. What is necessary is that there should be social practices by which there is selective advantage to those creatures who can turn their attention to themselves.

PART III

The Concept of Evolution in a Sociological Context

6 The Evolutionary Analogy in Social Explanation

R. Harré

THE fact of social change, change in institutions, in face-to-face relations, in social practices of all kinds, is a striking feature of contemporary views of human life. It has not always been so, since in the past either societies have had little idea of their origins, or in some cases they were, in some respects, more stable than those to which we have presently become accustomed. In this chapter, I want to explore the possibility of borrowing some aspects of the multiform conceptual system of evolutionary theory from its natural home in understanding the history of organic beings, for developing concepts for a similar role in the social sciences.

In order to develop the argument in detail, it is necessary to elaborate the central distinction necessary to our understanding of social life and to test our borrowed conceptual systems against it. The distinction I have in mind is that between the expressive aspects of action and practical aspects. I shall argue that any social event whatever must be considered to be located, at least potentially, in two social orders which are analytically distinct. The expressive order is that system of social relations, conventions, interpretations, and so on, which is concerned with the presentation of human beings to each other as of value and worth; important in it is the dramaturgy of self-presentation, the criteria of social respect and contempt and the ritual ways in which those are marked. In practice, the expressive order appears psychologically in a certain range of motivations. The practical order consists of those social relations which are involved in the system of work, as understood by, for example, Marx. These are the social processes involved in the transformation of material, originally at any rate, in the interests of sustaining life. The orders can be distinguished in another way. An action, say the planting of a seed, can be seen to be related to other things in the world, including the social world, by two

161

different kinds of relations. In considering the planting of the seed, one may be concerned with its consequences as mediated by natural mechanisms and described in the laws of nature; so that, for example, in planting a seed one expects to harvest a crop. On the other hand, this act may be considered with respect to certain conventions in which it is given an expressive meaning. For example, it may be that a seed is planted not only in expectation of a crop, but also in expectation of the act and its consequences being seen by neighbours as interpretable as a demonstration that one is ecologically aware, green-fingered, worthy in some way. It is most important in understanding the distinction, as I intend to use it, that it is seen not as an ontological pairing of categories, but as distinctive, analytical frameworks within which to see what considered neutrally would be one action. From the philosophical point of view, the distinction can be expressed in terms of a unity of action and a plurality of acts. The orders, though, are distinct, in that the consequences which flow from the unitary action via its plurality of act-interpretations, are themselves multiple and therefore can act back upon each other. Veblen,[1] for example, has pointed out how a social structure which might be considered to have had its origins in the practical order as an economic system, may require material symbols of its structure which then, motivated now expressively, puts demands upon the practical order and transforms it. For example, a railway baron in the United States at the turn of the century might require a mansion as an expressive representation of his standing, and thus encourage the quarrying of stone.

These orders, their interactions and their changes, I take to be the subject matter of any theory, or theories, of social change. It will emerge in the course of this chapter, that it is unlikely that changes in these orders can be adequately understood in terms of only one explanatory format. I shall argue that we need at least two, one of which will be the evolutionary format.

But, one might ask, would it not be best to investigate the changes in the complexly interacting dual orders naturalistically, and derive inductively some explanatory system in order to understand them? The difficulty with any such enterprise is the complexity and opacity of the material from which a theory is supposed to emerge. The sciences have been at their most fruitful when they have exploited analogies and borrowed conceptual systems, modifying them in the process. I hope to demonstrate that the social order and its understanding is no exception. But if I borrow from organic evolutionary theory there must be some preliminary adjustments of that theory. There are two ways in which general concepts figure in science. There are systems of concepts which constitute axiomatic sets of high order laws, general theories from which, by suitable insertions of particular conditions, descriptions of the matter under investigation, can be deduced. This is the deductive nomological conception of the use of explanatory concepts. It is altogether too crude a way of understanding the role of concepts to capture the points I wish to make. I do not propose in this paper to develop an independent argument against that way of looking at theorizing, but simply to note in passing that I shall not be using it in any substantial way. To identify the second way general concepts are used, I shall talk about the concepts constituting an explanatory format rather than an explanatory theory, since the notion of theory has unfortunately been spread across two very distinctive kinds of conceptual structure. The relation between the general theory of relativity and black hole dynamics is that of axiom system to deductive consequence. But the relation between Darwinian evolutionary theory and, say, the explanation of the diversity and distinction of beak shapes in Galapagos finches, is that of generic concepts to specific concepts. The *Origin of Species* is not a deductive structure. It is a philosophical analysis of the concepts of selection, change, etc., and a diverse collection of illustrative anecdotes which show the power of specific versions of those concepts to explain particular cases. The explanatory concepts I shall be developing in this chapter, are to be considered as at the level of explanatory formats, that is, they are generic concepts which are capable, I hope, of specific application to particular cases.

But why, in particular, should we attempt to set up a generic conceptual system derived from the theory of organic evolution? There are two main reasons. A cursory glance at the relation between social practices and local social requirements suggests that even the most pessimistic commentator must be impressed by the rather high degree to which practices are adapted to needs, whether this be practical, in the social organization of work in a particular geographical environment, or expressive in the development of symbolic practices which deal with particular consequences for particular groups of people in the practical order. For example, the expressive practices of football hooligans are very nicely adapted to resolving and remedying the humiliations they perceive themselves to have received in the world of work and school. The lesson biology learned from Darwin, that adaptation need not require some form of teleological explanation, can also be taken to heart by social theorists. Part of the charm of mutation/ selection systems is that they offer us the possibility of the explanation of adaptive change without positive causality for that change, and in particular they allow us to separate the processes by which mutant forms are created from these by which they are selected. I shall be developing this point of deep philosophical import in more detail below.

However, in the present state of knowledge and technique in the social sciences there is another issue which is contemporarily of at least as much importance, namely our incapacity to formulate adequate descriptions, well-grounded empirically, of the macro-social structures within which social practices occur. There have been various responses to the breakdown of confidence in the possibility of grasping macro-social structures. One might adopt the extreme positivism of the ethno-methodologists, effectively denying the existence and/or importance of such entities, seeing the social world as a moment-by-moment construction between face-to-face actors. This response seems to me ill considered. I can see no reason for denying the existence of macro-properties nor, indeed, of being sceptical about their efficacy. It seems to me quite clear that we must hypothesize collective attributes of various sorts which have considerable potency in the world. But how? If we know the macro only in its effects, then one solution to the problems posed by our ignorance of its structure, and perhaps in response to a recent scepticism about the possibility of there being a positive causality from collective features, would be to treat the macro-social structure as a selection environment. We could then consider it with respect to its power to inhibit the spread of certain novelties and not inhibit that of others. Thus the processes by which a practice spreads through a society could be looked at, even ethnomethodologically, as person-to-person, even institution-to-institution, different modes of copying, without committing ourselves thereby to an individualistic sociology. So spreading, or failing to spread, will have both a macro-feature in its explanation and a micro-explanatory aspect in the conditions for copying, that is, reproduction.

The argument sketched above justifies, at least provisionally, borrowing the evolutionary format for explaining social change. But I am satisfied that there are several basic processes, one of which seems to me to stand out clearly as distinctive from any evolutionary account of change. We are familiar from Marx's doctrine of the priority of the infra-structure, that is, the social system of production in explanations of social change, the idea of dialectic tension and resolution process. However, as I understand it, even though Marx in his mature work was willing to consider, and perhaps even emphasize, the reflexive and interactive relation between infrastructural and superstructural aspects of social formations, nevertheless, the dialectic, which one might say was the 'motor' of the machine, was located firmly in the practical order, and the fundamental tensions, whose resolution served as the dynamics of social change, were between distinctive human groups, having distinctive interests, defined with reference to the social order called into being in the system of production. Be that as it may, there is another kind of dialectical tension which seems to me empirically, at least, to be of greater significance, and that is the tension between the practical order and its system for identifying human beings as of certain categories, and the expressive order in which moral worth, value, dignity, and so on, are symbolically represented. These orders, being only analytically distinct, are capable of generating a tension within an individual human being as a typical member of some collective, so that the dialectical resolution may be psychological and this may fill the gap which yawns in Marxist theory between the collective, and the necessary individual level of motivation on which any causal hypothesis must, in the end, rest. A dialectical dynamics will, in general—though this is not a necessary feature—move from one equilibrium position to another. The equilibria that I presume in this chapter are defined simply by degree of coordinativeness between the system of representation in the expressive order, such as the symbolic marking of social standing, and the actual relations of, for example, relative capacity to consume, relative power, and so on, which might be defined in the practical order. So long as the expressive order and the practical order are coordinate, I would hold that conditions for a social equilibrium exist, though that equilibrium may not actually obtain for other reasons. By parity of reasoning, should there be a lack of coordinativeness between the orders, then conditions of disequilibria obtain, though whether there will be an actual social change to bring about a new equilibrium cannot, I think, be predicted from the mere existence of a tension between the two.

I presume, though I shall not argue it here (cf. my *Social Being*, Harré, 1979)[2], that the analytic independence of the orders allows for the possibility that in some historical conditions the practical order may lead the expressive, and in other conditions that priority may be reversed. For example, it seems to me clear that the transformation of the position of women in the practical order through the economic effects of the First World War, was prior to and led the transformations in the expressive order which have subsequently occurred, so that in the case of women's movements changes occurred in women's rights which were not at that time expressively represented. On the other hand, it seems clear that the rise of trade unions in nineteenth century Britain involved a social process of resolution in which the tension was generated by changes in the expressive order. The rise of Methodism and other nonconformist sects, with their ways of representing the relations between people, was quite out of key with the relations as generated in the practical order. In consequence, in nineteenth century industrial relations we see the expressive order leading the practical order, change in the former having to be equilibrated with change in the latter. These kinds of explanations I shall call explanations in accordance with the E/P format.

But it is insufficient to identify a tension resolution process in the relation between the expressive and practical orders, since there are times when innovations in the expressive order, introduced to represent changes in the practical order, do not survive, and some further explanatory format is necessary . For instance, changes in the expressive order which occurred during the French Revolution had distinctively different fates. The abandonment of the aristocratic way of travelling, namely down the left-hand side of the road, in favour of the proletarian, namely walking down the right-hand side of the road, has survived until the present day, whereas forms of address, novel religious or quasi-religious observances and other expressive innovations, very quickly perished during the Napoleonic imperium. How should this be explained? At this stage, we need to investigate the possibility of another format.

The most obviously available is that which I have already introduced through the suggestion that we should borrow from evolutionary biology the outline structure of its conceptual system, which I shall now call the M/S format. I owe to Phillipe van Parijs a distinction between two different kinds of evolutionary theory: those where the relation between mutant forms and selection environment is purely selective (that is, where the Darwinian conditions of independence between the causation of the new form and the process of its copying are strictly maintained), and reinforcement processes where there is a causal relation from the environment upon the practitioners, which directly leads to the encouragement of the novelty. This distinction has its analogue in evolutionary biology, though the analogue is of historical interest only. One could consider the reinforcement type of theory as approximating to a Lamarckian evolutionary format in which the environment was seen as causally efficacious in drawing out the possible mutation and amplifying such changes as had already occurred. It is worth remarking that Darwinism has, almost from its conception, been rigidly separatist on this matter. So, if van Parijs is right, there seems to be a case for saying that the evolutionary format, the M/S conceptual system, must be considered not as a single univocal set of generic notions, but as a spectrum of theory formats, ranging from the strictly Darwinian or selectional to the strictly Lamarckian, where the new social form is called into being by the conditions which favour it with van Parijs's reinforcement notion somewhere between. I shall proceed in the argument by taking the Darwinian form of evolutionary theory as fundamental and then defining deviant forms relative to that, so in looking for analogue concepts from organic evolution and its explanatory formats, I shall look only at forms of Darwinian theory.

But which form of Darwinian theory? Traditionally, the *locus* of change has been taken to be a species, and adaptation has been conceived of in terms of the relation of individual survival and reproductive capacity to the welfare of the species, measured, for example, in terms of relative population changes. But lately Darwinian theory has been refined by drawing out more precisely the consequences of unclarity with respect to the object of selection. This has led to the formulation of gene theory. I think it correct to say that gene theory is not a novel theory; rather it is a spelling out of consequences of the Darwinian explanatory format which had not been fully or adequately focused on before. And I think it also correct to say that gene selection theory was implicit in the way the Darwinian format was applied in recent times. There are two major notions in gene selection theory. One is that represented by the distinction between replicators (the physical entities which are actually copied in the passage of the generations), and inter-actors (the entities in which the interaction between environment and the biological entity takes place). The second feature of gene selection theory is the introduction of the idea of an evolutionarily stable strategy where the activities of interactors are seen to converge on certain equilibria which are advantageous to the spread of replicators through the population of interactors.

At this level of analysis, we are using only a very general form of the M/S structure. To examine the possibilities of the analogy between bio-evolution and socio-evolution, further details must be introduced. The gene selection theory can be represented in the following diagram:

Genes
↓
Epigenesis → (protein) = organism
/ | \
Species in eco-niche

The importance of epigenetic factors in the formation of an actual organism means that the relation between genes and organisms, or replicators and interactors is, in general, one : many.

It might be possible to formulate a version of a socio-evolutionary theory in a parallel manner, as in the following diagram:

Rules

Individual factors → (practices) = institutions

Culture in geo-niche

The possibility must be admitted that a stable rule system may, for all kinds of exogenous factors, issue in practices and be realized in institutions that are different from one another, so that the relationship between rule systems and institutions may be one : many.

Changes in these systems should occur in parallel ways; for instance, changes in genes will be spread through the population relative to the fate of corresponding organisms and changes in rules will spread through a society relative to the fate of corresponding institutions. So far the analogy looks quite plausible.

In order to identify more precisely the entities involved in these parallel theories, both need to be tightened up relative to the distinction between types and individuals; that is, relative to the distinction between the identity of a structure which is realized in many successive, numerically distinct, molecular instantiations, and the identity of those particular instantiations (see Jensen, Introductory Chapter, this volume). What are genes? Are they individual material realizations or are they abstract structural isomorphisms? It is quite unclear in the biological material, particularly as summarized by Dawkins, and equally unclear in cultural and social material, particularly as exemplified in the treatment of concepts by Toulmin in his *Human Understanding* (p. 197)[3].

I do not wish to deal with the problem of identity in the biological realm in this chapter, but only that problem as it appears in the social realm, the problematic identity in the rule or convention which is the social replicator corresponding to the gene. If rules are replicators, are they the individual or personal representations of the conventions governing practices, or could, for example, a hundred people instantiate the same rule? Similar problems beset the notion of practice. It seems clear that the relationship between practices and their socio-geographical environment must be considered in terms of individual instantiations. It is on this or that particular occasion that a practice seems bizarre, ill-adapted and unsatisfactory. So, my first proposal is that we should consider the identity of practices on the following model. Each instance is a distinct interactor and interactors form sets which are instances of a practice if they are sufficiently similar to one another. This argument would lead us back to the identity of rules along the same lines, in that one would suppose that the particular instantiation of a rule in an individual person ought to be taken to be the replicator unit whose identity is then determined by its particular existence. Rules, then, as so identified, will form sets according as the instantiations of each individual in a collective are similar, or sufficiently similar, to each other. A further advantage of taking this way out of the identity problem will appear in the discussion of mutation, since a new rule often appears in the course of an individual act of creation, or an individual error in the doing of a ceremony, let us say, or the playing of a game, as for instance the famous occasion when Ellis picked up the football and rugby was born.

However, the identity problem must be continually before us since there are further problems about the nature of rules as metaphysical entities. In general ethogenics, the most powerful analytical model for understanding social action and its correlative explanatory model requires us to consider certain social activities as if they were ceremonials, on the basis of an analogy with real ceremonials. Now, in the ceremonials that institutions perform, the identity of each individual instance of the performance of a ceremonial is guaranteed by the existence of a publicly represented manual of rules which maintain the identity by being individually decoded on each occasion. Of course, these decodings may be imperfect. But there is a sense of rule which we will have to take note of in which the rules are what are present in the public representation. In this case, we have a similar identity problem. Are the rules which are to be considered the fundamental entities each individual representation in each individual manual, or are the structural isomorphisms between manuals for the same ceremony to be the basis of a more abstract notion of rule identity? Whereas in the case of individual persons and their beliefs and social knowledge, it seemed advisable to treat the identity problem by locating identity in individuals, the opposite strategy will be seen to be necessary in other cases.

In order to identify the points of difference between socio- and bio-evolution we need to be able to compare the *locus* of mutation and the nature of selection in each case. It seems clear that mutation in bio-evolution must be strictly limited to cases of imperfect copying between replicators, however caused. In socio-evolution there is no doubt that a rule may be imperfectly learned and then become a new guiding principle, generating an institution or practice which is distinct from that generated by its predecessor. However, in the social case, there are innumerable instances of the invention of rules, the promulgation of inventions, the deliberate manufacture of ceremonials, and so on, which introduce novelty into the social order and succeed or fail through their relative adaptation to the problem they are designed to solve. For instance, in the French Revolution there was an effort to form a religion of rationality and, indeed, for a period Notre Dame became the home of just such a religion with its own acolytes, its own ceremonials. It failed to take.

Selection, on the other hand, is a much more complex issue. The first step is to identify, relative to the gene selection theory, just what selection might be. If we define, following Hull (this volume), a lineage as a temporal sequence of replicators, then it is a necessary condition for selection to have occurred that the identity relations between members of the lineage be interrupted in some way, that is, there must be a mutation. Now, in the biological case, Darwinian theory treats selection as the prevention of replication of naturally replicating individuals, so that the persistence of a character and its related gene or gene complex does not need to be explained and indeed is not explained by the theory; only its disappearance, through the failure of a sufficient number of members to reproduce. In the social case, selection indeed does occur in that mode. For instance, it may be that a natural tendency to imitate exists in all human beings, but that sometimes imitation fails, let us say through disgust, for instance, where some practice that is suggested is obnoxious to the sensibilities of those to whom it is proposed. But there are cases where there is deliberate encouragement of the replication of naturally non-replicating individuals. For examples, it seems to me that compulsory education is a case where the metaphysics behind educational programmes suggest that social change is possible through deliberately introducing new knowledge and new practices and requiring people to learn them, people who would not normally pick them up. In this way socio-evolution selection processes are radically different from biological.

We must also ask whether the location of selection pressure is similar. In the bio-evolutionary case selection pressure acts on interactors only, via their relationship with the environment. However, in socio-evolution, though indeed there is just that sort of process where practices are tested against the conditions of life, and the geographical possibilities of sustaining it, there are also selection pressures exercised directly on the rules, particularly innovative novelties. There is a great deal of human activity which, on this model, could be seen as the imaginative testing of institutions or practices which would exist were a rule which has been posed as an innovation actually to obtain. A great deal of parliamentary discussion, for example, seems to be capable of being interpreted in this way. We can use a commonplace anthropological distinction to identify this difference between biological and social evolution. When the practices of a society are the result of custom only, it seems that pressure will be brought to bear only on interactors, that is, social practices. But where custom has become law and law is an explicit formulation of the principles guiding conduct, then new laws can be proposed, examined and tested in imaginative examination of the possibilities and under those historical conditions the *locus* of selection pressure is on the replicators, not the interactors.

These differences are not fundamental. They preserve the schemata set out in the diagrams, and they allow, so far as I can see, for a fairly thoroughgoing analogy to be maintained, at least relative to these considerations. However, I want to add some rather serious reservations about the analogy carried through to this degree, since it seems to me clear that there are some deeper differences in socio-evolution and bio-evolution that are rather fundamental. To take some minor points first: the location of the point of change in a mutation-selection theory is rather different in the social from the biological. In general, in the biological realm, the change point is supposed to be that defined as the mutation, that is, in the replicator, which is tested against a relatively stable selection environment. Cases where the mutation is repeated and the selection-environment changes are admitted in biology but are rather rare. In socio-evolution, however, the case seems to be the reverse. There are cases where, against a fairly stable social and geographical background, there are innovations. The technical innovations in the nineteenth century would be an example. But much more frequently, it seems to me, human beings propose, over and over again, the same mutant practices, relative to the background against which they are conceived and the practices which are currently in force. New rules are often not so new, but the appearance of old ideas refurbished. However, there can be no doubt that the conditions against which they are tested, as realized in practice, are radically very different from one another. The best example I have come across is that between the coal strikes of 1926 and 1972 in Britain. In each case, more or less the same practice appeared, with behind it a novel conception of the social order, namely that manual workers' associations should be the dominant social force, but the quite different fate of these events in 1926 from those which occurred in 1972 can be explained largely through the radical difference in the socio-economic background. The failure of the coal strike in 1926 is to be put down to both social psychological attitudes of the day (expressive order) and the manner in which the energy system was organized in Britain (practical order). Very different conditions obtained in 1972, so that the miners were able to win a resounding victory and radically alter if only temporally the balance of influence in British society. This difference between the evolutionary schemes in each realm is one of emphasis only.

A further difference arises in the relation of the mutation/selection distinction to that between individual and collective. In the biological realm it seems clear that mutation is always, and necessarily, an individual event, whereas the selection conditions necessarily involve the collective. In the social realm there are indeed such cases, where individual innovation (for instance, the invention of a new way of letting the steam in and out of a steam engine), made on a particular occasion, spreads through a collective of production practices. On the other hand, it seems perfectly possible in the social case for there to be mutations at the collective level which are selected by the individual willingness of particular persons to continue the new arrangements. For instance, one can see something of this sort in the way in which classes are dealt with in human society. It might very well be, as Marx supposes, that classes are engendered by changes in the social relations of production, but whether any particular individual is going to show marks of respect to another who has the advantage over him socio-economically, is a matter of the individual's capacity, or willingness, to acquire a new practice. In so far as individuals refuse to accept these new practices, then the mutation may fail. Lastly, there is the relative Lamarckism of much that goes on in social change, where social knowledge from anthropology, history and social psychology may be used to develop new practices, well adjusted to the socio-economic conditions in which they must survive, or even the ambitions of governments to so alter the collective structure that individual practices will spread throughout it. Again, these differences seem minor and mark matters more of emphasis than of substance. However, there are some serious difficulties in the analogy.

So far we have been exploring the positive analogy and minor variations from it. There is one serious negative analogy which we must notice. Not only do record-keeping societies become more Lamarckian in their mode of social change but an important condition of gene-selection theory, as exemplified in the first diagram, cannot be assumed to obtain in the rule-selection theory as exemplified in the second. If we were to set out a lineage in the biological realm, the history of a biological type must be represented in such a way that the genes of ancestral forms can pass to descendents only through the genetic constitution of intermediate individuals. To put it mathematically, a lineage of genes in the biological world is a simple ordering. Every new individual must be produced by passing through a genetic node. The case is radically different for lineages of rules and conventions. In record-keeping societies the rules and conventions which obtained in the past are still available for copying in the remote future. For example, the rules prevailing in the days of the ancient Israelites have been the source of new social practices in England twice in recent history, once in the time of the Revolution, with the Diggers and Levellers, and again in the fundamentalism of the nineteenth century. It was not a lineage which had to pass through intermediate instantiations. Rather it was possible for the founding fathers of Methodism to go directly to the Old Testament and borrow from there descriptions of practices and the rules which went with them so that they could reproduce something like ancient Israelite society in an utterly new cultural framework. This difference is so radical that it seems to me, despite the relative strength of the positive analogies, we must say that borrowing from the biological to the social sphere requires a great deal of care and in the end, perhaps, must be undertaken with serious reservations.

While this last difficulty stands in the way of any simplistic borrowing I think there can be no doubt that the use of mutation/selection ideas is of the utmost value in the social sphere because it allows us, just as that conceptual scheme allowed in biology, to construct explanations of adaptation which do not entail any assumptions of a positive causality between the environment and practices which seem well adapted to it. As I pointed out, positive causality can be confined to the negative, to the elimination of unsatisfactory forms.

Notes

1 T. Veblen, *The Theory of the Leisure Class*, The Macmillan Company, New York, 1899.
2 R. Harré, *Social Being*, Blackwell, Oxford, 1979.
3 S. Toulmin, *Human Understanding*, Clarendon Press, Oxford, 1972, pp. 122 ff.

7 Human Adaptation

S. Toulmin

IN RECENT years, concepts of 'adaptation' have made their appearance at several points in the human sciences, and have begun to play a substantial part in the renewed efforts to develop adequate theories of social, cultural and political change. The most obvious and topical illustration of this is the recent controversy about 'socio-biology', which turned on the question how far the adaptedness of human populations and patterns of life can properly be analyzed in neo-Darwinian terms such as 'inclusive fitness' and 'group adaptation'.[1] But that dispute has been only the tip of a larger iceberg. Even before the publication of Wilson's book, Gerhard Lenski had argued a case for analyzing social change in 'populational' terms drawn from neo-Darwinian evolution theory;[2] Jean Piaget had characterized the development of human intelligence as 'a biological adaptation';[3] while, after relying for many years on a concept of 'social systems' modelled on the homeostatic 'adaptive mechanisms' of physiology, Talcott Parsons had moved back toward an evolutionary perspective on society;[4] . . . and so on.

All in all, therefore, this is a good time to take a fresh look at two questions: (1) How far, and in what respects, can such notions as adaptation, adaptiveness and adaptability contribute to our understanding of the human sciences? (2) What relation will our concepts of human adaptation bear to parallel concepts in other fields, especially those already well established within the biological sciences?

It should be noted that I have taken care to use the phrase 'concepts of adaptation' rather than 'the concept of adaptation', so as to avoid falling into the trap embodied in that little word 'the'. For it needs to be emphasized straight away that we shall have to concern ourselves, not with a single, univocal concept, for example, the concept of 'adaptation' as employed in elementary evolution theory and population dynamics, so much as with a family of related concepts which overlap and interconnect at

176

certain points, but nevertheless require analyzing in somewhat different terms.

Indeed, even biological theory itself (as we shall see) does not operate with *one and only one* concept of adaptation. Physiologists, developmental biologists and students of organic evolution, at least, use such notions as adaptiveness, adaptedness and adaptation in somewhat different ways. And the first goal of this present paper is, in fact, to sort out and characterize no less than *four* distinct modes of adaptation (or ways of adapting), all of which have legitimate parts to play in the biological and human sciences alike. Subsequently, having distinguished these modes of adaptation, we shall go on and consider how the four distinct ways of 'adapting' relate to one another in human affairs—whether on the plane of individual behaviour, or on that of collective practices and institutions. This will mean asking: If we describe human populations or institutions, societies or cultures, intellectual enterprises or technologies, languages or arts, as 'adapted', 'adaptive' or 'adaptable', what can we mean by those terms? And how do the different modes of human adaptation link up, within a truly comprehensive account of individual and collective experience?

By way of preface, we may briefly explore the basic etymology of the verb *adapt* and its cognates. Both historically and semantically, the theoretical uses of these words finally lead back to the adjective *apt*. That adjective is primarily used to mark off objects or actions as 'proper or appropriate' to the demands of particular situations, as judged by standards that are normally related to the specific character of those demands. Any systematic use of *apt* terminology needs, accordingly, to be understood in relation to the standpoint from which (and the purposes for which) this 'aptness' is to be judged. In brief, *aptness* involves some kind of 'match' or 'fit' between an object or action and its situation; and any judgement of aptness— whether concerned with an agent himself, or with his actions and their outcomes—must specify what exactly the action or product is supposedly apt *to* or apt *for*.

Notice that, in making such judgements, we are free to focus either on the agent who is responsible for 'fitting' or 'matching' his actions and their forseeable consequences to the current situation, or alternatively on the actions themselves, together with their actual outcomes and products. Colloquial English has, in fact, a richly developed vocabulary of cognate terms for expressing such judgements. In considering any human action, course of action, or policy, we have the choice between focusing on the 'aptitude' (or 'ineptitude') of the agent or agents concerned, and concentrating on the 'aptness' (or 'ineptness') of the actions they perform. The notion of *aptitude* is closely related to those of skilfulness and competence; an 'aptitude' is commonly a specific skill that is productive within some particular enterprise. (In earlier times, for instance, the term *adepts*, that is, 'adapts', was a euphemism for persons skilled in the arts of alchemy.) Correspondingly, the notion of *aptness* is closely related to those of appropriateness, effectiveness and/or propriety; and an action of remark (say) will be 'apt' or inept with reference to some specific purpose, and within an equally specific context.

On the general, pretheoretical level, accordingly, we can resist any invitation to assume that there is one and only one kind of *adaptation*, any more than there is one and only one kind of *aptness* or *aptitude*, or one and only one way of *adapting* actions and objects to all available occasions and purposes. In different situations and for different purposes, the specific task of 'adapting', that is, changing so as to become more apt, will obviously take quite different forms. (In colloquial parlance, 'adapting' always means becoming more apt *to* so-and-so *for* such-and-such purposes.) Similarly, those things, systems, people and populations that are 'adaptable' have the potentiality of 'adapting' in a number of different respects, with a variety of possible outcomes; and those outcomes have to be judged by correspondingly different criteria—depending, once again, on the situation *to* which, and the purposes *for* which, 'adaptability' is required. This point needs to be spelled out at the start, not from any exaggerated respect for colloquial parlance ('ordinary language'). Biological and social theory are perfectly entitled to set aside the constraints of everyday idiom, and to fashion their own neologisms and terms of art. But it can serve us, nonetheless, as a counterweight to a temptation that becomes powerful the moment we enter the world of theory, viz. the temptation to impose *one and only one* kind of 'adaptation', and *one and only one* set of criteria for judging 'adaptedness', on the entirety of biological and social theory.

In certain quarters, for instance, the traditional Darwinist notion of 'adaptation'—which refers, for example, to the differential reproduction rates of alternative, or coexisting, populations within a given habitat—has been accorded a kind of intellectual primacy over all other senses and uses of the term. Indeed, some evolutionary biologists have tended to talk as though the very word 'adaptation' were their private possession and people working in other fields must employ it in the same, strictly Darwinian manner. Still, however useful this family of terms may be in comparing the 'survival values' of different populations, or in accounting for the historical origins and transformations of particular organic species, two or three other kinds of adaptation, adaptiveness, etc. have won an equally legitimate and well established place in biological theory. Even for the purposes of a comprehensive biology, therefore, we must come to terms with the existence and characteristics of a variety of different 'adaptive' processes, having their own more or less 'well adapted' outcomes and displaying greater or lesser 'adaptability' to changes in the relevant situation.

To be specific: we may here distinguish and discuss, in turn, *four* kinds of adaptation, adaptiveness and adaptability, all of which play their parts in the biological and human sciences. These can be referred to as the 'calculative', 'homeostatic', 'developmental' and 'populational' modes of adaptation, respectively.

To explain them in turn: (1) In considering the problems of practical life, when people are faced by changes in their current situations; we may raise the question: How—and how well—did he/she/they *adapt to* those changes? In asking this question, we typically assume that the agents concerned can recognize the practical significance of those changes, and will alter their courses of action so as to make the best of them. ('He lost his job/his wife/his sight/his heating oil supply; and he adapted to the situation by retraining for a new career/selling his apartment and moving in with friends/taking a crash course in Braille/converting to natural gas.') In this first sense, *adapting* thus means choosing, as a result of a conscious calculation, to act differently *for a purpose*, viz., so as to maximize the gains and minimize the losses flowing from the changed situation.

(2) In studying the physiological functioning of organisms, or the physical working of machines that need to remain active or effective in the face of significant changes in the surroundings, we may similarly raise the question: By the operation of what mechanisms—and how effectively—does the organism or machine *adapt* its modes of operation to those environmental changes? In asking that question, we typically assume that the organism or machine is structured in ways that prevent external changes from disrupting its operations, and so help to maintain a 'normal' mode of operation (even a precise equilibrium) in the face of those external changes. ('When the weather heats up in summer, our bodies respond adaptively to the higher temperatures: the vaso-motor system enlarges our pores and more perspiration evaporates, so carrying heat away and maintaining the body at its normal temperature of 98.6°F.') In this second sense, *adapting* thus means responding functionally so as to maintain a 'normal' (equilibrium/healthy/preset/desired) condition in the organism or machine, viz., one that will preserve its normal functioning in the face of external changes.

(3) In studying the processes by which infants develop from a state of defenselessness to one in which they can fend for themselves, we may likewise ask: How—and how effectively— do young creatures succeed in developing from infancy to maturity, and so become *better adapted* to their conditions of life? In asking this third kind of question, we typically shift our attention to matters of heredity and to the developmental sequences or trajectories through which the genetic inheritance is physically expressed, as the developing individual becomes better equipped to cope with life in its given habitat. ('With the development of mobility, speech and deliberation, children become progressively less dependent on adults, and better adapted to their conditions of life.') In this third sense, *adapting* thus means becoming creatures of kinds that can cope effectively and independently with the problems of life—whether by 'adapting' in sense (1) or (2) or in other ways.

(4) In considering how populations of organisms (or other 'historical entities') come to change their character, and their manner of dealing with changes in their ecological and/or other

conditions, we may finally ask: Through what kinds of evolutionary processes—and how effectively—do these populations succeed in becoming *better adapted* to their habitats or milieux? In asking this last type of question, we typically regard adaptive changes as having a dual character—variation on the one hand, selective perpetuation on the other—and as being efficacious through the perpetuation and spread of novel, advantageous features. ('As the deserts enlarged, these plants adapted to the climatic change by developing hard seed pods that could survive prolonged extremes of heat, and would split open and germinate only after heavy rains.') In this final sense, accordingly, *adapting* means having some novel, advantageous feature appear and spread through the population concerned, viz., one that makes its members better equipped (fitter, better matched) to the novel conditions confronting them.

Each kind of 'adaptive process' is evidently most prominent in one particular field of science, area of experience, or type of activity: (1) conscious choice in rational human decisionmaking, (2) homeostatic responsiveness in the regulatory mechanisms of the body, (3) developmental preadaptation in morphogenesis, and (4) populational adaptation in organic evolution. Still, there is no way of cutting the different types off from one another, and separating them entirely. All four have some part to play in processes of many kinds: in biological functioning, in individual psychology, in social, economic and political affairs.

Within general biology, for example, physiological homeostasis, genetically controlled development and natural selection all represent well established modes of 'biological adaptation'; yet even Darwin himself recognized the significance of sexual selection ('choosing mating partners') as a factor in evolutionary change, so that some element of more or less 'conscious' choice cannot be ruled out even from this case. By contrast, in accounting for human conduct, we are sometimes inclined to focus on the role of rational thought (or conscious calculation) at the expense of all other modes of adapting. But, once again, the processes by which human beings become more effective in dealing with their situations typically involve elements of all four modes. The establishment of habits and customs, for instance, involves, in effect, novel adaptive responses that may parallel or reinforce the operation of physiological mechanisms (for example, the custom of taking an afternoon siesta in hot countries); our very ability to engage in calculative decisions or conscious choices at all depends on how successfully we 'grow up'; while the actual appearance of 'adaptive changes' in our behaviour is commonly associated with some selective ('trial and error') learning or experimentation.

Furthermore, just as adaptive changes of all four types are found in the conduct of individuals, so too corresponding elements can be expected in the behaviour of human collectives. Any comprehensive theory of social, economic and/or political change must, accordingly, identify the different roles of conscious, homeostatic, developmental and populational adaptation, respectively. In the political affairs of nation states, for instance, it is increasingly clear that the consequences of conscious government choices can be foreseen with real accuracy only for the short term. Longer-term 'social adaptation' proceeds, rather, in one or more of the other three modes. In the activities of bureaucracies, for instance, the self-maintaining character of those institutions, and their standard operating procedures testifies to the role of 'homeostasis' in social affairs; meanwhile, the possibility of providing for institutional self-modification in the charters or founding documents of such bureaucracies permits at least some element of 'developmental preadaptation' in the social realm; however, finally, a significant amount of social adaptation takes place (if at all) through 'populational' processes involving experimental innovation and the selection of advantageous novelties.

Concepts of *adaptation* can therefore play a constructive part in the human sciences, only if we are prepared to consider how far, and in what respects, human individuals and societies employ each of these four modes of adaptation, or ways of adapting, to ensure a 'match' or 'fit' between their activities and the current situation. What difference will these enquiries make to the ways in which we formulate our hypotheses and questions in (say) social philosophy and political theory, epistemology, linguistics and other human sciences? That is the question to be addressed in the rest of this chapter.

While this initial four-fold distinction is immediately before us, we can usefully begin by looking again at the problems that plagued traditional social and political philosophy. I would argue, for instance, that one of the principal weaknesses and sources of difficulty in much traditional social and political philosophy was its commitment to oversimplified ideas about 'social adaptation'. In earlier centuries (as in our own) social and political theorists tended to think and argue in terms of one single 'mode of adaptation' at a time; and they repeatedly ran into difficulties at just those points where they would otherwise have had to introduce the other modes of adaptive change. From the time of Plato on, for instance, the efficacy ('adaptedness') of human societies and institutions challenged the theoretical imagination and ingenuity of political theorists; and they met this challenge by interpreting that efficacy, either as resulting from foresight and calculated choice—our mode (1)—or else as being analogous to the homeostatic adaptation involved in normal physiological functioning—our mode (2).

Those political philosophers who emphasized calculative adaptation soon ran into difficulties. It is easy enough to understand how the conscious choices and foresight of human individuals or nations may, on occasion, play a decisive part in shaping the history of societies that already exist and are in full operation: the writings of Thucydides present a classic discussion of this possibility. Yet, given the short-term character of human foresight and calculation in the social realm, it is hard to see how any sort of conscious, deliberate, calculated human decisions could have brought effective social arrangements into existence in the first place. The political philosophers of the seventeenth and eighteenth centuries accounted for the origin of society by appealing to an hypothetical 'covenant' or 'contract' supposedly entered into by our forefathers, when they banded together to form the first 'societies'; and for a while this view had a certain blind charm.[5] But as Vico pointed out, rather unkindly, the binding force of any covenant or contract itself presupposes *the prior existence* of social mechanisms for entering into and honouring such agreements.[6] So, while it is possible to explain the 'adaptiveness' of social and political *change* (at least to some extent) as in the consequence of deliberate human choices, with humans consciously selecting the 'best adapted' options on the basis of explicit calculations, there seems no hope of explaining the very origins of social and political life in these terms. And, given the comparatively short term over which human foresight and conscious calculation prove really effective in actual practice, even middle- and longer-term changes in social institutions and political arrangements can scarcely be accounted for convincingly as the results of straightforward rational choices.

How have the political philosophers responded to the limitations of this 'calculative' mode? They have done so in a number of different ways. Some of them have continued to interpret social adaptation as resulting from 'calculated choice' but have shifted the responsibility for the relevant choices away from human beings themselves, and given it to Divine Providence. Others have reverted to Plato's 'organic' analysis, and have used homeostatic mechanisms as an alternative model for explaining social structure and processes. Others, again, have looked beyond our modes (1) and (2), and have hinted that some kind of overall, developmental preadaptation—our mode (3)—may govern the progressive unfolding of human history in its entirety.

Let us begin with the providentialists, particularly Vico.[7] Although Vico conceded that the effective modification of social institutions might, to some extent, be due to the ingenuity of human beings and the effectiveness of human foresight, such appeals to calculated choice (as he clearly saw) do not take us very far. If the larger-scale, longer-term history of social and political institutions is beyond human calculation, it is necessary to look elsewhere for the 'foresight' responsible for all the larger-scale, longer-term features of the *polis*. From this point of view, the adaptedness of human institutions may still be the outcome of foresight; but that foresight is no longer the finite, conditional foresight of human beings, who operate largely in ignorance of the future. Now, it is the infinite, unconditioned foresight of Divine Providence, which had the capacity to arrange, long in advance, for human beings to enter into 'well adapted' social institutions as soon as the historical conditions were right. Thus, for Vico, the operation of Divine Providence had ensured that human beings would eventually succeed in developing effective social arrangements, *if only unwittingly*, because God had fashioned both the World and Mankind in such a way as to guarantee this happy outcome.

By the year 1900, of course, most social scientists were

unhappy about appealing to Divine Providence in this way, and had begun looking around for other kinds of 'adaptive processes' in terms of which to account for the structure and efficacy of human institutions. At this point, two of the most eminent twentieth century sociologists set out to bring the traditional Organic Theory of the State up to date, by developing theoretical models of society patterned after the 'adaptive' mechanisms of late nineteenth century physiology. Emile Durkheim, for his part, was directly influenced by the great French physiologist, Claude Bernard.[8] The systemic interaction between different institutions and individuals responsible for the 'normal' or 'pathological' operation of any social phenomenon, as Durkheim explained it, strikingly recalls the analysis of, for example, the systemic interactions within the vaso-motor system, in terms of which Bernard had explained the normal or pathological functioning of the body's temperature regulation. Similarly, Talcott Parsons credited the stimulus for his own ideas about the homeostatic self-maintenance of 'social systems' to the influence of L. J. Henderson, who did much to put Bernard's ideas about functional homeostasis into circulation in the United States.[9] Both Durkheim and Parsons ended, as a result, by analyzing the 'normal' workings of society as depending on the operation of 'systems' that maintain 'healthy' equilibria, in the same general way that the normal operation of the digestive system (say) maintains healthy physiological equilibria in the human body.

Inevitably, however, such physiological analogies between society and the organism are partial and incomplete. As Claude Bernard saw quite clearly, framing our physiological explanations in terms of 'homeostatic systems' may enable us to account for the maintenance of equilibria in the workings of the body, for example, for the constant body temperature of warm-blooded animals, or the time patterns in the operation of the digestive system. But such explanations are quite unsuited to explaining either how organisms come to possess such physiological systems in the first place, or how they subsequently develop successful new forms and/or features.[10] By its very nature, any theory of 'homeostasis' is a theory of stasis, not of change; and, as a result, theories of social or political homeostasis, such as those of Durkheim and Parsons, cannot help but be *conservative* theories, which explain only how the existing institutions of a society adapt their operations in the face of external changes so as to defend themselves in their present forms, not how they can modify those forms to take better advantage of external conditions.

In what alternative direction, then, should we look for an account of the historical origins and subsequent development of 'well adapted' human societies? Having exhausted the scope of calculative adaptation—our mode (1)—and homeostatic adaptation—our mode (2)—we can look to the other two modes. The historicist philosophers of nineteenth century Germany opted for mode (3): they compared the entirety of human history to the ontogeny of an individual organism, and so viewed the history of society as the growing up of the human species. The adaptedness of a mature society was like the adaptedness of adult behaviour. Primitive society was like 'childhood'; feudalism, monarchy and/or early capitalism were the counterparts of 'adolescence'; Prussia (or Communism, or whatever) would then represent 'maturity'.[11] How did matters happen to arrive at this self-justificatory destination? In the last resort, it is hard to overlook the last echoes of earlier appeals to Divine (or Cosmic) Providence: certainly, it was not for nothing that, even in the 1960s, progressive-minded neo-Marxists in France could find grounds for a *rapprochement* with the liberal Catholic followers of Teilhard de Chardin.[12] Yet, there is surely something pat, smug and arbitrary about this ontogenetic model. It may provide us with an attractive enough image, or manner of speaking; but, if we press it in any specific detail, the parallels it draws between physiological development and social history yield no real understanding. Who are we, in any case, to credit ourselves with social adulthood or maturity, and to write the Classical Greeks and Romans down as the youngsters (or, at best, the teenagers) of history?

There remains the fourth, 'populational' mode of adaptation to consider. Within contemporary biology, functional and developmental physiology no longer stand on their own. Their necessary complement is an evolutionary account of the historical origin of physiological forms and structures. The existence of successful, well adapted homeostatic mechanisms (for instance) can no longer be accepted as self explanatory. Instead, it is one more phenomenon to be explained as the outcome of successive evolutionary adaptations to former conditions of life. And the same is true in the social realm. The existence of self-maintaining social and political 'structures' or 'systems' is no more self explanatory than that of physiological systems. This fact, too, calls for a properly historical theory of social and political evolution as its natural complement. The adaptedness of social forms can thus be compared, from this final standpoint, with the adaptedness of organisms and their populations. And, recalling the dual character of all evolutionary, mode (4) adaptation, we shall now need to ask, first, how institutional, conceptual and other social or cultural variants make their appearance in the first place; and, subsequently, how they show their merits as solutions to current social problems, and succeed in establishing themselves more widely.[13] As always in the case of mode (4) processes, these two sets of questions need to be looked at separately and independently. Social adaptation will depend on conditions that favour *both* the appearance of novel, experimental forms, *and also* a critical, discriminating selection between them.

Analyzing the different kinds of 'adaptation' involved in human affairs in richer and more realistic terms can bring other philosophical dividends, also. Consider, for instance, the issues that have bedevilled the philosophy of science over the last fifty or sixty years. For much of that time, philosophers set themselves the goal of accounting for the 'good' and 'bad' of science—explaining what justifies our incorporating novel scientific hypotheses and concepts into the currently accepted body of knowledge—in terms drawn from formal logic. The central tasks for the philosophy of science (they thought) were best tackled as requiring an 'inductive' logic: some 'confirmation theory' or other formal algorithm, by which we could measure the virtues and defects of new scientific ideas, and so assure the validity of novel theories.[14] This whole approach, however, depended for its correctness on a further, unstated assumption, viz., that scientific theories become better adapted (matched/fitted/appropriate) to nature wholly as the result of conscious foresight and calculation. The rationality of natural science, in short, was to be thought of as resting on a variety of mode (1) adaptation; and attempts to discuss the philosophy of science in terms of alternative, broader conceptions of rationality were met by accusations of 'irrationalism'.

During the last fifteen years, it has become increasingly clear that this assumption was always illusory, and the logicians' programme for philosophy of science a pipe dream.[15] Scientific ideas cannot be criticized and improved by calculative procedures alone. The virtues of scientific theories are functional, not formal; and we shall understand how novel concepts and hypotheses are rightly judged only if we look directly at the actual historical processes by which they in fact enter discussion and win a place in science. These processes, too, turn out to have the dual character of all evolutionary processes: they involve both variation and selective perpetuation, just like the processes of change that affect organic populations, linguistic forms, and other 'historical entities'. Novel concepts first enter a science tentatively, so forming a pool or 'population' of competing variants. Subsequently, they are selected among, as meeting the specific theoretical demands of a particular scientific situation, that is, as being 'better or worse adapted' than their competitors to the current problem situation. The historical evolution over time of scientific ideas—the phylogeny of science, so to say—is, as a result, a process of 'competitive adaptation' similar to other 'evolutionary' processes.[16]

What are the immediate implications of this change of approach in the philosophy of science? At bottom, it represents a broadening in our philosophical understanding of the *adaptive* character of scientific discovery. For the logical empiricists of the 1920s and 1930s—as for Francis Bacon earlier—the ambition was to produce an *organon*, or method, whose application would transform the 'improvement of the understanding' into a systematic and entirely explicit activity with its own formal algorithms and calculative procedures. For the logical empiricists, as for Francis Bacon, that is, good new scientific ideas and theories were 'better adapted' as being the outcome of human activities that were 'adaptive' in the first of our four senses alone. The true 'rationality' of the natural sciences did not (in their eyes) depend merely on their *success*: it rested quite as much on the fact that that success was achieved by conscious method, calculation and *foresight*. Unfortunately, however, the effective scope of human foresight and calculation in the natural sciences, quite as much as in social and political life, is very limited. Once we go beyond the most pedestrian scientific investigations, we have to proceed more tentatively and open-mindedly, and allow ourselves to be taken by surprise: working always with a variety of novel possibilities in mind, between which we shall finally choose, only in the light of essentially *un*foreseeable experiences. To suggest that scientific investigation could be 'rational' only if consciously directed towards a preconceived goal, in accordance with some explicit 'method', is thus not merely unrealistic: it is downright obsessional. It should not (I am tempted to say) have needed the Son of God to tell us that we cannot wish ourselves nine inches taller; nor, for that matter, should we need to be told that we cannot develop formal algorithms for predicting the intrinsically unforeseeable!

On the contrary: all these longstanding problems about 'adaptation'—in general philosophy, epistemology and the human sciences alike—will yield to theoretical analysis satisfactorily only if we take *all four* modes of adaptation seriously, and view the 'best adapted' forms of life and thought, scientific theories and social institutions, as the outcomes of historical processes involving *all four* of our modes of adapting. In discussing scientific ideas (for instance) we are not required to *choose between* explaining (1) by what formal algorithms 'good' ideas are to be told from 'bad' ones; (2) what functional equilibria are successfully maintained by 'good' ideas and not by 'bad' ones; (3) in what respects 'good' ideas properly reflect the natural self-unfolding of innate mental programmes; or, finally, (4) in what respects 'good' changes in ideas must prove themselves in competition with 'less good' ones. Rather, we may assume that teleological and adaptive processes of *all four* kinds play genuine parts in the operation and historical development of human thought; so that *all four* modes of adapting are relevant to any complete analysis of scientific 'success'.

Similarly, in other, parallel fields: social institutions, mechanisms of production, linguistic forms, cultural practices—all the diverse types of 'historical entities' that constitute the subject matter of the human sciences—will presumably turn out, in different respects, to be 'adaptive' not just in one of our senses, but in all four of them. There are, consequently, solid scientific reasons for believing that, in one respect or another, all our human modes of perceiving/dealing with/talking about the world are manifestations of conscious human choices and of functional equilibria, of innate, genetically preprogrammed capacities *and* of cultural evolution. So, the substantive question about 'adaptation' for human scientists to investigate is *not* which one of these four modes of adapting is operative in each particular case, but rather, how all four modes—calculation and homeostasis, genetic preadaptation and the selective perpetuation of fruitful variants—interdigitate and work together, within this or that particular field of human experience.

Let me add three last, briefer remarks by way of conclusion. First, if human scientists take the task of working out a *populational* account of social structure and social change (an account that pays attention to mode (4) adaptation) sufficiently seriously, the results will take them far beyond the limits of the *soi-disant* 'evolutionary' theories of nineteenth century social philosophy. A populational account of social, cultural, political or other kinds of change, given in terms of the appearance and selective perpetuation of 'better adapted' variants, rests on quite a different basis from the naive theories about 'evolutionary stages of social development' presented by Herder and Comte, Spencer, Marx and the early anthropologists. For those nineteenth century theories rested more or less openly on assumptions about the 'progressive' character of successive historical stages that were quite foreign—even antithetical—to the properly 'populational' arguments of Charles Darwin himself.

Modern evolutionary theories are theories about local, historically situated processes, not about the overall direction of cosmic development in its entirety. The central question, (1) 'How do evolutionary changes of any kind (whether in languages or animal populations, social institutions or cultural forms) take place in fact?', is closely linked to the question, (2) 'What makes some variants more successful than others in taking advantage of/adapting to the opportunities, meeting the challenges and/or responding to the demands, of *the current habitat and situation?*' Within any populational analysis of change in human affairs, therefore, we shall have to ask ourselves: What makes changes in human institutions/forms/ practices/modes of speech, etc. apt or appropriate to this given situation? And that question is quite distinct from the question,

'Does this change represent a further step forward in the march of history?' From a populational point of view (in short) the problems for the human sciences are not *teleological* but *ecological*: they are concerned, always, with 'aptness' and 'adaptedness' relative to *a given situation*, rather than with conformity to some overall direction of cosmic fulfilment. So it is particularly ironical that both Herbert Spencer and Karl Marx thought of Charles Darwin as an ally.[17]

Second, although a comprehensive account of change and adaptation in human affairs must provide elbow room for all four modes of 'adapting', it is, nevertheless, true to say that the historico-evolutionary (or populational) perspective must remain the governing one. Why should this be? The reasons are basically the same in the human realm as they are in the biological. In any given circumstances, we can normally abstract out biochemical and physiological, morphogenetic and evolutionary aspects of any particular biological phenomenon, and consider these aspects separately; but, the moment we start trying to fit the results of these separate inquiries back together, the necessary overall analytical framework has to be provided by the fourth, evolutionary aspect.[18] Many longstanding problems in general biology (e.g. in embryology and morphogenesis) finally proved soluble only as a result of viewing the phenomena concerned within their proper evolutionary contexts. When viewed in relation to the evolutionary history of the human species, for instance, the existence of *maladapted* features in the human body (e.g., the intervertebral discs of the spine) becomes as intelligible as the existence of *well adapted* features.

This is probably one of the factors that have lent plausibility and charm to recent speculations about 'socio-biology' and the genetic bases of human social behaviour. Yet, by arguing that the 'adaptedness' of human social behaviour (for example, our capacity for altruism) must be attributed, above all, to *genetic* factors, the socio-biologists put themselves at risk; since they are in danger of adopting too narrow a view, both of what constitutes 'adaptedness' in human social life, and of the processes by which the adaptedness of social behaviour is established and maintained. For (1) they oblige themselves to use the term 'adaptation' only in its strictest biological sense, as defined entirely in terms of the survival, or differential reproduction rates, of coexisting organic populations. Our social behaviour can have the 'adaptive' features it does (they imply) only because all other rival propulations of early hominids lacking those features are by now extinct. And (2) they go on to construe the existence and transmission of those particular 'adaptive' features as attributable directly to our genes.[19] On both accounts, however, their position is oversimplified. Even more than individual behaviour, social behaviour is *at most* the final expression of inborn genetic potentialities as qualified in the course of long sequences of development, within this or that particular culture and habitat; and we know so little about the manner in which human 'genes' do in fact come to achieve such final behavioural expression that we cannot afford any kind of dogmatism in discussing those outcomes. No doubt, sufficiently drastic genetic changes might destroy our capacity to develop into altruistic adults. But it is entirely premature to assert that this capacity is directly encoded, as such, in the DNA of our cell nuclei. In accounting for mature and altruistic adult social behaviour, plenty of other factors (including social and cultural factors, such as language) demand to be taken just as seriously as the 'genes' themselves.

More fundamentally, the *point* of 'well adapted' social and cultural forms is not merely to defend us against the risk of extinction. The value of 'adaptation' for human societies concerns quite other functions, apart from sheer survival. Even in biology, indeed, not all 'adaptation' is concerned with the differential reproduction rates of coexisting populations alone. The homeostatic 'adaptativeness' of physiological mechanisms, and the developmental 'adapting' of embryology and morphogenesis, are a reminder that biologists think of individual organisms and organs, also, as 'adapting'. Certainly, if some actual human population were to develop collective institutions, and reward individual personalities, of kinds that threatened its very chance of surviving at all, that population would indeed be gravely ill-adapted to its conditions of life. But survival alone—however indispensable—is not enough. Once the extreme threat of extinction is lifted, the 'adaptedness' of our modes of thought and practice need, surely, be measured in other ways, e.g. by the manner in which they protect us against want, and need, and ignorance of other kinds. The historical evolution of human culture and society has, in fact, generated individual activities and collective enterprises of many kinds; and, in a broad enough sense, all of these activities and enterprises have had their own 'evolutionary' histories, within which the dual processes of diversification and selective perpetuation have continually refined and 'adapted' human modes of thought and conduct to the current conditions of life. We have had, that is, the cultural option, of testing and abandoning ineffective modes of thought and action, not just the biological option of killing off all those who employ them!

Finally, in thinking about the human sciences, we must allow not just for a multiplicity in the *modes of adapting*, but also for a parallel multiplicity in the *criteria of adaptedness*. In human as much as in animal affairs, extinction is the ultimate threat, and survival the ultimate test. But, when we relax our abstractions and widen our perspectives, beyond the realm of 'natural selection' alone, it becomes clear that social and cultural evolution have resulted from human responses to a great variety and range of wants and needs. Both in the lives of individuals and the histories of societies and cultures, as a result, the ambition to arrive at a comprehensive understanding of 'human adaptation' will eventually raise questions about priorities. In the natural course of life, human individuals face choices among the different lives there are for them to live; and in the natural course of history, human collectivities likewise face choices among the different possible directions in which it is open to them to change. In both cases, alternative lines of development or evolution frequently present themselves; and which of these lines holds out a promise of being the most fully *adaptive* will depend—at least in part—on how the agents involved order their priorities and 'criteria of adaptive success'.

At this concluding point, we are trembling on the brink of *ethics*. Given the variety of different goals, or adaptive outcomes, among which we may choose by ordering our priorities differently, how are we then to decide either what kind of life to live as individuals, or alternatively which directions of social and cultural change to encourage as collectivities? Here there is room only to state this question, not to discuss it, still less answer it. Stating it in these terms does not, however, imply that our choice of priorities is free, arbitrary and unrestricted. Both on the personal and on the collective level, the scope for ethical decision takes us *beyond* the facts of human development and social evolution alone; but this does not mean that, on either level, ethical and social decisions can properly be taken *in disregard of* those facts.

To deal with the questions that arise at this point would take us far outside the limits of the present essay. If I have managed to throw some fresh light on the meaning (or meanings) of the terms *apt, adapt, adaptive, adaptation* and *adaptability*, in their application to human affairs, that is sufficient for one chapter. To go on and ask, in addition, what kinds of things are *in fact* 'well adapted' or 'successful' or 'worthwhile' in human affairs of one kind or another would be to raise broad, complex and substantive issues of a highly practical, rather than an academic sort; and these are the bread and butter concern of working scientists and politicians, artists and entrepreneurs, rather than of philosophers or other theoretically minded onlookers.

Notes

1 See E. O. Wilson, *Sociobiology* (1975), and the extensive debate to which that book gave rise.
2 See G. Lenski, *Human Societies* (1970).
3 See, for example, J. Piaget, *Biologie et Connaissance* (1966).
4 Contrast T. Parsons, *The Structure of Social Action* (1937), with his much later book, *The Evolution of Societies* (1977).
5 Thomas Hobbes's *Leviathan* established, in this respect, a tradition that continued through John Locke's two essays on government right down to Jean Jacques Rousseau's *Du Contrat social*.
6 See, for example, G. G. Vico, *La Scienza Nuova* (Naples, 1725, 1740).
7 *ibid., passim.*
8 As Paul Q. Hirst argues in *Durkheim, Bernard & Epistemology* (1975), the arguments of Durkheim's *Les Règles de la Méthode sociologique* (1895) were greatly indebted to Claude Bernard's discussion of homeostasis, in, for example, *Introduction à l'Etude de la Médecine experimentale* (1865) and *Leçons sur la Chaleur animale* (1876).
9 See Parson's own account in the essay, 'On Building Social Systems Theory: a Personal History', in *Daedalus*, 99:4 (1971), esp. pp. 828, 830-1.
10 See, for example, Bernard's *Experimental Medicine* (n. 8 above), Pt. II, Ch. II, Sec. I, and the commentary in G. J. Goodfield, *The Growth of Scientific Physiology* (1960), esp. Ch. 8.
11 In this respect, Hegel and Marx alike follow Saint Simon, Comte and Lamarck, rather than Darwin.
12 See the discussion in my *Human Understanding*, Pt. I (1972), esp. Ch. 5, pp. 324–56.
13 *ibid.*
14 See, for example, Carl G. Hempel, *Aspects of Scientific Explanation* (1959).

15 See, for example, Frederick Suppe's excellent editorial introduction and discussion, in *The Structure of Scientific Theories* (1974).
16 See *Human Understanding* (n. 12 above), Pt. I, Sec. B., pp. 133–318.
17 After all, Karl Marx even decided to dedicate *Kapital* to Darwin, while Spencer's highly Lamarckian ideas about sociology, for example, in *The Principles of Sociology* (1876), did not stop him from claiming to be a Darwinist!
18 See J. B. S. Haldane, 'Time in Biology', *Science Progress*, 44 (1956), pp. 385–402.
19 While most of Richard Dawkins, *The Selfish Gene* (1976), argues a fairly straightforward case for socio-biology, the final chapter (like the final chapter of Wilson's own book) relaxes and admits the possibility of other kinds of 'evolutionary' processes.

The Consequences of Socio-Evolutionary Concepts for Naturalism in Sociology: Commentaries on Harré and Toulmin

R. Bhaskar

Men make their own history but they do not make it just as they please; they do not make it under circumstances chosen by themselves, but under circumstances directly encountered, given and transmitted from the past.[1]

1. *Introduction*

WHAT ARE the implications of a populational or evolutionary approach for the possibility of a naturalistic sociology? Rom Harré and Stephen Toulmin both contend that an ecological model furnishes *one* of the explanatory frameworks or conceptual schemes in terms of which social change must be understood. I agree. But I want to suggest that the evolutionary analogy presupposes what I have called the *transformational model of social activity* (TMSA);[2] and that this model, in entailing a new (anti-positivist, non-reductionist, transcendental realist) *critical naturalism*, shows the conditions and limits of evolutionary schemata in social science in a clearer light.

The context in which socio-evolutionary concepts are mooted today differs in two important respects from that of the closing trine of the nineteenth century. It is informed, on the one hand, by a much fuller understanding of the basis of the Darwinian revolution, and, on the other, by extended critiques of positivist and historicist philosophies of science and history. Thus while the internal coherence and explanatory power of evolutionary theory have been enhanced by gene-theoretic elaborations of it,[3] it is now clear that Darwinism is not, in any simple sense, a doctrine of progress, or even (for any nominated species) of survival. Rather, in retrospect, Darwin's great significance can be seen to lie in the way in which, in proposing adequate explanations of natural functionality or adaptiveness without invoking the notion of a purposive being or implying either consciousness or design, he undermined the idea of teleology in nature. Since Darwin, we know that the reason for the apparent 'original complicity' or preestablished harmony between species and environment (or subject and object, or part and whole)—that primal mystery, which is such a prevalent feature of our experience of nature—is simply that, if and when the pair are ill-suited or mismatched, the species (or subject or part) dies away; so that, as Andrew Collier has remarked, 'nature will always produce the appearance of design *if* it produces the appearance of anything'.[4]

At the same time, it has become clear that the actualist (deductivist and determinist) ontologies characteristically underpinning positivist and historicist philosophies are fundamentally flawed; and that, indeed, they are inconsistent with the very possibilities of experimental and applied sciences, which presuppose ontological distinctions between structures and events and open systems and closed, and *a fortiori* epistemological ones between statements of causal laws and empirical regularities and the activities of explanation and prediction.[5] This critique of received theories of knowledge entails *inter alia* a radical reappraisal of the concept and structure of scientific explanations. On the new philosophy of science, explanation consists essentially in the *resolution* of puzzles (problems) by novel *concepts*, designating newly discovered *real* aspects or interconnections, not in the deductive subsumption of those puzzles under more general ones! *Theoretical explanations* typically assume an *analogical-retroductive* form, in which antecedently available cognitive resources are used as the building blocks of knowledge to construct plausible models of the mechanisms producing identified patterns of phenomena, which are then empirically tested, and in turn explained. *Practical explanations* involve the *transfactual* application of theoretical knowledge in the reconstruction of the formation of events, etc. as conjunctures, that is, as products of a multiplicity of different determinations. These theories of explanation imply the untenability of both ontological reductionism and epistemological monism, exemplified here by Wilson's biologism[6] and the unilinear and monocausal approaches (for example, of functionalism and historicist Marxism) criticized by Toulmin. A non-reductionist realism presupposes commitment to the existence of some kind of emergence. The most plausible position is, perhaps, that social objects are the emergent powers of material ones, subject to continual conditioning by nature.[7] On this analysis, the socio sphere appears as a taxonomically and causally irreducible but dependent mode of matter.

On the TMSA social structure and human agency are ontologically irreducible but mutually interdependent. Society both preexists and is necessary for any intentional action, but it exists and persists only in virtue of intentional activity, which thereby reproduces or transforms it. Social forms are thus both the ever-present *condition* and the continually reproduced *outcome* of human praxis. And praxis is both production and reproduction of the conditions of production, namely social forms. Thus agents reproduce (or to a greater or lesser extent, transform), in their substantive motivated actions, the unmotivated conditions necessary for, as the means of, those actions; and society is both the medium and result of their activity. The TMSA can be represented as in Diagram 1.

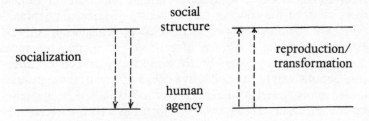

Diagram 1: The transformational model of social activity

On this model, unintended consequences and unacknowledged conditions limit the actor's understanding of his social world, while unconscious motivation and tacit skills limit his understanding of himself.

If the question, 'how is a scientific sociology possible?', is addressed against the background of classical physics and chemistry then the *activity-*, *concept-* and *space-time-* dependent and *relational* nature of social forms can be immediately derived from this model as ontological limits on naturalism.[8] An investigation of the negative analogy in evolutionary biology, which is already historical and relational, should then cross-confirm the practical and conceptual character of the socio-sphere. Note that, to the extent that evolutionary biology is conceived as a source of *analogy*, two forms of reductionism—of content, in biologism, and of form, in functionalism—are straightaway preempted.

2. *Natural functions and human adaptations*

What is involved in the scientific explanation of some pheno-menon or feature, A, in terms of its function, F? I suggest the following four analytically distinct steps:

(i) *functional claim* (for example, a cow's tail is useful for swishing away flies);

(ii) consequence claim[9] (it is because of this fact (i) that cows possess—*came to possess*—long tails);

(iii) *theoretical elaboration* of the mode of connection presupposed in (ii), that is, between functional fact and consequent, or of adaptation or functionality (for example, Darwin's theory of natural selection);

(iv) detailed *natural history* of specific case, presupposing (iii) (short-tailed cows perished).

Stephen Toulmin's paper bears mainly on phases (i) and (iii) of this schema.

A functional fact, F, such as the propensity of increasing size to yield economies of scale up to a point in the car industry, may be analyzed quite simple as (a) a dispositional property (b) which is 'functional' for some end (for example, economy); that is, as A tends to do B, under conditions C_1 . . . . C_n in virtue of its nature N, where B is a (or the) 'function' of A, given the context D (including C_1 . . . . . C_n) and end (or end-function) E. What is meant by 'functional' or 'adaptive' here? Toulmin argues that the root notion is the idea of 'aptness', 'match' or 'fit' between an object and its situation—for example, species/environment, agent/actvity (of aptitude), action/con-text (cf. aptness)—'adapting' signifying changing so as to become more apt. Clearly, as Toulmin indicates, 'fit' is always relative to a particular environment (D) and for a particular end

(E). Obviously, from a naturalistic perspective, ends must be sought immanently, *within* the context of fit itself. But is there a most general criterion of fit such as, for example, the Darwinian measure of adaptation as the differential reproduction rates of alternative or coexisting populations within a given habitat? Toulmin makes the very important point that in the human realm a multiplicity of criteria of adaptedness must be budgeted for, assuming that the end of existence (survival)—a condition for any other end (save extinction)—is satisfied. In social life such 'surplus' criteria are of course chronically, and even fatally, *contested.*

A consequence statement may be analyzed equally straight-forwardly as A exists (develops, etc.) because of F, or as F tends to produce A; that is, if A tends to do B, then A tends to exist, occur, survive, flourish, etc. This does not involve any mysteri-ous 'backwards causation'. In a consequence statement it is the prior or concurrent existence of a dispositional property which explains the existence (development, etc.) of the feature men-tioned in the antecedent of the tendency statement specifying the disposition. (In a Darwinian context it is the past, not the current, adaptive value of a feature which is causally relevant to its occurrence.) Three other points should be noticed about (ii). First a functional consequence claim is *contingent*: it is de-feasible—both because A may not be useful in the specified way (failure of functional condition) and because its usefulness may not account for its existence (failure of consequence condition). Second, a functional consequence claim, although it does not state what the consequence-producing mechanism is (that is, explain the mode of connection between functional fact and consequent), is, nevertheless, *regulatively useful* precisely in indicating the need for a theoretical elaboration of it, so pointing science towards (iii). Finally, (ii) may be justified even in the absence of knowledge of the mechanism of adaptation, provided we have grounds for supposing that such a mechanism exists (we may know *that* F caused A without knowing *how*). In each of these respects a functional consequence claim is on a par with a causal power one.[10] Indeed, on this analysis, the 'double causality' of a functional consequence claim just consists in the property that the existence (development, etc.) of some feature is causally explained by a causal disposition of it.

The error of functionalism can now be quickly isolated: it consists in the supposition that the mere fact that if a feature existed it would play some useful role accounts for its existence. Instead, what one requires to be justified in making a functional consequence claim are grounds for supposing that functional fact and consequent are nominally connected. Darwin's theory of natural selection specifies *one* mode in which consequence claims of the 'cow's tail' type can be defended: alternative, for example, providential and quasi-purposive explanatory sketches, can easily be constructed. The gene-complex selection theory constitutes a further (second-order) elaboration on the mechanism of natural selection. The mutation/selection (M/S) and replicator) interactor (R/I) conceptual frameworks are 'explanatory formats' in Harré's sense, which must be applied to concrete natural-historical circumstances for the explanation of particular cases (cf. (iv) above).

Toulmin, showing that 'adaptation' and its cognates are not univocal (even in biology), argues that the core notion of 'fit' is theoretically realized in both the biological and human realms in four relatively distinct modes: (1) calculative, (2) homeostatic, (3) developmental (lately in vogue with the work of Piaget, Chomsky and Habermas) and (4) populational. These may be regarded as four different ways of elaborating a claim to natural functionality. It is not clear if Toulmin intends the list to be exhaustive. Certainly the calculative paradigm seems too narrow to encompass all the modalities of intentional action and adaptation—for these include the non-calculative, non-discursive modes of acting and adapting *tacitly, practically* and *unconsciously*. Further, if the developmental model is defined in terms of the causal independence of variation and selective perpetuation then the possibility of quasi-Lamarckian and other populational modes would seem to be prematurely ruled out. In both cases, the effect is to veer Toulmin's account in an excessively naturalist direction.

Toulmin identifies a weakness of much traditional social theory, for example, that of utilitarian, organicist (functional-ist), historicist and biologistic cast, in its one-sided commitment to one or other mode of elaboration to the exclusion of all others. *Au contraire*, Toulmin contends that reference to all four modes will in general be necessary for any piece of practical historiography, whether in the biological or social domains. Nevertheless, within this necessary eclecticism, the fourth-populational-mode takes epistemic precedence—both because explanations in the other modes logically presuppose it and because it uniquely accommodates dis- as well as eu- (and, one might add, a-) functionality, maladaptation alongside it.

This vista raises the large question of the internal relations between the modes (is a reflexively self-regulated, developing, maladapted practice possible?), which cannot be considered here. Rather, I want to draw out two disanalogies of the populational paramorph, as presented by Toulmin, for the social sciences.

In the social arena, reproduction is neither 'automatic' nor 'blind'. On the contrary, it depends upon the accomplishments of skilled agents about their tasks, accounting for them, themselves and the social order in which they exist in very definite ways. The 'calculative'—or rather 'intentional'—mode is much more centrally implicated in the social than in the biological domain. Biological models in the social sciences have been prone to stress unintended consequences at the expense of human subjectivity; so it is important to emphasize that real history—the place, time and meaning of selection pressure on practices—consists, as Marx put it, in '*nothing* but the activity of men in pursuit of their ends'.[11] Such activity is the medium of the reproduction and transformation alike of the social world. Hence the mode of reproduction of the social system cannot be treated as a parameter *external* to the historical (evolutionary, selective, transformative) process: rather it just is that process considered under its transcendental aspect. The form of social replication is the way, whatever it happens to be, individuals collectively live their lives. And the activity—and concept-dependent nature of the processes of social reproduction—renders social forms liable to critique and conscious change.

Moreover, social relations are typically internal, so that neither changes in selection nor changes in mutation conditions can be conceived as completely exogenous. In strict Darwinian theory, mutation (M) and selection (S) conditions are totally independent. In Lamarckian theory, the mutation conditions are 'coupled on' (to use Toulmin's useful concept[12]) selection conditions (that is, $S \rightarrow M$). Consideration of such phenomena as market research suggests that much social evolution is quasì-Lamarckian in form.[13] Conversely, selection conditions may be coupled on mutation conditions (that it, M → S), as for example, in advertizing. More generally, mutant (mutations in) practices are intelligible in context, which they actively transform, producing, as Harré indicates, weaker or stronger 'reinforcement' (or resistance!). So in the socio-evolutionary case we need a theory (i) of the mode of interaction or interinfluence between relatively independent M- and S- conditions, given that socio-evolution can be neither completely Darwinian (on pain of a voluntaristic account of practices) nor wholly Lamarckian (on pain of a determinisitic account of processes) in form; and (ii) of the 'dialectic' (for want of a better term) of mutual accommodation and destabilization, adjustment and tension, fitting and slipping, conflict, subversion and replacement between social 'subject' and 'object', form of life and setting, given that adaptation can be neither perfect (on pain of the end of [pre- !] history) nor so imperfect as to render social reproduction impossible (which, when it verges, issues in an actual substantive revolution). Both desiderata point to the need for a socio-psychological theory of agency—or more precisely, of *agents* (their classes, relations and interests)—as the mediating link between selecting environments and mutating practices.[14]

These remarks may be summed up by saying that whereas the Darwinian model upholds a rigid separation between the modes of replication and of interaction, and between mutation and selection conditions, in the social world these poles are causally interdependent and mutually interpenetrating. A third major categorical difference, highlighted by Toulmin, concerns the insufficiency of survival, and the possibility of multiple (and conflicting) criteria of adaptation in the human context. I will return to this later. However it is worth noting here that this consideration carries ontological import, only in as much as differential criteria are or might be *acted upon*: that is, in virtue of the activity- and concept-dependence of memetic,[15] in contrast to genetic, codes. Together these differentiae restore the *practical, conceptual, totalizing* and *critical* tasks of the socio-evolutionary, in contradistinction from the bio-evolutionary, sciences.

3. *The limits of the evolutionary analogue*

Rom Harré argues that an evolutionary model provides, in consort with a dialectical one, an indispensable matrix for the understanding of social change. I do not wish to discuss here his very fruitful practical/expressive couplet[16] or to comment on his notion of dialectic, as the generation and resolution of tensions between structures or orders. Instead I will restrict my remarks to his development of the R/I format as an analogue of the socio-evolutionary process and his motivation for an essentially Darwinian social historiography.

Pursuing the implications of the gene-theoretic elaboration of the M/S framework, Harré suggests that the social analogues of genes (replicators) and organisms (interactors) are rules and practices (or institutions) respectively. I want to propose, without offering any detailed justification here, the following alternative interpretation of the model:

lineage	= history
replicator	= social structure
interactor$_1$	= practice/institution
interactor$_2$	= agent
environment	= ensemble of interactors$_1$, embedded in biosphere.

I prefer the category of social structure to that of rule, both because only causally efficacious rules are replicators, and because social replicators must involve resources in addition to rules (memetic matter as well as form). And I distinguish two types of social interactors, and *a fortiori* of collectives: practices are generated by social structures, but it is through the medium of human agency that selection pressure operates.

In the social case, the mode of replication is activity-(interactor$_1$ and$_2$) dependent, and, in particular, just is the mode of reproduction of the lineage: that is, the mode of reproduction of the population (of practices) is the very process of 'copying', the mode of replication of the social structure (memetic code) itself. Now a species is a naturally self-producing system, but society is *neither naturally reproduced* (in contrast with the biological case, in socio-evolution there is no physical basis for continuity) nor *self-reproducing* (social structures are not self-generating). So if the R/I theory is not to lapse into *reification* (meme as self-reproducing) or to collapse into *reductionism* (memes as genes), it must presuppose the TMSA, that is, human agency as the medium and vehicle of replication, without of course seeing replication as the consciously intended outcome of human agency. As Harré notes elsewhere, 'all populational theories conceive of change as defined in terms of the replacement of a population of one type by a collection of individuals of another; under the condition that there exists a *real relation* between the members of the successive populations'.[17] It is the role of the TMSA to specify this real relation of replication, on which human agents reproduce the codes governing their activities, in the course of, and as the necessary means of, those very same activities they govern.

However it does not follow from the fact that the M/S framework presupposes the TMSA that it can be replaced by it. On the contrary, the great merit of the M/S system is that it allows us to delineate the way in which the environment, the ensemble of internally related interactors, in their physical setting, mediated by the practical activity and consciousness of interactors$_2$, may exert selection pressure on particular interactors$_1$, whether preexisting or new, so as either to inhibit (Darwinian mechanism) or to encourage (Lamarckian mechanism) them. As such, it situates a range of modes of selection, out of a wider array of possible modes of determination,[18] in which endogenously determined 'adaptive' transformations in the social structure can occur.

Harré's discussion of the disanalogies between socio- and bio-evolution throws the transformational character of the social process into heightened relief. For the phenomena of non-simple lineage ordering, replicative innovation, selection on replicators, causal interaction between replicators, direct causal relations between interactors, Lamarckism and 'reinforcement' all turn on the concept- and activity-dependence of social evolution.

It should be noted that the duality and interdependence of structure and praxis means that there can be only a virtual distinction between replicators and interactors$_1$, that these are not distinct 'things', but different (real) aspects of the same process. Further the preexisting (continuous) and holistically changing (space-time-dependent) character of the social world implies that no transformation is total and all reproduction is transformation, so that there can be at most only a heuristic distinction between synchrony and diachrony. Hence theoretical sociology must be *historical* in character. The internality of the relationship between social objects and social science implies that it must be *reflexive* (contingently critical and totalizing), while the inadequacy of both traditional individualist and collectivist ('holist') conceptions of its subject matter suggests that it must be *relational*, casting doubt on standard formulations of the micro/macro contrast. Moreover the TMSA implies that there is neither a logical nor an epistemic asymmetry between the explanation of (relative) stasis, that is, of continuity, and of (relative) change. Specifically, to the extent that either are seen under the aspect of adaptation, or more generally of a consequence explanatory scheme (of the type sketched in section 2), an elaboration is required of the mode of connection between the (dys)functional property and the concomitant or consequent continuity or change (which, to the extent that the elaboration is not itself a simple purposive or intentional one, must of course be mediated by an account of the conscious practical/expressive activity of agents, as always in the sociosphere). It is a mistake to suppose an ontological asymmetry by hypostatizing the social system as something which would (somehow) reproduce itself *unless* prevented. Both tradition and convention, whether as general phenomena or in particular instances, require social explanation (even if the explanations should turn out to be obvious or trivial or take the form of a principle of least action). Change and unchange in the social world are on a par.

This bears directly, I think, on the first part of Harré's dual motivation of the evolutionary analogue: namely the capacity of the M/S format to accommodate the explanation of adaptive change without any 'positive causality' for those changes. Now while it is the case that adaptation, in whatever mode it is elaborated, presupposes a causal connection between features, whether functional or dysfunctional, and consequences, it does not of course follow that this connection involves either (a) teleology or (b) 'causal influence' from the environment on the genesis, as distinct from selection and perpetuation, of those changes. (I take (a) and (b) to be the two most plausible explications of 'positive causality'). However, in the social case, teleology in the form of intentional agency *is* involved as a condition, and part-cause of adaptive changes. Moreover, as Harré points out elsewhere,[19] mutations, that is, transformations in practices, must normally be seen as at least weakly coupled on their selection environment, so that they cannot be treated as random, as in the Darwinian prototype. Nor, as I have just argued, can the selective perpetuation of selected variants be regarded as self-explanatory.

It seems to me that Harré's pessimism about our capacity to form empirically well-grounded descriptions of 'macro-structures' is also unfounded. For we can certainly retrodict from the explananda of sociological inquiry viz. practices as conceptualized by agents, to their possible causes or conditions of possibility along the lines indicated in section 1 for the theoretical natural sciences in general. To be sure, there are differences (and difficulties!) here. For one thing, the relevant generative mechanisms not only cannot be identified, but do not exist independently of their effects, so confirmation of them will always be *indirect*. For another, social mechanisms only (just as bio-evolutionary ones normally) manifest themselves in *open* systems, where decisive test situations, of the classical laboratory-experimental sort, will rarely if ever be possible—from which it follows that criteria for the rational assessment and development of theories (for the adaptiveness of social science to its subject matter) cannot be predictive and so must be exclusively *explanatory*. These are the most salient *epistemological* limits on naturalism.

As already stressed, a major ontological peculiarity of the social world consists in the conceptualized, preinterpreted, character of its object domain. Now social science may come to reveal a discrepancy between social objects and beliefs about those objects; and if such a discrepancy can be socially explained (as in the patterns of the explanation of ideological mystification, psychological rationalization or socio-psychological counterfinality) then we may pass, as I have shown in detail elsewhere,[20] to a critical assessment of the (social) object responsible for it. At this stage, we are now no longer 'trembling on the brink of ethics' (Toulmin), but have plunged straight into it . . . and come out of it again, in practice. Such a critique, in as much as it casts light on unsuspected or recondite sources of determination, facilitates the development of emancipatory practice oriented to emancipated (free) action. And in this process implicit selection criteria—criteria of adaptiveness—are brought to consciousness, subject to critical scrutiny and themselves more or less transformed. When unreflected processes are rendered amenable to conscious control, we are free to fulfil our nature.

4. *Conclusion*

Human history is faster, more interconnected and complex, praxis- and concept-dependent and value-impregnated than biological history (some of these differences are relative, some appear absolute); biological time is itself a fleeting now in the longer curve of natural history, in turn a flash in the hollow sound of eternity. Much, but not all, human history can be modelled on a populational schema which respects the interdependence of social replication and interaction and social selection and mutation and presupposes in its elaborations of the modes of connection between adaptive (and maladaptive) features and their historical consequences a transformational and relational view of activity. If this is done, social 'evolution' will take on a new meaning, just as 'mass' has done in twentieth century physics, as the model gradually severs its connections with its parent-source and comes to acquire an autonomous life of its own. This said, it is important to stress, by way of conclusion, that much human history just *is* (and will always be) natural history, both in the sense that the human species is evolving biologically and in the sense that the natural and social life of the species is continually subject to the determinations of our ecological environment, in which we have been lately so dramatically intervening.

Notes

1 K. Marx, 'The 18th Brunaire of Louis Bonaparte', *Collected Works*, London, 1968, p. 97.
2 See my *The Possibility of Naturalism*, Sussex and New Jersey.

3 See, for example, R. Dawkins, *The Selfish Gene*, Oxford, 1976, for a popular exposition.

4 A. Collier, 'In Defence of Epistemology', *Issues in Marxist Philosophy Vol ?II*, J. Mepham and D. Ruben (eds), Sussex, 1979, p. 85 (my italics).

5 See my *A Realist Theory of Science*, 2nd edn, Sussex and New Jersey, 1978, for a full elaboration of this argument.

6 See E. O. Wilson, *Sociobiology*, Cambridge, 1975.

7 See my 'Emergence, Explanation and Emancipation', *Conceptual Issues in the Human Sciences*, P. Secord (ed.), Oxford, 1981.

8 See *The Possibility of Naturalism*.

9 See G. A. Cohen, *Karl Marx's Theory of History*, Oxford, 1978, Ch. 9.

10 See R. Harré and E. H. Madden, *Causal Powers*, Oxford, 1975, for a full analysis of the logic of causal power statements.

11 K. Marx, 'The Holy Family', *Selected Writings*, ed T. Bottomore and M. Rubel, Harmondsworth, 1963, p. 78.

12 S. Toulmin, *Human Understanding*, Vol. I, Oxford, 1972, p. 338.

13 Cf. R. Harré, *Social Being*, Oxford, 1979, p. 366.

14 As Harré expresses it, we need a theory of 'how large-scale phenomena are represented in individual consciousness and . . . how a myriad of interpersonal interactions form collectives', *ibid*.

15 See *The Selfish Gene*.

16 It may be instructively contrasted with Bourdieu's material/symbolic and Habermas's instrumental/practical [hermeneutic] distinctions.

17 *ibid.*, p. 368 (my italics).

18 Cf. E. O. Wright, *Class, Crisis and the State*, London, 1978, Ch. 1.

19 See *Social Being*, Ch. 16.

20 See my 'Scientific Explanation and Human Emancipation', *Radical Philosophy*, 26, (Winter 1980).

PART IV

Approaches to the Growth of Knowledge

8 Towards a Normative Conception of the Growth of Knowledge

J. Mittelstrasse

IN THIS essay I will plead in favour of an attempt to see things differently from the way they are seen by many philosophers of science at the moment. It is not a matter of claiming to present developed insights but of reestablishing a certain *speculative unclarity* where clarity appears to reign today. Hence there is no promise of a new theoretical happiness put within the grasp of philosophers and historians of the evolution of science, but rather an appeal to go back along the path that the theory of scientific evolution has taken in the last few years, with the intention of considering whether the decision to depart from certain older assumptions was not, in some points, illconsidered and, possibly, dogmatic.

The chapter is in three parts. The first contains an attempt to describe what *really is*. As it is easy to make mistakes in talking about what is the case, this is the most difficult part. The second part introduces some *distinctions*. As one is usually on one's own with one's proposals at first, this is the easiest part. The third part is aimed at the *changing* of what really is. And because what is usually wants to remain as it is, this is the most uncertain part. Hence the reference to a certain speculative freedom which makes it easier for both sides.

1. *Historicism and formalism*

1.1 I shall begin by recalling something that is perhaps self-evident: *the concept of science in scientific praxis determines its relationship to its own history*. What belongs to this history and what does not, what is to be classified as progress or as reaction, is judged not only in terms of what science today knows, but much more in terms of what science today regards as *scientific*. Wherever the history of science is written, it is not just a matter of providing the prehistory of scientific praxis; it is rather the case that this prehistory is always written in the terms and concepts of an understanding of science assumed to be common to all. It is not just scientific knowledge itself that elucidates the earlier history of science, but, above all, the concept of science that is embedded in this knowledge and organizes it methodically. And this is true both of every individual strand of history and also of scientific development as a whole. This means that the *factum science* not only determines the habits of a scientific community; through its concept of science it also asserts itself in the sphere of scientific history and, in particular, in theories of scientific evolution.

The methodological self-conception which the modern empirical sciences have of themselves can serve as an example. This conception refers to a procedure leading from the provision of *measurements* (data acquisition) via the formulation of *theoretical statements* and the derivation of conclusions (equations) from these statements, which reestablish the original data, to an *explanation* of the process which underlies these data. Such a procedure is termed *empirical* because it is based upon measurements (data) and it is also termed *hypothetical* because the theoretical statements made are mere assumptions which, through the conclusions drawn from them, have to stand up to empirical testing. A consequence of the identification of this method with *scientific rationality* is, for example, the disqualification under suspicion of rationalism or deductivism of endeavors to formulate non-empirical conditions for empirical sciences.

Whether one is an empiricist or a rationalist has, of course, an effect upon one's judgement of scientific developments. If Bacon and Descartes had been historians of science they would perhaps have based their judgements on the same facts, but they would certainly not have written the same history. However, their history would have been a *progressive history*. The contemporary belief that a progressive history can no longer be written is not primarily the result of 'higher' insights that would turn Bacon and Descartes into our pupils if they were to write today, but, again, of a changed concept of science. In other words: *there can be no judgement of scientific evolution that is independent of the epistemology of science.*

1.2 The contemporary concept of science that substantially

determines the judgement of scientific developments has its roots in logical empiricism (Carnap) on the one hand, and critical rationalism (Popper) on the other. Logical empiricism represents a foundational programme in the classical sense, critical rationalism the thesis that it cannot be realized. Popper's explication of the so-called problem of basic sentences and his characterization of basic statements as premises of an empirical falsification won by means of conventions forbids the assumption that reconstructions could ever grasp 'reality' adequately, that is, definitively. But this, precisely, was the core of Carnap's endeavours in so far as they were directed towards solving problems of adequacy occurring in connection with his system of basic concepts (constitutive system) in regard to the 'structure of reality'.[1] Popper replaces empirically well-established scientific constructions (by virtue of the so-called empiricist meaning criterion) by a *beginning from above*: because of the supposed logical impossibility of inductive conclusions in empirical sciences and of the consequent lack of symmetry between verification and falsification, the possibility of falsification of a statement becomes the defining criterion of scientific rationality. But this means that theories are not built up 'from below' in well-founded steps, involving, in particular, the establishment of language norms. Instead, the attempt is made merely to fit the theories subsequently into a hierarchy of theories. Claims to validity remain tied to the postulate of possible falsification and to a kind of corroborational record: 'We choose the theory which best holds its own in competition with other theories; the one which, by natural selection, proves itself the fittest to survive. This will be the one which not only has hitherto stood up to the severest tests, but the one which is also testable in the most rigorous way'.[2]

In the final analysis, when decisions for or against a theory are taken on a basis which is itself the product of a theoretical development, and without any possibility of intervention directed towards the foundation of science, then the concept of *rational explanation* and, finally, therefore, the concept of science itself takes on a *historical* character. The fact that in Popper (and in Carnap) only *theories* and not *empirical conditions* or *historical developments* are to be reconstructed in no way changes this. Within the frame of reference of the genesis and corroboration of theories, as developed in Popper's logic of discovery, a reconstruction of the claims of scientific theories to validity can, in the final analysis, only be made on the basis of *actual theoretical developments*. But this means that the concept of science itself is historicized, and historical reflections begin to replace the older endeavours towards a rational foundation of science.

This orientation is characteristic of Kuhn's theory of scientific evolution. According to Kuhn's conception, scientific developments cannot be written about either as *progressive history* or as *foundational history*. Not only because this does not accord with the facts (which might be an historically accurate statement), but because a judgement of the historical forms of scientific knowledge depends upon criteria which are themselves a part of these historical developments. In the framework of this model of rationality, to stand outside developments in such judgements would mean succumbing again to the illusions of older foundational programmes (as, for example, logical empiricism). For this reason, Popper's accusation that Kuhn has turned his 'logic of discovery' into a 'logic of historical relativism'[3] is unjustified. Popper overlooks the fact that his 'logic of discovery' had always been relativistic in regard to method-oriented foundational claims. Kuhn only draws from this fact the consequences for the history of science.

Kuhn's ideas are widely accepted today. Concepts like the *dynamization* of scientific evolution in Sneed and Stegmüller[4] are only variations upon them, and have become the theoretical basis of entire disciplines, for example, modern science of science.[5] Thus, *historicism*, in the form described above, also enters the philosophy of science. Actual developments, including those which have led to the dominant theories, decide upon the treatment and judgement of basic problems.

This development, which began as '*logic of discovery*' (Popper) and, as logic of scientific evolution (Kuhn), has now begun to replace the philosophy of science in the older sense, is a step in the wrong direction. It is not Kuhn's *analytical* achievements, documented particularly in the elaboration of the concept of normal science, which are at issue here, but the *normative implications* that result from this approach. These lie in the *historicization* of knowledge and the corresponding appearance of a *natural historical* conception of scientific praxis. A 'struggle of the theories for existence' (as in Popper and Toulmin[6]) is written basically as the variation and selection of theory formation in relation to the 'natural' conditions of scientific praxis.

Kuhn has himself tried to answer the question of the normative implications of his approach:

The structure of my argument is simple and, I think, unexceptionable: scientists behave in the following ways; those modes of behaviour have (here theory enters) the following essential functions; in the absence of an alternate mode that would serve similar functions, scientists should behave essentially as they do if their concern is to improve scientific knowledge.[7]

The norm recommended here states that as a rule everything can remain as it is as long as it meets the demands of scientific research as these are found in the expectations of the participants. Of course, this also includes the event of irrational praxis. However, the concept of irrational praxis cannot be formed according to this approach because it assumes the existence of judgemental criteria outside actual developments in the sciences. So everything appears to be in the best possible order, to the advantage of existing scientific praxis.

If (in accordance with a widespread linguistic habit) one characterizes as analytical an understanding of science that orients itself normatively to the *factum* science, that is, to an established scientific praxis, then analytical concepts of science must necessarily result in an historicist understanding of the evolution of science.

1.3 The reference to Kuhn's theory of scientific evolution has served up to now as evidence for the thesis that the *factum* science not only determines the habits of a scientific community but also asserts itself, by means of its concept of science, in approaches to and theories of scientific evolution. In spite of the objective relief from constraints that a theory of scientific evolution like Kuhn's has vis-à-vis evaluations of scientific theories which were originally foundationally oriented, the starting point was a fundamental *historical* interest in scientific evolution. This interest now seems increasingly to be giving way to a logic of scientific evolution having as much to do with history as mathematics has to do with the life of Euclid. For example, the dynamization of the concept of theory formation mentioned above has led to the interpretation of scientific developments using *model theory*. In this *meta-theoretical* treatment of theory formation 'historical' occurs as a property of theories affecting their *dynamic* aspect (extension and suppression of theories).[8] Thus, alongside the transition to historicism (Kuhn), the dissolution of history into *theoretically reflected structures* brings a new *formalism*, which, as Stegmüller himself notes, can be understood as a consequent realization of Carnap's formal intentions (the transfer of conceptual determinations into formal structures).[9] The reconstruction of Kuhn's conceptions in a logic of scientific evolution leads, it seems, over the graves of historically oriented endeavours to a remarkable reconciliation of the positions of Popper and Carnap.

Taking his orientation from *actual* scientific evolution (and thus with an historical interest), Kuhn had questioned the taboo of the consistent rationality of scientific praxis ('gaps of rationality' between successive paradigms). It seems that the philosophy of science is now concerned to reestablish that rationality by means of structure theory, but also with the help of a so-called 'sophisticated falsificationism' of Lakatos.[10] And it appears that Kuhn today agrees more and more with this trend, at the expense, among other things, of the *sociological* components of his approach. But this means that the enlightening effect of Kuhn's approach, which continued even in its historist elaboration, has been finally abandoned in favour of a merely *formal description* of the development of theories. This logic of scientific evolution does not have a normative content in the narrow, praxis oriented sense.

In contrast to a mere description of existing conditions and developments, a *normative* consideration involves their evaluation against the background of *well-founded* orientations for acting. The use of the word 'normative' assumes, therefore, that judgements both of conditions of which what is judged is a part and of other general conditions can be kept independent. The so-called 'normative character of what is', which should not be confused with this concept, refers on the other hand to the validity of certain rules of action or to institutions which regulate action. In this sense, conditions are always *subject to norms*. This is also true, for example, of Popper's logic of discovery, which can be termed normative in the sense that it attempts to subject scientific praxis to norms in accordance with a certain model of rationality. Within this model of rationality scientific statements and judgements always refer to a theoretical framework, which is not available in the sense of a methodical step-by-step development (particularly of the scientific language used). This is also the case with recent efforts to close gaps of rationality between incommensurable paradigms. Models of theory dynamics present the process of theory formation as determined by rules, that is, as subject to norms. In their limitation to the analysis of structural properties, however, these models are no more *normative* vis-à-vis claims to validity than the historicism mentioned above. Historicism and formalism, in the forms discussed here, are thus both representative of an analytical concept of science.

2. *Reasons and effects*

2.1 The limitation to an analytical understanding of scientific praxis and its evolution is due essentially to the assumption that theoretically determined misunderstandings and dogmatic assertions in scientific conditions can be avoided by abandoning the distinction between well-founded and unfounded orientations altogether or by grasping them merely as part of the self-understanding of the historical praxis one is studying empirically and historically. Both theoretical orientations and the theories examined are set in quasi-natural historical conditions; in view of this equal treatment of theories and the understanding of theories, normative judgements are regarded as *dogmatic*.

Whoever argues in this way has accepted that historical genesis and existing scientific praxis can only be understood as *causal relationships*. The ends and rules of action included within these relationships are only *stated* and related to actual developments in a *causal-genetic* way. This means that they occur as a part, namely as the 'causative part', of developments that are *explained* in this way, but not *reflected upon normatively*. The historicist and formalist appearances overlay scientific praxis and promote all those prejudices which permit the individual scientist to make himself permanently at home in the established praxis.

The task of removing these appearances from scientific praxis can only be fulfilled by developing a concept of a *foundational history* which is free of one-sided causal and structuro-theoretical conceptions of scientific history, and which enables us to recognize in the *effectual history* of scientific conditions stages in a foundational development of science.[11] Whereas causal reconstructions at best explain the *self-understanding* and the *situational understanding* of those active in scientific praxis and structurally oriented reconstructions at best *confirm* what one in any case already knows, reconstructions that work with such a concept could put us in a position to speak of *well-founded developments* within scientific theory formation.

From a methodological point of view, such a procedure requires that a distinction be made between an *actual* and a *critical* history in a heuristic framework. It is assumed that an essential part of human work, namely scientific work, has not occurred simply naturally, without well-founded steps, and, on the other hand, that a methodically developed praxis such as scientific praxis includes stages that can be historically reconstructed. If such a heuristic becomes part of scientific orientations, it will be possible to avoid the continuation of mistaken developments or genetically unreflected corrections which, in a certain sense, remain naive.[12]

To this extent, the concept of a theoretical heuristic of rational reconstructions in Lakatos also corresponds to the conceptions developed here, in so far as the latter are concerned with the distinction between an actual history and a critical history and their 'dialectical' relationship within the framework of an historical analysis. In such a heuristic Lakatos distinguishes two steps:

(1) one gives a rational reconstruction; (2) one tries to compare this rational reconstruction with actual history and to criticize both one's rational reconstruction for lack of historicity and the actual history for lack of rationality. Thus any historical study must be preceded by a heuristic study: history of science without philosophy of science is blind.[13]

'One gives a rational reconstruction' means here that one gives the *logic* with which one intends to analyze the historical theory formations. In Lakatos, this is essentially Popper's logic, and for this reason the dialectic of actual and critical history, according to Lakatos, includes among its constitutive elements a *conventionalistic* description of *beginnings* and a restriction of effectual history. In this way the history of science does not perhaps remain blind, but it remains mute; it is silent on the point of the *methodical reorganization* of existing scientific praxis. The distinction between effectual history and foundational history, or the demand that scientific history as effectual history should be supplemented by foundational history 'constructed' from a heuristic standpoint, emphasizes this point.

2.2 At first sight it might appear that the concept of effectual history refers to science as a politico-juridical institution, the concept of foundational history to science as a particular form of the formation of knowledge. In the sphere of science, a distinction must in fact be made between science as part of a juridico-political context (including nature and society) and, in this sense, as an *institution*, and science as the systematic relationship of statements and foundational actions, that is, as the (institutionalized) form of the formation of knowledge. On the one hand, therefore, science can be understood as activity distinguished from the forms of so-called everyday knowledge by certain norms of rationality or, on the other hand, as the social form of the activity which produces scientific knowledge.

Today, the research programme of the (historically and empirically oriented) science of science is directed towards the social form of the formation of knowledge. Above all, this research is interested in questions of the control of science for social ends.[14] In so far as it also aims at an integration of the social and cognitive factors of scientific evolution, this programme usually assumes the acceptance of Kuhn's model of scientific rationality in its analysis of scientific developments. Thus, in a concealed fashion, in the framework of science of science not only research into the institution of science (as the social form of the formation of knowledge) but also research into scientific knowledge itself becomes an empirico-historical question.

The distinction between effectual history and foundational history is directed against this research programme, which was discussed earlier under the concept of historicism. But not in a way that science as an institution (in the sense explained) can be classified under the concept of effectual history and science as scientific knowledge under the concept of foundational history. Against this it can be argued, for example, that not only *dogmatizations* have effects, but also *arguments*, that not all dogmatizations (in the terminology used here) are *institutional* and that speaking about well-founded developments, the methodical foundation of which is at issue, cannot be restricted to non-institutional contexts. Finally, it ought, for example, to be possible to speak of a well-founded development of the institution school within the European educational system. Thus the concepts of effectual history and foundational history can be applied both to the institutional form of science and to scientific knowledge itself. The decisive point is that the concept of effectual history is indeed supplemented by the concept of foundational history.

This supplementation also enables us to provide a framework for a distinction between various tasks in science of science and philosophy of science. It is the task of science of science to deal with the *social forms* of the formation of knowledge and, therefore, with science as an *institution*; and it is the task of the philosophy of science to achieve *methodological reflection upon the formation of knowledge*. In this sense science of science is empirical and historical, philosophy of science analytical and normative. In other words: there are two tasks which have to be achieved by a division of labour: the task of enlightening science about itself, that is, institutionally, and the task of determining the methods and goals of an enlightened science. One is served by science of science, the other by philosophy of science.

If this proposal were, in its turn, to have institutional effects, a misunderstanding that threatens to develop within science of science would also be warded off. This misunderstanding rests upon the assumption that the theoretical means used in the enlightenment of science about itself are also the most suitable means for the enlightenment of science in respect of methods and goals. I have tried to show that such a misunderstanding is itself a product of certain opinions in the philosophy of science.

2.3 As is well known, the distinction between the 'internal' and the 'external' history of the formation of knowledge, particularly as elaborated by Lakatos, is also based upon the possibility of distinguishing between the social form of the formation of knowledge and the methodological norms (procedural norms) of scientific praxis. According to Lakatos, rational reconstructions of scientific developments refer primarily to *methodological* developments ('internal history'). Empirical anomalies, which cannot be explained methodologically, are, on the other hand, shown to be part of the historical conditions to which scientific developments are subject ('external history'): 'rational reconstructions remain for ever submerged in an ocean of anomalies. These anomalies will eventually have to be explained either by some better rational reconstruction or by some 'external' empirical theory'.[15] In this way Lakatos opposes Kuhn and tries to hold on to an assumption of rationality in regard to (some) scientific developments.

The distinction between an 'internal' and an 'external' history sounds very plausible, but it is in fact problematical. For it assumes that a fundamental distinction can be made in scientific praxis between *internal* norms and ends on the one hand, and *external* norms and ends on the other. However, this is not the case. This is already expressed by the fact that, in this connection, the norms of scientific praxis are often declared as special *methods* and the ends often defined as *subsequent ends* of a scientific praxis that is already regarded as legitimated. The relationship of scientific norms (for example, norms of discussion or norms of reproduction) and scientific ends (for example, the establishment of an overall view of the formation of antibodies or of the possible solutions of algebraic equations) with the corresponding everyday or social norms and ends is often denied, in spite of the availability of better insights. The reason for this lies in the attempt to isolate scientific and nonscientific rationality from each other in such a way that the usual foundational obligation to provide normative orientations (ends and rules of actions) does not occur in the sciences.

I think that the unsuitable attempt to distinguish fundamentally between internal and external norms and ends in scientific praxis should be replaced by a characterization of the different research approaches of science of science and philosophy of Science: an analysis directed towards the methodological norms of the formation of knowledge is called *internalistic*, an analysis of the social forms of the formation of knowledge, that is, of science as an institution, is termed *externalistic*. This says nothing about the structure of scientific praxis according to norms and ends (for example, with separate responsibility for 'rational reconstruction' and an 'empirical theory') but merely points yet again to the twofold task in the sphere of science that can be solved by a division of labour.

3. *Knowledge which stabilizes praxis*

3.1 The fact that one cannot fundamentally distinguish between *internal* and *external* norms and ends of a scientific praxis leads to the expression of *social conditions* of science. A methodological argument (that is, the reconstructable relationship between scientific and everyday norms and ends) underlines the *reality* of relationships between scientific and social praxis emphasized in a different context of discussion. The emergence of modern natural science from the situation of material (particularly agrarian and artisan) production in the sixteenth and seventeenth centuries may serve as an example of this context. Thus Borkenau holds that 'the mechanistic world picture consists of transferring the events within a manufacture to the entire universe'.[16]

But speaking about *conditions*, as is usual in such a context, is problematical—quite apart from the fact that in this case a concept of manufacture with the division of labour is assumed that is not historically applicable to Italian workshops in Galileo's times. That is, very often a *logical* meaning of *necessary* conditions (borrowed from an analysis of if-then-sentences) is assumed here, that is not clearly enough distinguished from a causal use of the expression 'condition'. The result is either too strong an assertion ('the social circumstances *a* produce necessarily the scientific forms *b* as their effects') or a trivial assertion: in regard to *factual* developments the statement that what happened happened upon 'necessary' (even 'sufficient') conditions is, because of the implications of the concept of 'happening', analytical.[17]

There are, indeed, real relationships between social and scientific developments which cannot be denied. It is a fact that within the organization of a society ends exist which, like nautical or irrigation requirements, cannot be gained without 'theoretical' efforts. Scientific developments (in this case astronomy, hydrostatics and hydrodynamics) follow relationships of this kind. Furthermore, it is also the case that certain arguments are rendered taboo in the framework of legitimation requirements (for instance, the treatment of the thesis of the eternity of the world in medieval scholasticism). In the first case we are dealing with a *finalizing relationship*,[18] in the second case with a *dogmatizing relationship*. The examples of a finalizing relationship make it clear that it is not an individual theory but the institutionalization of a science which in analysis leads to 'social conditions'. In this sense the analysis of the relationship between social and scientific developments has to pay attention to the *institutional* character of science. To put it differently: this is no *direct* route from the social circumstances to particular theories.

Incidentally, in *methodological* as well as in *institutional* respects, Kuhn's sociological concept of a scientific community proves to be essentially a *monadic construction*. This scientific community is a community within a community; according to Kuhn, it always knows what the world is like and it is only connected to it by personal and historical accident.[19] On the other hand, it is exactly Kuhn's ideas that make it possible to give a more radical meaning to the talk of 'social conditions' of science: if one does not think any longer in the categories of a *progressive history* one can, indeed, no longer adhere to the concept of a development that is also systematically well-founded. What sorts of theory one has, depend then obviously on the society, that is, an institutional system of needs, in which one pursues science.

Everything depends here on a good sense of proportion. It is generally true that we live in mixed conditions, that is, in social processes which are still partly operating in a quasi-natural way, partly in contexts of action which are consciously planned. Hence the task arises not only of enlarging our knowledge of the laws of social natural growth (valid only if not interfered with) but also of analyzing socially relevant ways of acting with respect to their factual orientations, and of reorganizing them if need be. Science is also one of these socially relevant ways of acting. In its historical praxis, it represents the product of scientific reason and unreason. These elements are typical of any historical praxis (mixed conditions) and have to be recognized. If this is not done, or if it even is considered to be impossible for systematic reasons, analyses of the history of science actually serve to stabilize a mixed scientific praxis.

3.2 It was the weakness of previous history of science to have confined itself essentially to a *history of theory*, and by doing this to have delegated everything that did not fit directly into theory or into a theoretical development either to the history of technology (as application of theory), or to political history (as contemporary historical background). The methodological and the institutional relationships between social and scientific praxis were left out of consideration.

Certainly, this must not obscure the fact that in considering such a relationship one could not hitherto rely on an elaborated theory of the structure of knowledge which leads to construction of language and science that have been justified step by step. For the reasons given above a historicist and formalist point of view is not in a position to achieve such an elaboration. To do justice to the relationship between social and scientific norms and ends, above all *methodologically*, the elaboration ought to take *practical* and *pragmatic* aspects into equal consideration.

Let us assume that we already have such a theory. Within its framework a theory in its original sense ought to be representable as *knowledge which stabilizes praxis*. This concept means, in outline, the following: (1) *theoretical* relationships, including the sciences, are *means* which serve *practical* orientations; (2) in these relationships a practical relationship (preceding any formation of theory in a narrow sense) between purposeful reflection and actual acting, which, again, is intent on the adequacy of its single steps, can be constructed in a well-founded way. Accordingly, theory whose object is praxis turns out to be, on the one hand, a *constructive part* of praxis, on the other hand, however, dependent upon praxis in that it has to be conceived at the same time as *theory reconstructing praxis*.[20]

I have here sketched an outline of a programme for the elaboration of the theory of knowledge formation we are seeking.[21] After what has been said, it is clear that such an elaboration would have to take the *institutional* framework of science into account, that is, the praxis we are speaking of here is always institutionally constituted. For science as an institution (the social form of the formation of knowledge) and science as a system of statements and foundational actions means that both aspects are in a *dialectical* relationship to each other. Here, 'dialectical' is not meant as a contrast to 'methodological', but in an original sense, namely as derived from the *reciprocity of dialogus relationships*. This, again, is not in contrast to, but stands at the *beginning* of all *methodological* enlightenment.

3.3 Theories of scientific evolution claim to extend our knowledge of the methodological and institutional organization of scientific praxis. For reasons already given, it should not be a question of increasing our knowledge only of those laws of scientific natural growth that are *valid when not interfered with*. What is, rather, at issue is always a better understanding of one's own praxis, that is, what we expect is knowledge that *guides action*. Now, we only *learn* in a sense which is really oriented towards action, which aims at the reorganization of one's own scientific praxis, when we understand, or at least try to understand how scientific praxis can be organized in a well-founded way. This requires both methodological and teleological efforts which, in the sense of the concept of knowledge which stabilizes praxis sketched above, goes beyond empirical historical data. In other words, what matters is an understanding of science that is both *genetically* and *normatively reflective*.

A genetically and normatively reflective understanding of science makes it necessary to examine thoroughly the departure from the concept of *progressive history*. This departure occurred in the framework of the historicist consequences which Kuhn drew from Popper's model of rationality. The concept of development-by-accumulation[22] was replaced by the concept of a procedural development, which restricted the concept of progress to the concept that one theory can be reduced 'structurally' to another. In fact, however, there is also *cumulative* knowledge that cannot be reduced to Kuhn's concept of normal science or to what the Greeks called 'historia' (ἱστορία), accumulative extension of knowledge. Examples are provided by the development of logic, the philosophy of language or mathematics (one need only call to mind, for example, the development of the infinitesimal calculus). In all cases it can be shown that, over and above certain 'paradigmatic' theory formations, progress is made in the sense that *developments orient us better and better*. This is meant not only in the sense that we know more than our predecessors but that we know what we know in a way that is more and more well-founded.

In order to speak of *well-founded scientific developments*, both points are important: the proof that certain developments orient us better and better, and the proof that certain developments can be understood as *stages in a systematic structuring* of scientific knowledge. Finally, to speak in terms of cause and effect, not only finalizing and dogmatizing relationships exist, but also *constructive* relationships. For example, the development from Euclidean geometry through Galilean kinematics to Newtonian dynamics is not only *historical*, but also *systematic*. Systematic developments assume the observation of a principle of method-ological order;[23] but, as in the case of physics, they also often assume the existence of a technology serving to show that elements of social praxis can also enter directly into the methodological structure. Instead of a procedural model of evolution that has for its part replaced a naive cumulative model, we can speak here of a *constructive* model of evolution.

Whether (some) scientific developments can be seen as foundational relationships unfolding step by step, that is, as stages of a well-founded structuring of science, is a question which cannot be answered in advance (or in general). At this point I usually (and some of my colleagues believe rashly) quote Hegel: 'The only idea which philosophy brings with it is, however, the simple idea of *reason*, that reason rules the world and that the course of world history has run reasonably. This conviction and insight is indeed a precondition with regard to history as such'.[24] The reasonable nature of developments is not asserted here, but assumed in the sense of a hermeneutic principle. According to Hegel (but also Kant[25]), this is necessary before even a start can be made with endeavours to reconstruct the past, in which history is not only to be *related* but also *judged* in respect of claims to validity. And this is, quite simply, true.

In the concepts of effectual history and foundational history, and with reference to the division of labour in the relationship between philosophy of science and science of science it can be said that it is the task of philosophy of science to prove that foundational history is *possible*, and it is the task of science of science to examine whether it *really exists*, that is, whether it can be shown that effectual history can be replaced, at least in part, by foundational history. What is *assumed*, in Hegel's sense, is merely (I repeat this) that an essential part of human work has not arisen purely naturally. Again, it becomes *methodologically possible*, first, to distinguish developments in *effectual history*, for which arguments can no longer be presented in regard to well-founded scientific orientation, from other developments realizing parts of a well-founded praxis; second, to spot *mistaken developments* and to characterize them as such; third where necessary, to grasp parts of the dominant scientific praxis, even in its standard works, as part of such a mistaken historical development and to *reorganize* them with the help of proposals directed towards a well-founded structuring of science.

Only when what we wish to make possible has been achieved will it be possible to speak of an adequately *understood history*. History has not been adequately understood when the historical material submits to the application of certain theories of scientific history (for example, historicist or formalist theories), but only when reconstructions can be supported by *constructive plans* of well-founded relationships and *critical judgements* of actual relationships. As Hegel so laconically puts it: 'Thought must be applied (here). The world reveals itself as reasonable to whoever sees the world as reasonable'. And if the world does not immediately appear as reasonable, as we would like to assume more cautiously today, it at least appears in such a way that we can gradually learn to distinguish the interwoven paths of reason and unreason.

Notes

1 See *Der logische Aufbau der Welt*, 2nd edn, Hamburg, Felix Meiner, 1961, p. 139.
2 *The Logic of Scientific Discovery*, London, Hutchinson & Co. (Publishers) Ltd., 1959, p. 108.
3 'Normal Science and its Dangers', in *Criticism and the Growth of Knowledge: Proceedings of the International Colloquium in the Philosophy of Science, London, 1965, Volume 4*, Imre Lakatos and Alan Musgrave (eds), Cambridge, Cambridge University Press, 1970, p. 55.
4 Joseph D. Sneed, *The Logical Structure of Mathematical Physics*, Dordrecht, D. Reidel Publishing Company, 1971; Wolfgang Stegmüller, *Probleme und Resultate der Wissenschaftstheorie und Analytischen Philosophie*, Vol. II/2: *Theorienstrukturen und Theoriendynamik*, Berlin, Heidelberg and New York, Springer-Verlag, 1973.

230   *Philosophy of Evolution*

5 Cf. Peter Weingart, 'Wissenschaftsforschung und wissenschaftssoziologische Analyse', in *Wissenschaftssoziologie I (Wissenschaftliche Entwicklung als sozialer Prozess)*, Peter Weingart (ed.), Frankfurt, Athenäum Verlag, 1973, pp. 20 ff.; Ina S. Spiegel-Rösing, *Wissenschaftsentwicklung und Wissenschaftssteuerung: Einführung und Material zur Wissenschaftsforschung*, Frankfurt, Athenäum Verlag, 1973, pp. 57 ff. For a critical discussion of the dependence of modern science of science on a Kuhnian model of scientific evolution see Jürgen Mittelstrasse, 'Theorie und Empirie der Wissenschaftsforschung', in *Grundlagung der historischen Wissenschaftsforschung*, Clemens Burrichter (ed.), Basel and Stuttgart, Schwabe & Co. AG, 1979, pp. 71–106.

6 Stephen Toulmin, *Foresight and Understanding: An Enquiry into the Aims of Science*, London, Hutchinson & Co. (Publishers) Ltd. 1961, pp. 110–11. Kuhn just gives a variation of Popper's statement quoted above in his *The Structure of Scientific Revolutions*, 2nd edn, Chicago, University of Chicago Press, 1970, p. 146. ('Verification is like natural selection: it picks out the most viable among the actual alternatives in a particular historical situation. Whether that choice is the best that could have been made if still other alternatives had been available or if the data had been of another sort is not a question that can usefully be asked'.)

7 'Reflections on my Critics', in *Criticism and the Growth of Knowledge*, p. 237.

8 Cf. Note 4 and Wolfgang Stegmüller, 'Theoriendynamik und logisches Verständnis', in *Theorien der Wissenschaftsgeschichte: Beiträge zur diachronen Wissenschaftstheorie*, Werner Diederich (ed.), Frankfurt, Suhrkamp Verlag, 1974, pp. 167–209.

9 Wolfgang Stegmüller, *Probleme und Resultate der Wissenschaftstheorie und Analytishcen Philosophie*, Vol. IV/1: *Personelle Wahrscheinlichkeit und Rationale Entscheidung*, Berlin, Heidelberg and New York, Springer Verlag, 1973, p. 21. Carnap defends the thesis 'dass die Wissenschaft nur die Struktureigenschaften der Gegenstände behandelt' (*Der logische Aufbau der Welt*, p. 11).

10 'Falsification and the Methodology of Scientific Research Programme', in *Criticism and the Growth of Knowledge*, pp. 116 ff.

11 I have argued in favour of this distinction at greater length in *Die Möglichkeit von Wissenschaft*, Frankfurt, Suhrkamp Verlag, 1974, pp. 106–44, 234–44 (Ch. 5: 'Prolegomena zu einer konstruktiven Theorie der Wissenschaftsgeschichte').

12 For a general argument concerning this heuristic procedure, see Friedrich Zambartel, 'Wie ist praktische Philosophie Konstruktiv möglich? Über einige Missverständnisse eines methodischen Verständnisses praktischer Diskurse', in *Praktische Philosophie und konstruktive Wissenschaftstheorie*, Friedrich Kambartel (ed.), Frankfurt, Suhrkamp Verlag, 1974, p. 23.

13 'Falsification and the Methodology of Scientific Research Programmes', in *Criticism*, p. 138.

14 Cf. E. G. Skolnikoff, 'Report: International Commission for Science Policy Studies', *Science Studies*, 3, 1973, pp. 89–90, and Ina S. Spiegel-Rösing, *Wissenschaftsentwicklung und Wissenschaftssteuerung*, p. 28. (Die Aufgabe der Wissenschaftsforschung ist die theoretische und empirische Analyse der Bedingungen Wissenschaftsentwicklung und ihrer Steuerbarkeit auf verschiedene Ziele sowie die kritische Reflexion der gesellschaftlichen Voraussetzungen und Konsequenzen von Wissenschaft'.)

15 Imre Lakatos, 'History of Science and its Rational Reconstructions', *Boston Studies in the Philosophy of Science*, VIII, 1971, p. 118; cf. pp. 105–8.

16 Franz Borkenau, *Der Übergang vom feudalen zum bürgerlichen Weltbild*, Paris, Librairie Félix Alcan, 1934, p. 12.

17 Similar assertions to those of Borkenau's can be found, for example, in Peter Bulthaup, *Zur gesellschaftlichen Funktion der Naturwissenschaften*, Frankfurt, Suhr-

kamp Verlag, 1973, and Wolfgang Lefèvre, *Naturtheorie und Produktionsweise: Probleme einer materialistischen Wissenschaftsgeschichtsschreibung—Eine Studie zur Genese der neuzeitlichen Naturwissenschaft*, Darmstadt and Neuwied, Hermann Luchterhand Verlag GmbH & Co. KG, 1978.

18 For this concept, see Gernot Böhme and Wolfgang van den Daele and Wolfgang Krohn, 'Die Finalisierung der Wissenschaft', *Zeitschrift für Soziologie*, 2, 1973, pp. 128–44.

19 *The Structure of Scientific Revolutions*, pp. 4–5.

20 For a more detailed account of this interrelation between theory and praxis, see my *Das praktische Fundament der Wissenschaft und die Aufgabe der Philosophie*, Konstanz, Universitätsverlag GmbH, 1972, pp. 44–52.

21 This programme can be seen as part of a constructivist approach to the philosophy of science. Cf. Paul Lorenzen, *Normative Logic and Ethics*, Mannheim, Bibliograph-isches Institut AG, 1969; Paul Lorenzen and Oswald Schwemmer, *Konstruktive Logik, Ethik und Wissenschaftstheorie*, 2nd edn, Mannheim, Bibliographisches Institut AG, 1975, Peter Janich, Friedrich Kambartel and Jürgen Mittelstrasse, *Wissenschaftstheorie als Wissenschaftskritik*, Frankfurt: Aspekte Verlag GmbH, 1974.

22 Thomas S. Kuhn, *The Structure of Scientific Revolutions*, p. 2.

23 A principle of methodological (or pragmatic) order commits theory construction to the following rules: (a) to use only means which are already constructed; (b) to rely only on results which are already proved. Again, the observance of this principle marks a constructivist approach to the philosophy of science. See Note 21 and Jürgen Mittelstrasse, *Die Möglichkeit von Wissenschaft*, pp. 56–83, 221–9 (Ch. 3: 'Erfahrung und Begründung').

24 *Vorlesungen über die Philosophie der Geschichte*, in Georg Wilhelm Friedrich Hegel, *Sämtliche Werke*, Hermann Glockner (ed.), Vol. XI, Stuttgart, Fr. Frommanns Verlag, 1928, pp. 34–5.

25 'Lose Blätter zu den Fortschritten der Metaphysik', in *Kants gesammelte Schriften*, Königlich Preussische Akademie der Wissenschaften (ed.), Vol. XX, Berlin, Walter de Gruyter & Co., 1942, p. 341; cf. p. 343. Kant is dealing here with the concept of a *philosophical* history of philosophy.

9 A Refutation of Convergent Realism

L. Laudan*

The positive argument for realism is that it is the only philosophy that doesn't make the success of science a miracle.

H. Putnam[1]

1. *The problem*

IT is becoming increasingly common to suggest that epistemological realism is an empirical hypothesis, grounded in, and to be authenticated by its ability to explain, the workings of science. A growing number of philosophers (including Boyd, Newton-Smith, Shimony, Putnam, Friedman and Niiniluoto) have argued that the thesis of epistemic realism is open to empirical test. The suggestion that epistemological doctrines have much the same empirical status as the sciences is a welcome one; for, whether it stands up to detailed scrutiny or not, it marks a significant facing-up by the philosophical community to one of the most neglected (and most notorious) problems of philosophy: the status of epistemological claims.

But there are potential hazards as well as advantages associated with the 'scientizing' of epistemology. Specifically, once one concedes that epistemic theses are to be tested in the court of experience, it is possible that one's favourite epistemic theories may be refuted rather than confirmed. It is the thesis of this chapter that precisely such a fate afflicts a form of realism advocated by those who have been in the vanguard of the move to show that realism is supported by an empirical study of the development of science. Specifically, I shall show that epistemic realism, at least in certain of its extant forms, is neither supported by, nor can it make sense of, much of the available historical evidence.

* I am indebted to all of the following for clarifying my ideas on these issues and for saving me from some serious errors: P. Achinstein, R. Buri, C. Glymour, A. Grünbaum, G. Gutting, A. Janis, L. Kruger, J. Lennox, A. Lugg, P. Machamer, N. Maull, E. McMullin, I. Niiniluoto, N. Rescher, K. Schaffner, S. Wykstra.

2. *Convergent realism*

Like other philosophical *-isms*, the term 'realism' covers a variety of sins. Many of these will not be at issue here. For instance, 'semantic realism' (in brief, the claim that all theories have truth values and that some theories—we know not which— are true) is not in dispute. Nor shall I discuss what one might call 'intentional realism' that is, the view that theories are generally intended by their proponents to assert the existence of entities corresponding to the terms in those theories). What I shall focus on instead are certain forms of epistemological realism. As Hilary Putnam has pointed out, although such realism has become increasingly fashionable, 'very little is said about what realism *is*'.[2] The lack of specificity about what realism asserts makes it difficult to evaluate its claims, since many formulations are too vague and sketchy to get a grip on. At the same time, any efforts by the critic to formulate the realist position with greater precision lay the critic open to charges of attacking a straw man. In the course of this chapter, I shall attribute several theses to the realists. Although there is probably no realist who subscribes to all these theses, most of them have been defended by some self-avowed realist or other; taken together, they are perhaps closest to that version of realism advocated by Putnam, Boyd and Newton-Smith. Although I believe the views I shall be discussing can be legitimately attributed to certain contemporary philosophers (and shall frequently cite the textual evidence for such attributions), it is not crucial to my case that such attributions can be made. Nor will I claim to do justice to the complex epistemologies of those whose work I will criticize. My aim, rather, is to explore certain epistemic claims which those who are realists might be tempted (and in some cases have been tempted) to embrace. If my arguments are sound, we shall discover that some of the most intuitively tempting versions of realism prove to be chimeras.

The form of realism I shall discuss involves variants of the following claims:

(R1) scientific theories (at least in the 'mature' sciences) are typically approximately true and more recent theories are closer to the truth than older theories in the same domain;

(R2) the observational and theoretical terms within the theories of a mature science genuinely refer (roughly, there are substances in the world that correspond to the ontologies presumed by our best theories);

(R3) successive theories in any mature science will be such that they 'preserve' the theoretical relations and the apparent referents of earlier theories (that is, earlier will be 'limiting cases' of later theories);[3]

(R4) acceptable new theories do and should explain why their predecessors were successful insofar as they were successful.

To these semantic, methodological and epistemic theses is conjoined an important meta-philosophical claim about how realism is to be evaluated and assessed. Specifically, it is maintained that:

(R5) theses (R1)–(R2) entail that ('mature') scientific theories should be successful; indeed, these theses constitute the best, if not the only explanation, for the success of science. The empirical success of science (in the sense of giving detailed explanations and accurate predictions) accordingly provides striking empirical confirmation for realism.

I shall call the position delineated by (R1) to (R5) *convergent epistemological realism*, or CER for short. Many recent proponents of CER maintain that (R1), (R2), (R3) and (R4) are empirical hypotheses which, via the linkages postulated in (R5), can be tested by an investigation of science itself. They propose two elaborate abductive arguments. The structure of the first, which is germane to (R1) and (R2), is this:

1. If scientific theories are approximately true, they will typically be empirically successful;
2. If the central terms in scientific theories genuinely refer, those theories will generally be empirically successful;
3. Scientific theories are empirically successful.

4. (Probably) Theories are approximately true and their terms genuinely refer.

The argument relevent to (R3) is of slightly different form, specifically:

1. If the earlier theories in a 'mature' science are approximately true and if the central terms of those theories genu-

inely refer, then later more successful theories in the same
science will preserve the earlier theories as limiting cases;
2. Scientists seek to preserve earlier theories as limiting cases
and generally succeed.

3. (Probably) Earlier theories in a 'mature' science are
approximately true and genuinely referential.

Taking the success of present and past theories as given,
proponents of CER claim that *if* CER were true, it would follow
that the success and the progressive success of science be a
matter of course. Equally, they allege that if CER were false, the
success of science would be 'miraculous' and without explanation.[4] Because (on their view) CER explains the fact that science
is successful, the theses of CER are thereby confirmed by the
success of science and non-realist epistemologies are discredited
by the latter's alleged inability to explain both the success of
current theories and the progress which science historically
exhibits.

As Putnam and certain others (for example, Newton-Smith)
see it, the fact that statements about reference (R2, R3) or about
approximate truth (R1, R3) function in the explanation of a
contingent state of affairs, establishes that 'the notions of
"truth" and "reference" have a causal explanatory role in
epistemology.'[5] In one fell swoop, both epistemology and
semantics are 'naturalized' and, to top it all off, we get an
explanation of the success of science into the bargain!

The central question before us is whether the realist's
assertions about the interrelations between truth, reference and
success are sound. It will be the burden of this chapter to raise
doubts about both I and II. Specifically, I shall argue that *four*
of the five premises of those abductions are either false or too
ambiguous to be acceptable. I shall also seek to show that even if
the premises were true, they would not provide a warrant for the
conclusions which realists draw from them. Sections (3)
through (5) of this chapter deal with the first abductive
argument; section (6) deals with the second.

3. *Reference and success*

The specifically referential side of the empirical argument for realism has been developed chiefly by Putnam, who talks explicitly of reference rather more than most realists. On the other hand, reference is usually implicitly smuggled in, since most realists subscribe to the (ultimately referential) thesis that 'the world probably contains entities very like those postulated by our successful theories'.

If R2 is to fulfil Putnam's ambition that reference can explain the success of science, and that the success of science establishes the presumptive truth of R2, it seems he must subscribe to claims similar to these:

(S1) the theories in the advanced or mature sciences are successful;

(S2) a theory whose central terms genuinely refer will be a successful theory;

(S3) if a theory is successful, we can reasonably infer that its central terms genuinely refer;

(S4) all the central terms in theories in the mature sciences do refer.

There are complex interconnections here. (S2) and (S4) explain (S1), while (S1) and (S3) provide the warrant for (S4). Reference explains success and success warrants a presumption of reference. The arguments are plausible, given the premises. But there is the rub, for with the possible exception of (S1), none of the premises is acceptable.

The first and toughest nut to crack involves getting clearer about the nature of that 'success' which realists are concerned to explain. Although Putnam, Sellars and Boyd all take the success of certain sciences as a given, they say little about what this success amounts to. So far as I can see, they are working with a largely *pragmatic* notion to be cashed out in terms of a theory's workability or applicability. On this account, we would say that a theory is successful if it makes substantially correct predictions, if it leads to efficacious interventions in the natural order, if it passes a battery of standard tests. One would like to be able to be more specific about what success amounts to, but the lack of a coherent theory of confirmation makes further specificity very difficult.

Moreover, the realist must be wary—at least for these purposes —of adopting too strict a notion of success, for a highly robust and stringent construal of 'success' would defeat the realist's purposes. What he wants to explain, after all, is why science in general has worked so well. If he were to adopt a very demanding characterization of success (such as those advocated by inductive logicians or Popperians) then it would probably turn out that science has been largely 'unsuccessful' (because it does not have high confirmation) and the realist's avowed explandum would thus be a non-problem. Accordingly, I shall assume that a theory is 'successful' so long as it has worked well, that is, so long as it has functioned in a variety of explanatory contexts, has led to confirmed predictions and has been of broad explanatory scope. As I understand the realist's position, his concern is to explain why certain theories have enjoyed this kind of success.

Construing 'success' in this way, (S1) can be conceded. Whether one's criterion of success is broad explanatory scope, possession of a large number of confirming instances, conferring manipulative or predictive control, it is clear that science is, by and large, a successful activity.

What about (S2)? I am not certain that any realist would or should endorse it, although it is a perfectly natural construal of the realist's claim that 'reference explains success'. The notion of reference that is involved here is highly complex and unsatisfactory in significant respects. Without endorsing it, I shall use it frequently in the ensuing discussion on the whole. The realist sense of reference is a rather liberal one, according to which the terms in a theory may be genuinely referring even if many of the claims the theory makes about the entities to which it refers are false. Provided that there are entities which 'approximately fit' a theory's description of them, Putnam's charitable account of reference allows us to say that the terms of a theory genuinely refer.[6] On this account (and these are Putnam's examples), Bohr's 'electrons', Newton's 'mass', Mendel's 'gene', and Dalton's 'atom' are all referring terms, while 'phlogiston' and 'aether' are not.[7]

Are genuinely referential theories, (that is, theories whose central terms genuinely refer) invariably or even generally successful at the empirical level, as (S2) states? There is ample evidence that they are not. The chemical atmoic theory in the eighteenth century was so remarkably unsuccessful that most chemists abandoned it in favour of a more phenomenological, elective affinity chemistry. The Proutian theory that the atoms of heavy elements are composed of hydrogen atoms had, through most of the nineteenth century, a strikingly unsuccessful career, confronted by a long string of apparent refutations. The Wegenerian theory that the continents are carried by large subterranean objects moving laterally across the earth's surface was, for some thirty years in the recent history of geology, a strikingly unsuccessful theory until, after major modifications, it became the geological orthodoxy of the 1960s and 1970s. Yet all of these theories postulated basic entities which (according to Putnam's 'principle of charity') genuinely exist.

The realist's claim that we should expect referring theories to be empirically successful is simply false. And, with a little reflection, we can see good reasons why it should be. To have a genuinely referring theory is to have a theory which 'cuts the world at its joints', a theory which postulates entities of a kind that really exist. But a genuinely referring theory need not be such that all—or even most—of the specific claims it makes about the properties of those entities and their modes of interaction are true. Thus, Dalton's theory makes many claims about atoms which are false; Bohr's early theory of the electron was similarly flawed in important respects. Contra-(S2), genuinely referential theories need not be strikingly successful, since such theories may be 'massively false' (that is, have far greater falsity content than truth content).

(S2) is so patently false that it is difficult to imagine that the realist need be committed to it. But what else will do? The (Putnamian) realist wants attributions of reference to a theory's terms to function in an explanation of that theory's success. The simplest and crudest way of doing that involves a claim like (S2). A less outrageous way of achieving the same end would involve the weaker,

(S2′) a theory whose terms genuinely refer will usually (but not always) be successful.

Isolated instances of referring but unsuccessful theories, sufficient to refute (S2), leave (S2′) unscathed. But if we were to find a broad range of referring but unsuccessful theories that would be evidence against (S2′). Such theories can be generated at will. For instance, take any set of terms which one believes to be genuinely referring. In any language rich enough to contain negation, it will be possible to construct indefinitely many unsuccessful theories, all of whose substantive terms are genuinely referring. Now, it is always open to the realist to claim that such 'theories' are not really theories at all, but mere conjunctions of isolated statements—lacking that sort of conceptual integration with 'real' theories. Sadly, a parallel argument can be made for genuine theories. Consider, for instance, how many inadequate versions of the atomic theory there were in the 2000 years of atomic 'speculating', before a genuinely successful theory emerged. Consider how many unsuccessful versions there were of the wave theory of light before the 1820s, when a successful wave theory first emerged. Kinetic theories of heat in the seventeenth and eighteenth century, developmental theories of embryolgy before the late nineteenth century sustain a similar story. (S2′), every bit as much as (S2), seems hard to reconcile with the historical record.

As Richard Burian has pointed out to me (in personal communication), a realist might attempt to dispense with both of those theses and to simply rest content with (S3) alone. Unlike (S2) and (S2′), (S3) is not open to the objection that referring theories are often unsuccessful, for it makes no claim that referring theories are always or generally successful. But (S3) has difficulties of its own. In the first place, it seems hard to square with the fact that the central terms of many relatively successful theories (for example, aether theories, phlogistic theories) are evidently non-referring. I shall discuss this tension in detail below. More crucial for our purposes here is that (S3) is *not strong enough* to permit the realist to utilize reference to explain success. Unless genuineness of reference entails that all or most referring theories will be successful, then the fact that a theory's terms refer scarcely provides a convincing explanation of that theory's success. If, as (S3) allows, many (or even most) referring theories can be unsuccessful, how can the fact that a successful theory's terms refer be taken to explain why it is successful? (S3) may or may not be true; but in either case it arguably gives the realist no explanatory access to scientific success.

A more plausible construal of Putnam's claim that reference plays a role in explaining the success of science involves rather more indirect argument. It might be said (and Putnam does say this much) that we can explain why a theory is successful by assuming that the theory is true or approximately true. Since a theory can only be true or nearly true (in any sense of those terms open to the realist) if its terms genuinely refer, it might be argued that reference gets into the act willy-nilly when we explain a theory's success in terms of its truth(like) status. On this account, reference is piggy-backed on approximate truth. The viability of this indirect approach is treated at length in section 4 below so I shall not discuss it here except to observe that if the only contact point between reference and success is provided through the medium of approximate truth, then the link between reference and success is extremely tenuous.

What about (S3), the realist's claim that success creates a rational presumption of reference? We have already seen that (S3) provides no explanation of the success of science, but does it have independent merits? The question specifically is whether the success of a theory provides a warrant for concluding that its central terms refer. Insofar as this is—as certain realists suggest—an empirical question, it requires us to inquire whether past theories which have been successful are ones whose central terms genuinely referred (according to the realist's own account of reference).

A proper empirical test of this hypothesis would require extensive sifting of the historical record of a kind that is not possible to perform here. What I can do is to mention a wide range of once successful, but (by present lights) non-referring, theories. A fuller list will come later (see section 5), but for now we shall focus on a whole family of related theories, namely, the subtle fluids and aethers of eighteenth and nineteenth century physics and chemistry.

Consider specifically the state of aetherial theories in the 1830s and 1840s. The electrical fluid, a substance which was generally assumed to accumulate on the surface rather than permeate the interstices of bodies, had been utilized to explain *inter alia* the attraction of oppositely charged bodies, the behaviour of the Leyden jar, the similarities between atmospheric and static electricity and many phenomena of current electricity. Within chemistry and heat theory, the caloric aether had been widely utilized since Boerhaave (by, among others, Lavoisier, Laplace, Black, Rumford, Hutton, and Cavendish) to explain everything from the role of heat in chemical reactions to the conduction and radiation of heat and several standard problems of thermometry. Within the theory of light, the optical aether functioned centrally in explanations of reflection, refraction, interference, double refraction, diffraction and polarization. (Of more than passing interest, optical aether theories had also made some very startling predictions, for example, Fresnel's prediction of a bright spot at the centre of the shadow of a circular disc; a surprising prediction which, when tested, proved correct. If that does not count as empirical success, nothing does!) There were also gravitational (for example, LeSage's) and physiological (for example, Hartley's) aethers which enjoyed some measure of empirical success. It would be difficult to find a family of theories in this period which were as successful as aether theories; compared to them, nineteenth century atomism (for instance), a genuinely refer-ring theory (on realist accounts), was a dismal failure! Indeed, on any account of empirical success which I can conceive of, non-referring nineteenth century aether theories were more successful than contemporary, referring atomic theories. In this connection, it is worth recalling the mark of the great theoretical physicist, J. C. Maxwell, to the effect that the aether was better confirmed than any other theoretical entity in natural philo-sophy!

What we are confronted by in nineteenth century aether theories, then, is a wide variety of once highly successful theories, whose explanatory concept Putnam singles out as a prime example of a non-referring one.[8] What are (referential) realists to make of this historical case? On the face of it, it poses two rather different kinds of challenge to realism: (1) it suggests that (S3) is a dubious piece of advice in that *there can be* (and have been) *highly successful theories some central terms of which are non-referring*; and (2) it suggests that *the realist's claim that he can explain why science is successful is false at least in so far as a part of the historical success of science has been success exhibited by theories whose central terms did not refer.*

But perhaps I am being less than fair when I suggest that the realist is committed to the claim that *all* the central terms in a successful theory refer. It is possible that when Putnam, for instance, says that 'terms in a mature [or successful] science typically refer',[9] he only means to suggest that *some* terms in a successful theory or science genuinely refer. Such a claim is fully consistent with the fact that certain other terms (for example, 'aether') in certain successful, mature sciences (for example, nineteenth century physics) are nonetheless non-referring. Put differently, the realist might argue that the success of a theory warrants the claim that at least some (but not necessarily all) of its central concepts refer.

But such a weakening of (S3) entails a theory of evidential support which can scarcely give comfort to the realist. After all, part of what separates the realist from the positivist is the former's belief that the evidence for a theory is evidence for *everything* which the theory asserts. Where the stereotypical positivist argues that the evidence selectively confirms only the more 'observable' parts of a theory, the realist generally asserts (in the language of Boyd) that:

the sort of evidence which ordinarily counts in favor of the acceptance of a scientific law or theory is, ordinarily, evidence for the (at least approximate) truth of the law or theory as an account of the causal relations obtaining between the entities ['observation or theoretical'] quantified over in the law or theory in question.[10]

For realists such as Boyd, either all parts of a theory (both observational and non-observational) are confirmed by success-ful tests or none is. In general, realists have been able to utilize various holistic arguments to insist that it is not merely the lower level claims of a well-tested theory which are confirmed but its deep-structural assumptions as well. This tactic has been used to good effect by realists in establishing that inductive support 'flows upward' so as to authenticate the most 'theoretical' parts of our theories. Certain latter-day realists (such as Glymour) want to break out of this holist web and argue that certain components of theories can be 'directly' tested. This approach runs the very grave risk of undercutting what the realist desires most: a rationale for taking our deepest-structure theories seriously, and justification for linking reference and success. After all, if the tests to which we subject our theories only test *portions* of them, then even highly successful theories may well have central terms which are non-referring and central tenets which, because untested, we have no grounds for believing to be approximately true. Under those circumstances, a theory might be highly successful and yet contain important constituents which were patently false. Such a state of affairs would wreak havoc with the realist's presumption (R1) that success betokens approximate truth. In short, to be less than a holist about theory testing is to put at risk precisely that predilection for deep-structure claims which motivates much of the realist enterprise.

There is, however, a rather more serious obstacle to this weakening of referential realism. It is true that by weakening (S3) to only certain terms in a theory, one would immunize it from certain obvious counterexamples. But such a manoeuvre has debilitating consequences for other central realist theses. Consider the realist's thesis (R3) about the retentive character of intertheory relations (discussed below in detail). The realist both recommends as a matter of policy and claims as a matter of fact that successful theories are (should be) rationally replaced only by theories which preserve reference for the central terms of their successful predecessors. The rationale for the normative version of this retentionist doctrine is that the terms in the earlier theory, *because it was successful, must* have been referential and thus a constraint on any successor to that theory is that reference should be retained for such terms. This makes sense just in case success provides a blanket warrant for presumption of reference. But if (S3) were weakened so as to say merely that it is reasonable to assume that *some* of the terms in a successful theory genuinely refer, then the realist would have no rationale for his retentive theses (variants of R3), which have been a central pillar of realism for several decades.[11]

Something apparently has to give. A version of (S3) strong enough to license (R3) seems incompatible with the fact that many successful theories contain non-referring central terms. But any weakening of (S3) dilutes the force of, and removes the rationale for, the realist's claims about convergence, retention and correspondence in intertheory relations.[12] If the realist once concedes that some unspecified set of the terms of a successful theory may well not refer, then his proposals for restricting 'the class of candidate theories' to those which retain reference for the *prima facie* referring terms in earlier theories is without foundation.[13]

More generally, we seem forced to say that such linkages as there are between reference and success are rather murkier than Putnam's and Boyd's discussions would let us to believe. If the realist is going to make his case for CER, it seems that it will have to hinge on approximate truth, (R1), rather than reference, (R2).

4. *Approximate truth and success: the 'downward path'*

Ignoring the referential turn among certain recent realists, most realists continue to argue that, at bottom, epistemic realism is committed to the view that scientific theories, even if strictly false, are nonetheless 'approximately true' or 'close to the truth' or 'verisimilar'.[14] The claim generally amounts to this pair:

(T1) if a theory is approximately true, then it will be explanatorily successful; and

(T2) if a theory is explanatorily successful, then it is probably approximately true.

What the realist would *like* to be able to say, of course, is:

(T1′) if a theory is true, then it will be successful.

(T1′) is attractive because self-evident. But most realists balk at invoking (T1′) because they are (rightly) reluctant to believe that we can reasonably presume of any given scientific theory that it is true. If all the realist could explain were the success of theories which were true *simpliciter*, his explanatory repertoire would be acutely limited.

As an attractive move in the direction of broader explanatory scope, (T1) is rather more appealing. After all, presumably many theories which we believe to be false (for example, Newtonian mechanics, thermodynamics, wave optics) were— and still are—highly successful across a broad of applications.

Perhaps, the realist evidently conjectures, we can find an *epistemic* account of that pragmatic success by assuming such theories to be approximately true. But we must be wary of this potential sleight of hand. It may be that there is a connection between success and approximate truth; *but if there is such a connection it must be independently argued for*. The acknowledgedly uncontroversial character of (T1′) must not be surreptitiously invoked—as it sometimes seems to be—in order to establish (T1). When (T1¹)'s antecedent is appropriately weakened by speaking of approximate truth, it is by no means clear that (T1) is sound.

Virtually all the proponents of epistemic realism take it as unproblematic that if a theory were approximately true, it would deductively follow that the theory would be a relatively successful predictor and explainer of observable phenomena. Unfortunately, few of the writers of whom I am aware have defined what it means for a statement or theory to be 'approximately true'. Accordingly, it is impossible to say whether the alleged entailment is genuine. This reservation is more than perfunctory. Indeed, on the best-known account of what it means for a theory to be approximately true, it does *not* follow that an approximately true theory will be explanatorily successful.

Suppose, for instance, that we were to say in a Popperian vein that a theory, T_1, is approximately true if its truth content is greater than its falsity content, that is, $Ct_T(T_1) \gg Ct_F'(T_1)$.[15] (Where $Ct_T(T_1)$ is the cardinality of the set of true sentences entailed by T_1 and $Ct_F(T_1)$ is the cardinality of the set of false sentences entailed by T_1.) If approximate truth is so construed, it does *not* logically follow that an arbitrarily selected class of a theory's entailments (namely, some of its observable consequences) will be true. Indeed, it is entirely conceivable that a theory might be approximately true in the indicated sense and yet be such that *all* of its thus far tested consequences are *false*.[16]

Some realists concede their failure to articulate a coherent notion of approximately truth or verisimilitude, but insist that this failure in no way compromises the viability of (T1). Newton-Smith, for instance, grants that 'no one has given a satisfactory analysis of the notion of verisimilitude',[17] but insists that the concept can be legitimately invoked 'even if one cannot at the time give a philosophically satisfactory analysis of it'.[18] He quite rightly points out that many scientific concepts were explanatorily useful long before a philosophically coherent analysis was given for them. But the analogy is unseemly, for what is being challenged is not whether the concept of approximate truth is philosophically rigorous but rather whether it is even clear enough for us to ascertain whether it entails what it purportedly explains. Until some realist provides a clearer analysis of approximate truth than is now available, it is not even clear whether truthlikeness would explain success, let alone whether, as Newton-Smith insists, 'the concept of verisimilitude is *required* in order to give a satisfactory theoretical explanation of an aspect of the scientific enterprise'.[19] If the realist would demystify the 'miraculousness' (Putnam) or the 'mysteriousness' (Newton-Smith[20]) of the success of science, he needs more than a promissory note that somehow, someday, someone will show that approximately true theories must be successful theories.[21]

Whether there is some definition of approximate truth which does indeed entail that approximately true theories will be predictively successful (and yet still probably false) is not clear.[22] What can be said is that, pious promises to the contrary notwithstanding, *none* of the proponents of realism has yet articulated any coherent account of approximate truth which entails that such theories will, across the range where we can test them, be successful predictors. Further difficulties abound. Even if the realist had a semantically adequate characterization of approximate or partial truth, and even if that semantics entailed that most of the consequences of an approximately true theory would be true, he would still be without any criterion that would *epistemically* warrant the ascription of approximate truth to a theory. As it is, the realist seems to be long on intuitions and short on either a semantics or an epistemology of approximate truth.

These should be urgent items on the realists' agenda since, until we have a coherent account of what approximate truth is, central realist theses like (R1), (T1) and (T2) are just so much mumbo-jumbo.

5. *Approximate truth and success: the 'upward path'*

Despite the doubts voiced in section 4, let us grant for the sake of argument that if a theory is approximately true, then it will be successful. Even granting (T1), is there any plausibility to the suggestion of (T2) that explanatory success can be taken as a rational warrant for a judgement of approximate truth? The answer, I submit, is an unambiguous negative.

To see why, we need to explore briefly one of the connections between 'genuinely referring' and being 'approximately true'.

However the latter is understood, I take it that *a realist would never want to say that a theory was approximately true if its central theoretical terms failed to refer*. If there were nothing like genes, then a genetic theory, no matter how well confirmed it was empirically, would not be approximately true. If there were no entities similar to atoms, no atomic theory could be approximately true; if there were no sub-atomic particles, then no quantum theory of chemistry could be approximately true. In short, a necessary condition—especially for a scientific realist— for a theory being close to the truth is that its central explanatory terms must genuinely refer. (An *instrumentalist*, of course, could countenance the weaker claim that a theory was approximately true so *long* as its directly testable consequence were close to the observable values. But, as I argued above, the realist must take claims about approximate truth to refer alike to the observable and the deep-structural dimensions of a theory.)

Now, what the history of science offers us is a plethora of theories which were both successful and (so far as we can judge) non-referential with respect to many of their central explanatory concepts. I discussed earlier one specific family of theories which fits this description. Let me add a few more prominent examples to the list: the crystalline spheres of ancient and medieval astronomy; the humoral theory of medicine; the effluvial theory of static electricity; 'catastrophist' geology, with its commitment to a universal (Noachian) deluge; the phlogiston theory of chemistry; the caloric theory of heat; the vibratory theory of heat; the vital force theories of physiology; the contact-action gravitational aether of Fatio and LeSage; the electromagnetic aether; the optical aether; the theory of circular inertia. This list, which could be extended *ad nauseam*, involves in every case a theory which was once successful and well confirmed, but which contained central terms which (we now believe) were non-referring. Anyone who imagines that the theories which have been successful and long-lived in the history of science have also been, with respect to their central concepts, genuinely referring theories has studied only the more 'whiggish' versions of the history of science (that is, the ones which recount only those past theories which are referentially similar to currently prevailing ones).

It is true that proponents of CER sometimes hedge their bets by suggesting that their analysis applies exclusively to 'the mature sciences' (for example, Putnam and Krajewski). This distinction between mature and immature sciences proves convenient to the realist since he can use it to dismiss any *prima facie* counterexample to the empirical claims of CER on the grounds that the example is drawn from an 'immature' science. But this insulating manoeuvre is unsatisfactory in two respects. In the first place, it runs the risk of making CER vacuous, since these authors generally define a mature science as one in which correspondence or limiting case relations obtain invariably between any successive theories in the science once it has passed 'the threshold of maturity'. Krajewski grants the tautological character of this view when he notes that 'the thesis that there is [correspondence] among successive theories becomes, indeed, analytical'.[23] Nonetheless, he believes that there is a version of the maturity thesis which 'may be and must be tested by the history of science'. That version is that 'every branch of science crosses at some period the threshold of maturity'.[24] But the testability of this hypothesis is dubious at best. There is no historical observation which could conceivably *refute* it since, even if we discovered that no sciences yet possessed 'corresponding' theories, it could be maintained that eventually every science will become corresponding. It is equally difficult to *confirm* it since, even if we found a science in which corresponding relations existed between the latest theory and its predecessor, we would have no way of knowing whether that relation will continue to apply to subsequent changes of theory in that science. In other words, the much-vaunted empirical testability of realism is seriously compromised by limiting it to the mature sciences.

But there is a second unsavoury dimension to the restriction of CER to the 'mature' sciences. The realists' avowed aim, after all, is to explain why science is successful: that is the 'miracle' which they allege the non-realists leave unaccounted for. The fact of the matter is that parts of science, including many 'immature' sciences, have been successful for a very long time; indeed, many of the theories I alluded to above were empirically successful by any criterion I can conceive of (including fertility, intuitively high confirmation, successful prediction, etc.). If the realist restricts himself to explaining only how the 'mature' sciences work (and recall that very few sciences indeed are yet 'mature' as the realist sees it), then he will have completely failed in his ambition to explain why science in general is successful. Moreover, several of the examples I have cited above come from the history of mathematical physics in the last century (for example, the electromagnetic and optical aethers) and, as Putnam himself concedes, '*physics* surely counts as a "mature" science if any science does'.[25] Since realists would presumably insist that many of the central terms of the theories enumerated above do not genuinely refer, it follows that none of those theories could be approximately true (recalling that the former is a necessary condition for the latter). Accordingly, cases of this kind cast very grave doubts on the plausibility of (T2), that is, the claim that nothing succeeds like approximate truth.

I daresay that for every highly successful theory in the past of science which we now believe to be a genuinely referring theory, one could find half a dozen successful theories which we now regard as substantially non-referring. If the proponents of CER are the empiricists they profess to be about matters epistemological, cases of this kind and this frequency should give them pause about the well-foundedness of (T2).

But we need not limit our counterexamples to non-referring theories. There were many theories in the past which (so far as we can tell) were both genuinely referring and empirically successful which we are nonetheless loathe to regard as approximately true. Consider, for instance, virtually all those geological theories prior to the 1960s which denied any lateral motion to the continents. Such theories were, by any standard, highly successful (and apparently referential); but would anyone today be prepared to say that their constituent theoretical claims—committed as they were to laterally stable continents—were close to the truth? Or what about the chemical theories of the 1920s which assumed that the atomic nucleus was structurally homogeneous? Or those chemical and physical theories of the late nineteenth century which explicitly assumed that matter was neither created nor destroyed? I am aware of no sense of approximate truth (available to the realist) according to which such highly successful, but evidently false, theoretical assumptions could be regarded as 'truthlike'.

More generally, the realist needs to find a riposte to the *prima facie* plausible claim that there is no necessary connection between increasing the accuracy of our deep-structural characterizations of nature and improvements at the level of phenomenological explanations, predictions and manipulations. It *seems* entirely conceivable intuitively that the theoretical mechanisms of a new theory, T_2, might be closer to the mark than those of a rival, T_1, and yet T_1 might be more accurate at the level of testable predictions. In the absence of an argument that greater correspondence at the level of unobservable claims is more likely than not to reveal itself in greater accuracy at the experimental level, one is obliged to say that the realist's hunch that increasing deep-structual fidelity must manifest itself pragmatically in the form of heightened experimental accuracy has yet to be made cogent. (Equally problematic, of course, is the inverse argument to the effect that increasing experimental accuracy betokens greater truthlikeness at the level of theoretical, that is, deep-structural, commitments.)

6. *Confusions about convergence and retention*

Thus far, I have discussed only the static or synchronic versions of CER, versions which make absolute rather than relative judgements about truthlikeness. Of equal appeal have been those variants of CER which invoke a notion of what is variously called convergence, correspondence or cumulation. Proponents of the diachronic version of CER supplement the arguments discussed above ((S1)–(S4) and (T1)–(T2)) with an additional set. They tend to be of this form:

(C1) if earlier theories in a scientific domain are successful and thereby, according to realist principles (for example, (S3) above), approximately true, then scientists should only accept later theories which retain appropriate portions of earlier theories;

(C2) as a matter of fact, scientists do adopt the stragegy of (C1) and manage to produce new, more successful theories in the process;

(C3) the 'fact' that scientists succeed at retaining appropriate parts of earlier theories in more successful successors shows that the earlier theories did genuinely refer and that they were approximately true. And thus, the strategy propounded in (C1) is sound.[26]

Perhaps the prevailing view here is Putnam's and (implicitly), Popper's according to which rationally-warranted successor theories must (a) contain reference to the entities apparently referred to in the predecessor theory (since, by hypothesis, the terms in the earlier theory refer), and (b) contain the 'theoretical laws' and 'mechanisms' of the predecessor theory as limiting cases. As Putnam tells us, a 'realist' should insist that *any* viable successor to an old theory T_1 must 'contain the laws of T_1 as a limiting case'.[27] John Watkins, a like-minded convergentist, puts the point this way:

It typically happens in the history of science that when some hitherto dominant theory T is superceded by T^1, T^1 is in the relation of correspondence to T [that is, T is a 'limiting case' of T^1].[28]

Numerous recent philosophers of science have subscribed to a similar view, including Popper, Post, Krajewski, and Koertge.[29]

This form of retention is not the only one to have been widely discussed. Indeed, realists have espoused a wide variety of claims about what is or should be retained in the transition from a once successful predecessor (T_1) to a successor (T_2) theory. Among the more important forms of realist retention are the following cases: (1) T_2 entails T_1 (Whewell); (2) T_2 retains the true consequences or truth content of T_1 (Popper); (3) T_2 retains the 'confirmed' portions of T_1 (Post, Koertge); (4) T_2 preserves the theoretical laws and mechanisms of T_1 (Boyd, McMullin, Putnam); (5) T_2 preserves T_1 as a limiting case (Watkins, Putnam, Krajewski); (6) T_2 explains why T_1 succeeded insofar as it succeeded (Sellars); (7) T_2 retains reference for the central terms of T_1.

The question before us is whether, when retention is understood in *any* of these senses, the realist's theses about convergence and retention are correct.

6.1 *Do scientists adopt the 'retentionist' strategy of CER?*   One crucial part of the convergent realist's argument is a claim to the effect that scientists generally adopt the strategy of seeking to preserve earlier theories in later ones. As Putnam puts it:

preserving the *mechanisms* of the earlier theory as often as possible, which is what scientists try to do. . . . That scientists try to do this . . . is a fact, and that this strategy has led to important discoveries . . . is also a fact.[30]

Similarly, Szumilewicz insists that many eminent scientists made it a main heuristic requirement of their research programmes that a new theory stand in a relation of correspondence with the theory it supercedes.[31] If Putnam and the other retentionists are right about the strategy which most scientists have adopted, we should expect to find the historical literature of science abundantly provided with (a) proofs that later theories do indeed contain earlier theories as limiting cases, or (b) outright rejections of later theories which fail to contain earlier theories. Except on rare occasions (coming primarily from the history of mechanics), one finds neither of these concerns prominent in the literature of science. For instance, to the best of my knowledge, literally no one criticized the wave theory of light because it did not preserve the theoretical mechanisms of the earlier corpuscular theory; no one faulted Lyell's uniformitarian geology on the grounds that it dispensed with several causal processes prominent in catastrophist geology; Darwin's theory was not criticized by most geologists for its failure to retain many of the mechanisms of Lamarckian 'evolutionary theory'.

For all the realist's confident claims about the prevalence of a retentionist strategy in the sciences, I am aware of *no* historical studies which would sustain as a *general* claim his hypothesis about the evaluative strategies utilized in science. Moreover, insofar as Putnam and Boyd claim to be offering 'an explanation of the [retentionist] behaviour of scientists',[32] they have the wrong explanandum, for if there is any widespread strategy in science, it is one which says, 'accept an empirically successful theory, regardless of whether it contains the theoretical laws and mechanisms of its predecessors'.[33] Indeed, one could take a leaf from the realist's (C2), and claim that the success of the strategy of assuming that earlier theories do not always refer shows that it is true that earlier theories do not!

(One might note in passing how often, and on what flimsy evidence, realists imagine that they are speaking for the scientific majority. Putnam, for instance, claims that 'realism is, so to speak, "science's philosophy of science"' and that 'science taken at "face value" *implies* realism.'[34] Hooker insists that to be a realist is to take science 'seriously',[35] as if to suggest that conventionalists, instrumentalists and positivists such as Duhem, Poincaré, and Mach did not take science seriously. The willingness of some realists to attribute realist strategies to working scientists—on the strength of virtually no empirical research into the principles which *in fact* have governed scientific practice—raises serious doubts about the genuineness of their avowed commitment to the empirical character of epistemic claims.)

6.2 Do later theories preserve the mechanisms, models, and laws of earlier theories?   Regardless of the explicit strategies to which scientists have subscribed, are Putnam and several other retentionists right that later theories 'typically' entail earlier theories, and that 'earlier theories are, very often, limiting cases of later theories'.[36] Unfortunately, answering this question is difficult, since 'typically' is one of those weasel words which allows for much hedging. I shall assume that Putnam and Watkins mean that 'most of the time (or perhaps in most of the important cases) successor theories contain predecessor theories as limiting cases'. So construed, the claim is patently false. Copernican astronomy did not retain all the mechanisms of Ptolemaic astronomy (for example, motion along an equant); Newton's physics did not retain all (or even most of) the 'theoretical laws' of Cartesian mechanics, astronomy and optics; Franklin's electrical theory did not contain its predecessor (Nollet's) as a limiting case. Relativistic physics did not retain the aether, nor the mechanisms associated with it; statistical mechanics does not incorporate all the mechanisms of thermodynamics; modern genetics does not have Darwinian pangenesis as a limiting case; the wave theory of light did not appropriate the mechanisms of corpuscular optics; modern embryology incorporates virtually none of the mechanisms prominent in classical embryological theory. As I have shown elsewhere,[37] loss occurs at virtually every level: the confirmed predictions of earlier theories are sometimes not explained by later ones; even the 'observable' laws are not always retained, not even as limiting cases; theoretical processes and mechanisms of earlier theories are, as frequently as not, treated as flotsam.

The point is that some of the most important theoretical innovations have been due to a willingness of scientists to violate the cumulationist or retentionist constraint which realists enjoin 'mature' scientists to follow.

There is a deep reason why the convergent realist is wrong about these matters. It has to do, in part, with the role of ontological frameworks in science and with the nature of limiting case relations. As scientists use the term 'limiting case', T_1 can be limiting case of T_2 only if (a) *all* the variables (observable and theoretical) assigned a value in T_1 are assigned a value by T_2 and (b) the values assigned to every variable of T_1 are the same as, or very close to, the values T_2 assigns to the corresponding variable when certain initial and boundary conditions—consistent with T_2[38]—are specified. This seems to require that T_1 can be a limiting case of T_2 only if *all* the entities postulated by T_1 occur in the onology of T_2. Whenever there is a change of ontology accompanying a theory transition such that T_2 (when conjoined with suitable initial and boundary conditions) fails to capture T_1's ontology, then T_1 *cannot* be a limiting case of T_2. Even where the ontologies of T_1 and T_2 overlap appropriately (that is, where T_2's ontology embraces all of T_1's), T_1 is a limiting case of T_2 only if *all* the laws of T_1 can be derived from T_2, given appropriate limiting conditions. It is important to stress that *both* these conditions (among others) must be satisfied before one theory can be a limiting case of another. Where 'closet positivisis' might be content with capturing only the formal mathematical relations or only the observable consequences of T_1 within a successor, T_2, any genuine realist must insist that T_1's underlying ontology is preserved in T_2's, *for it is that ontology above all which he alleges to be approximately true.* Too often, philosophers (and physicists) infer the existence of a limiting case relation between T_1 and T_2 on substantially less than this. For instance, many writers have claimed a theory to be a limiting case of another when only some, but not all, of the laws of the former are 'derivable' from the latter. In other cases, one theory has been said to be a limiting case of a successor when the mathematical laws of the former find homologies in the latter but where the former's ontology is not fully extractable from the latter's.

Consider one prominent example which has often been misdescribed, namely, the transition from the classical aether theory to relativistic and quantum mechanics. It can, of course, be shown that some 'laws' of classical mechanics are limiting cases of relativistic mechanics. But there are other laws and general assertions made by the classical theory (for example, claims about the density and fine structure of the aether, general laws about the character of the interaction between aether and matter, models and mechanisms detailing the compressibility of the aether) which could not conceivably be limiting cases of modern mechanics. The reason is a simple one: a theory cannot assign values to a variable which does not occur in that theory's language (or, more colloquially, it cannot assign properties to entities whose existence it does not countenance). Classical aether physics contained a number of postulated mechanisms for dealing *inter alia* with the transmission of light through the aether. Such mechanisms could not possibly appear in a successor theory like the special theory of relativity which denies the very existence of an aetherial medium and which accomplishes the explanatory tasks performed by the aether via very different mechanisms.

Nineteenth century mathematical physics is replete with similar examples of evidently successful mathematical laws which, because some of their variables refer to entities whose existence we now deny, cannot be shown to be limiting cases of our physics. As Adolf Grünbaum has cogently argued, when we are confronted with two incompatible theories, T_1 and T_2, such that T_2 does not 'contain' all of T_1's ontology, then not all the mechanisms and theoretical laws of T_1 which involve those entities of T_1 not postulated by T_2 can possibly be retained—not even as limiting cases—in T_2.[39] This result is of some significance. What little plausibility convergent or retentive realism has enjoyed derives from the presumption that it correctly describes the relations between classical and post-classical mechanics and gravitational theory. Once we see that even in this *prima facie* most favourable case for the realist (where *some* of the laws of the predecessor theory are genuinely limiting cases of the successor), changing ontologies or conceptual frameworks make it impossible to capture many of the central-theoretical laws and mechanisms postulated by the earlier theory, then we can see how misleading is Putnam's claim that 'what scientists try to do' is to preserve 'the *mechanisms* of the earlier theory as often as possible—or to show that they are "limiting cases" of new mechanisms . . .'[40] Where the mechanisms of the earlier theory involve entities whose existence the later theory denies, no scientists does (or should) feel any compunction about wholesale repudiation of the earlier mechanisms.

But even where there is no change in basic ontology, many theories (even in 'mature sciences' like physics) fail to retain all the explanatory successes of their predecessors. For instance, statistical mechanics has yet to capture the irreversibility of macro-thermodynamics as a genuine limiting case. Classical continuum mechanics has not yet been reduced to quantum mechanics or relativity. Contemporary field theory has yet to replicate the classical thesis that physical laws are invariant under reflection in space. If scientists had accepted the realist's constraint (viz., that new theories must have old theories as limiting cases), neither relativity nor statistical mechanics would have been viewed as viable theories. It has been said before, but it needs to be reiterated over and again: *a proof of the existence of limiting relations between selected components of two theories is a far cry from a systematic proof that one theory is a limiting case of the other*. Even if classical and modern physics stood to one another in the manner in which the convergent realist erroneously imagines they do, his hasty generalization that theory successions in all the advanced sciences show limiting case relations is patently false.[41] But, as this discussion shows, not even the realist's paradigm case will sustain the claims he makes about it.

What this analysis underscores is just how reactionary many forms of convergent epistemological realism are. If one took seriously CER's advice to reject any new theory which did not capture existing theories as referential and existing laws and mechanisms as approximately authentic, then any prospect for deep-structure, ontological changes in our theories would be foreclosed. Equally outlawed would be any significant repudiation of our theoretical models. In spite of his avowed commitment to the growth of knowledge, the realist would unwittingly freeze science in its present state by forcing all future theories to accommodate the ontology of contemporary science and by foreclosing the possibility that some future generation may come to the conclusion that some (or even most) of the central terms in our best theories are no more referential than was 'natural place', 'phlogiston', 'aether', or 'caloric'.

6.3 *Could theories converge in ways required by the realist?* These instances of violations in genuine science of the sorts of continuity usually required by realists are by themselves sufficient to show that the forms of scientific growth which the convergent realist takes as his explicandum are often absent, even in the 'mature' sciences. But we can move beyond these specific cases to show in principle that the kind of cumulation demanded by the realist is unattainable. Specifically, by drawing on some results established by David Miller and others, the following can be shown:

(a) the familiar requirement that a successor theory, T_2, must both preserve the true consequences of its predecessor, T_1, and explain T_1's anomalies is contradictory;

(b) that if a new theory, T_2, involves a change in the ontology or conceptual framework of a predecessor, T_1, then T_1 will have true consequences not entailed by T_2;

(c) that if two theories, T_1 and T_2, disagree, then each will have true consequences not entailed by the other;

(d) that one theory, T_2, will possess all the *true* observational consequences of another, T_1, just in case they are *observationally equivalent*. Even if T_2 and T_1 are mutually consistent (that is, if T_2 does not contradict T_1), T_2 will not be able to explain all the true observational consequences of T_1 unless T_2 and T_1 are observationally equivalent.

In order to establish these conclusions, one needs to utilize a 'syntactic' view of theories according to which a theory is a conjunction of statements and its consequences are defined à la Tarski in terms of content classes. Needless to say, this is not the only, nor necessarily the best, way of thinking about theories; but it happens to be the way in which most philosophers who argue for convergence and retention (for example, Popper, Watkins, Post, Krajewski, and Niiniluoto) tend to conceive of theories. What I want to show is that if one utilizes the Tarskian conception of a theory's content and its consequences as they do, then the familiar convergentist theses alluded to in (a) through (d) make no sense.

These results can be proved, given two relatively uncontroversial assumptions: (i) that the theories under consideration are empirically incomplete in the sense that there is at least one true 'observational statement' which is logically independent of them, and (ii) that disjunction introduction is a legitimate operation in constituting the class of consequences of a theory. Taking these as given, the argument for (a) to (d) is straightforward.

To show that (a) is true, consider the following: since T_2 is incomplete, there is some true observational statement, p, such that T_2 does not entail p. Let us call T_1's anomaly, $-a$, and since $-a$ is an anomaly for T_1, it is clear that $T_1 \rightarrow a$. Since by hypothesis, T_2 explains T_1's anomaly, $T_2 \rightarrow -a$. Since $T_1 \rightarrow a$, $T_1 \rightarrow (a \vee p)$ by disjunction introduction. Because p is true, 'a v p' is a true consequence of T_1. But since $-(T_2 \rightarrow p)$ and $-(T_2 \rightarrow a)$, the true statement 'a v p' is no consequence of T_2. Hence incomplete successor theories which correct anomalies of their predecessors cannot have all the true observational consequences of their refuted predecessors.

For (b), I assume that if T_2's ontology does not fully include T_1's then there will be a statement, a, which is entailed by T_1, which is not well formed in T_2. As before, let p be a true statement independent of T_2. Then T_1 has the true consequence 'a v p' which is not a consequence of T_2.

The proof of (c) is similar to (a)'s. If T_2 is incomplete, p—independently of T_2—will be true. If T_2 and T_1 disagree, there must be some statement a such that $(T_1 \rightarrow a)$ and $(T_2 \rightarrow -a)$. The true statement 'a v p' is a consequence of T_1 but not of T_2. Similarly if T_1 is incomplete, T_2 will have true consequences not entailed by T_1.

As for (d), it follows straightforwardly from the above. Suppose T_1 and T_2 are mutually consistent but such that neither entails all the observational consequences of the other. Then there must be some observational statement, s, such that $(T_1 \rightarrow s)$ and $-(T_2 \rightarrow s)$. Assuming T_2 is incomplete, there is a true p independent of T_2. 's v p' is a true consequence of T_1 but not T_2.

Similarly, if T_1 is incomplete and does not entail all the observational consequences of T_2, then T_2 will have true observational consequences not entailed by T_1.

What these elementary but devastating results establish is that virtually any effort to link scientific progress or growth to the wholesale retention of a predecessor theory's Tarskian content *or* logical consequences *or* true consequences *or* observed consequences *or* confirmed consequences is evidently doomed. Realists have not only got their history wrong in so far as they imagine that cumulative retention has prevailed in science, but we can see that—given their views on what should be retained through theory change—history could not possibly have been the way their models require it to be. The realists' strictures on cumulativity are as ill-advised normatively as they are false historically.

Along with many other realists, Putnam has claimed that 'the mature sciences do converge . . . and that that convergence has great explanatory value for the theory of science'.[42] As this section should show, Putnam and his fellow realists are arguably wrong on *both* counts.

Popper once remarked that 'no theory of knowledge should attempt to explain why we are successful in our attempts to explain things'.[43] Such a dogma is too strong. But what the foregoing analysis shows is that an occupational hazard of recent epistemology is imagining that convincing explanations of our success come easily or cheaply.

6.4 *Should new theories explain why their predecessors were successful?* An apparently more modest realism than that outlined above is familiar in the form of the (Sellarsian) requirement (R4) that every satisfactory new theory must be able to explain why its predecessor was successful in so far as it was successful. On this view, viable new theories need not preserve all the content of their predecessors, nor capture those predecessors as limiting cases. Rather, it is simply insisted that a viable new theory, T_N, must explain why, when we conceive of the world according to the old theory T_O, there is a range of cases where our T_O-guided expectations were correct or approximately correct.

What are we to make of this requirement? In the first place, it is clearly *gratuitous*. If T_N has more confirmed consequences (and greater conceptual simplicity) than T_O, then T_N is preferable to T_O even if T_N cannot explain why T_O is successful. Contrariwise, if T_N has fewer confirmed consequences than T_O, then T_N cannot be rationally preferred to T_O even if T_N explains why T_O is successful. In short, a theory's ability to explain why a rival is successful is neither a necessary nor a sufficient condition for saying that it is better than its rival.

Other difficulties likewise confront the claim that new theories should explain why their predecessors were successful. Chief among them is the ambiguity of the notion itself. One way to show that an older theory, T_1, was successful is to show that it shares many confirmed consequences with a newer theory, T_2, which is highly successful. But this is not an 'explanation' that a scientific realist could accept, since it makes no reference to, and thus does not depend upon, an epistemic assessment of either T_1 or T_2. (After all, an instrumentalist could quite happily grant that if T_2 'saves the phenomena' then T_1—insofar as some of its observable consequences overlap with or are experimentally indistinguisable from those of T_2—should also succeed in saving the phenomena.)

The intuition being traded on in Sellars' persuasive account is that the pragmatic success of a new theory, combined with a partial comparison of respective consequences of the new theory and its predecessor, will sometimes put us in a position to say when the older theory worked and when it failed. But such comparisons as can be made in this manner do not involve *epistemic* appraisals of either the new or the old theory *qua* theories. Accordingly, the philosophy of such comparisons provides no argument for epistemic realism.

What the realist apparently needs is an *epistemically* robust sense of 'explaining the success of a predecessor'. Such an epistemic characterization would presumably begin with the claim that T_2, the new theory, was approximately true and would proceed to show that the 'observable' claims of its predecessor, T_1, deviated only slightly from (some of) the 'observable' consequences of T_2. It would then be alleged that the (presumed) approximate truth of T_2 and the partially overlapping consequences of T_1 and T_2 jointly explained why T_1 was successful in so far as it was successful. But this is a *non sequitur*. As I have shown above, the fact that a theory, T_2, is approximately true does not even explain why T_2 is successful; how, under those circumstances, can the approximate truth of T_2 explain why some theory different from T_2 is successful? Whatever the nature of the relations between T_2 and T_1 (entailment, limiting case, etc.), the epistemic ascription of approximate truth to either T_1 or T_2 (or both) apparently leaves untouched questions of how successful T_1 or T_2 are.

The idea that new theories should explain why older theories were successful (in so far as they were) originally arose as a rival to the 'levels' picture of explanation according to which new theories fully explained—because they entailed—their predecessors. It is clearly an improvement over the levels picture (for it does recognize that later theories generally do not entail their predecessors). But as a general thesis about intertheory relations, designed to buttress a realist epistemology, it is difficult to see how this position avoids difficulties similar to those discussed in earlier sections.

Like other aspects of convergent realism, this requirement is highly *historicist*. It insists that the adequacy of a theory is not primarily a matter of the relationship between that theory and the data but that it is, as well, a function of what theories immediately preceded the theory under appraisal. Considering how many epistemic realists are in the vanguard of the fight against historicism, it is with some dismay that one discovers how much of epistemic realism (for example, the requirement that new theories must preserve reference for their rivals, that they must contain their predecessors as limiting cases, that new theories must explain why the old were successful) is linked to the thesis that the accidents and vicissitudes of the temporal sequence of theories in any given domain are central to theory assessment.

7. *The realists' ultimate 'petitio principii'*

It is time to step back a moment from the details of the realists' argument to look at its general strategy. Fundamentally, the realist is utilizing, as we have seen, an abductive inference which proceeds from the success of science to the conclusion that science is approximately true, verisimilar, and referential (or any combination of these). This argument is meant to show the sceptic that theories are not ill-gotten, the positivist that theories are not reducible to their observational consequences, and the pragmatist that classical epistemic categories (for example, 'truth', 'falsehood') are a relevant part of meta-scientific discourse.

It is little short of remarkable that realists would imagine that their critics would find the argument compelling. As I have shown elsewhere,[44] ever since antiquity, critics of epistemic realism have based their scepticism upon a deep-rooted conviction that the fallacy of affirming the consequent is indeed fallacious. When Sextus or Bellarmine or Hume doubted that certain theories which saved the phenomena were warrantable as true, their doubts were based on a belief that the exhibition that a theory had some true consequences left entirely open the truth-status of the theory. Indeed, many non-realists have been non-realists precisely because they believed that false theories, as well as true ones, could have true consequences.

Now enters the new breed of realist (such as Putnam, Boyd and Newton-Smith) who wants to argue that epistemic realism can reasonably be presumed to be true by virtue of the fact that it has true consequences. But this is a monumental case of begging the question. The non-realist refuses to admit that a *scientific* theory can be warrantedly judged to be true simply because it has some true consequences. Such non-realists are not likely to be impressed by the claim that a *philosophical* theory like realism can be warranted as true because it arguably has some true consequences. If non-realists are chary about first-order abductions to avowedly true conclusions, they are not likely to be impressed by second-order abductions, particularly when, as I have tried to show above, the premises and conclusions are so indeterminate.

But, it might be argued, the realist is not out to convert the intransigent sceptic or the determined instrumentalist.[45] He is perhaps seeking, rather, to show that realism can be tested like any other scientific hypothesis, and that realism is at least as well confirmed as some of our best scientific theories. Such an analysis, however plausible initially, will not stand up to scrutiny. I am aware of no realist who is willing to say that a *scientific* theory can be reasonably presumed to be true or even regarded as well confirmed just on the strength of the fact that its thus far tested consequences are true. Realists have long been in the forefront of those opposed to *ad hoc* and *post hoc* theories. Before a realist accepts a scientific hypothesis, he generally wants to know whether it has explained or predicted more than it was devised to explain; he wants to know whether it has been subjected to a battery of controlled tests; whether it has successfully made novel predictions; whether there is independent evidence for it.

What, then, of realism itself as a 'scientific' hypothesis?[46] Even if we grant (contrary to what I argued in section 4) that realism entails and thus explains the success of science, ought that (hypothetical) success warrant, by the realist's own construal of scientific acceptability, the acceptance of realism? Since realism was devised in order to explain the success of science, it remains purely *ad hoc* with respect to that success. If realism has made some novel predictions or been subjected to carefully controlled tests, one does not learn about it from the literature of contemporary realism. At the risk of patent inconsistency, the realist rejects the instrumentalist's view that saving the phenomena is a significant form of evidential support while endorsing realism itself on the transparently instrumentalist grounds that it is confirmed by those very features it was invented to explain. The fact of the matter seems to be that no proponent of realism has sought to show that realism satisfies those stringent empirical demands which the realist himself minimally insists on when appraising scientific theories. The latter-day realist often calls realism a 'scientific' or 'well-tested' hypothesis, but seems curiously reluctant to subject it to those controls which he otherwise takes to be a *sine qua non* for empirical well-foundedness.

8. *Conclusion*

The arguments and cases discussed above seem to warrant the following conclusions:

(1) The fact that a theory's central terms refer does not entail that it will be successful; and a theory's success is no warrant for the claim that all or most of its central terms refer.

(2) The notion of approximate truth is presently too vague to

permit one to judge whether a theory consisting entirely of approximately true laws would be empirically successful; what is clear is that a theory may be empirically successful even if it is not approximately true.

(3) Realists have no explanation whatever for the fact that many theories whose laws are not approximately true and whose terms seemingly do not refer are nonetheless often successful.

(4) The convergentist's assertion that scientists in a 'mature' discipline always preserve, or seek to preserve, the laws and mechanisms of earlier theories in later ones is false; his assertion that when such laws are preserved in a successful successor, we can explain the success of the latter by virtue of the truthlikeness of the preserved laws and mechanisms, suffers from all the defects noted above confronting approximate truth.

(5) Even if it could be shown that referring theories and approximately true theories would be successful, the realists' argument that successful theories are approximately true and genuinely referential takes for granted precisely what the non-realist denies (vis., that explanatory success betokens truth).

(6) It is not clear that acceptable theories either *do* or *should* explain why their predecessors succeeded or failed. If a theory is better supported than its rivals and predecessors, then it is not epistemically decisive to its appraisal whether it explains why its rivals worked.

(7) If a theory, T, has once been falsified, it is completely unreasonable to expect that a successor should retain either all of T's content *or* its confirmed consequences *or* its theoretical mechanisms.

(8) Nowhere has the realist established—except by fiat—that non-realist epistemologies lack the resources to explain the success of science.

With these specific conclusions in mind, we can proceed to a more global one: it is not yet established—contra-Putnam, Newton-Smith and Boyd—that realism can explain *any* part of the success of science. What is very clear is that realism *cannot*, even by its own lights, explain the success of those many theories whose central terms have evidently not referred and whose theoretical laws and mechanisms were not approximately true. The inescapable conclusion is that in so far as many realists are concerned—as several profess to be—with explaining how science works and with measuring the adequacy of their epistemology by that standard, they have thus far failed to explain very much and their epistemology is confronted by anomalies which seem beyond its resources to grapple with. Whether this state of affairs will temper the current enthusiasm for realism is rather unclear since, judging by the track record, criticizing realism is rather like condemning sin: those who are addicted to it will probably ignore the criticism; those who do not accept it in the first place scarcely need to be reminded of its pitfalls.

Notes

1 H. Putnam, *Mathematics, Matter and Method*, Cambridge, 1975, vol. 1, p. 69.
2 H. Putnam, *Meaning and the Moral Sciences*, London 1978, p. 18. (Hereafter I will refer to this work as '*MMS*'.)
3 Putnam, evidently following Boyd, sums up (R1) to (R3) in these words:

  1.) Terms in a mature science typically *refer*.
  2.) The laws of a theory belonging to a mature science are typically approximately *true* . . . I will only consider [new] theories . . . which have this property—[they] contain the [theoretical] laws of [their predecessors] as a limiting case. (*MMS*, pp. 20–1.)

4 Putnam insists, for instance, that if the realist is wrong about theories being referential, then 'the success of science is a miracle'.
5 H. Putnam, *MMS*, p. 21. Boyd remarks: 'scientific realism offers an *explanation* for the legitimacy of ontological commitment to theoretical entities'. (*op. cit.*, Note 10, p. 2a). It allegedly does so by explaining why theories containing theoretical entities work so well: because such entities genuinely exist.
6 Whether one utilizes Putnam's earlier or later versions of realism is irrelevant for the central arguments of this chapter.
7 Cf. Putnam, *MMS*, pp. 20–2.
8 Cf. Putnam, *MMS*, p. 22.
9 Putnam, *MMS*, p. 20.
10 R. Boyd, 'Realism, Underdetermination, and a Causal Theory of Evidence', *Nous*, 1973, p. 1. Cf. also *ibid.*, p. 3: 'experimental evidence for a theory is evidence for the truth of even its non-observational laws'. See also W. Sellars, *Science, Perception and Reality*, New York, 1962, p. 97.
11 A caveat is in order here. *Even if* all the central terms in some theory refer, it is not obvious that every rational successor to that theory must preserve all the referring terms of its predecessor. One can easily imagine circumstances when the new theory is preferable to the old one even though the range of application of the new theory is less broad than the old. When the range is so restricted, it may well be entirely appropriate to drop reference to some of the entities which figured in the earlier theory.
12 For Putnam and Boyd both 'it will be a constraint on T_2 [that is, any new theory in a domain] . . . that T_2 must have this property, the property that *from its standpoint*

one can assign referents to the terms of T_1 [that is, an earlier theory in the same domain].' (*MMS*, p. 22). For Boyd, see *op. cit.*, p. 8: 'new theories should, *prima facie*, resemble current theories with respect to their accounts of causal relations among theoretical entities'.

13 Cf. Putnam, *MMS*, p. 22.

14 For just a small sampling of this view, consider the following: McMullin: 'The claim of a realist ontology of science is that the only way of explaining why the models of science function so successfully . . . is that they approximate in some way the structure of the object', (*Minn. Stud.*, V, 1970, pp. 63–4; Niiniluoto: 'the continued success [of confirmed theories] can be *explained* by the hypothesis that they are in fact close to the truth . . .', 'Scientific Progress', forthcoming, p. 21; Putnam: the claim that 'the laws of a theory belonging to a mature science are typically approximately *true* . . . [provides] an *explanation* of the behaviour of scientists and the success of science', *MMS*, pp. 20–1. Smart, Sellars, and Newton-Smith, among others, share a similar view.

15 Although Popper is generally careful not to assert that actual historical theories exhibit ever increasing truth content (for an exception, see his *Conjectures and Refutations*, New York, 1963, p. 220), other writers have been more bold. Thus, Newton-Smith writes that 'the historically generated set of theories in a mature science . . . is a sequence in which succeeding theories have greater truth-content and less falsity content than their predecessors' ('The Underdetermination of Theories by Data', *Proceedings of the Aristotelian Society, Supplementary Volume L II*, 1978, p. 72.).

16 On the more technical side, Niiniluoto believes he has shown that a theory's degree of corroboration covaries with its 'estimated verisimilitude'. (Cf. I. Niiniluoto, 'On the Truthlikeness of Generalizations', in Butts & Hintikka (eds.), *Basic Problems in Methodology and Linguistics*, Dordrecht, 1977, pp. 121–47 and 'Scientific Progress', forthcoming.) Roughly speaking, 'estimated truthlikeness' is a measure of how closely (the content of) a theory corresponds to *what we take to be* the best conceptual systems that we so far have been able to find ('Scientific Progress', typescript, p. 18). If Niiniluoto's measures work (which is doubtful since their languages are not rich enough to formulate 'real' theories), it follows from the above-mentioned convariance that an empirically successful theory will have a high degree of estimated truthlikeness. But because estimated truthlikeness and genuine verisimilitude are not necessarily related (the former being parasitic on existing evidence and available conceptual systems), it is an open question whether—as Niiniluoto asserts—the 'continued success' of highly confirmed theories 'can be *explained* by the hypothesis that they in fact are close to the truth at least in the relevant respects', *ibid.*, p. 21. Unless I am mistaken, this remark betrays a confusion between 'true verisimilitude' (to which we have no epistemic access) and 'estimated verisimilitude' (which is accessible but non-epistemic).

17 W. Newton-Smith, 'In Defense of Truth', manuscript, p. 16.

18 *ibid.*

19 *ibid.*

20 Newton-Smith claims that the increasing predictive success of science through time 'would be totally mystifying . . . if it were not for the fact that theories are capturing more and more truth about the world', *ibid.*, p. 15.

21 I must stress again that I am not denying that there *may* be a connection between approximate truth and predictive success. I am only observing that until the realists show us what that connection is, they should be more reticent than they are about claiming that realism can explain the success of science.

22 A *non-realist* might argue that a theory is approximately true just in case all its *observable* consequences are true or within a specified interval from the true value.

Theories that were 'approximately true' in this sense would indeed be demonstrably successful. But, the realist's (otherwise commendable) commitment to taking seriously the theoretical claims of a theory precludes him from utilizing any such construal of approximate truth, since he wants to say that the theoretical as well as the observational consequences are approximately true.

23 W. Krajewski, *Correspondence Principle and Growth of Science*, Dordrecht, 1977, p. 91.

24 *ibid.*

25 Putnam, *MMS*, p. 21.

26 If this argument, which I attribute to the realists, seems a bit murky, I challenge any reader to find a more clearcut one in the literature! Overt formulations of this position can be found in Putnam, Boyd and Newton-Smith.

27 Putnam, *MMS*, p. 21.

28 John Watkins, 'Corroboration and the Problem of Content-Comparison', in Radnitzky and Andersson (eds.), *Progress and Rationality in Science*, Dordrecht, 1978, pp. 376-7.

29 Popper: 'a theory which has been well corroborated can only be superceded by one . . . [which] *contains* the old well-corroborated theory—or at least a good approximation to it' (*LSD*, p. 276); Post: 'I shall even claim that, as a matter of empirical historical fact, [successor] theories [have] always explained the *whole* of [the well confirmed part of their predecessors]' (*Stud. Hist. Phil. Sci.*, 2, 1971, p. 229; Koertge: 'nearly all pairs of successive theories in the history of science stand in a correspondence relation and . . . where there is no correspondence to begin with, the new theory will be developed in such a way that it comes more nearly into correspondence with the old' (*Conceptual Change*, Dordrecht, 1973). Among other authors who have defended a similar view, one should mention A. Fine ('Consistency, Derivability and Scientific Change', *J. Phil.*, 64, 1967, pp. 231 ff.), C. Kordig ('Scientific Transitions, Meaning Invariance, and Derivality', *Southern Journal of Philosophy*, 1971, pp. 119-25), H. Margenau (*The Nature of Physical Reality*, New York, 1950), E. Nagel and L. Sklar ('Types of Inter-Theoretic Reductions', *Brit. J. Phil. Sci.*, *18*, 1967, pp. 190-24).

30 Putnam, *MMS*, p. 20. Putnam fails to point out that it is also a fact that many scientists do *not* seek to preserve earlier mechanisms and that theories which have not preserved earlier theoretical mechanisms (whether the germ theory of disease, plate tectonics, or wave optics) have led to important discoveries is also a fact.

31 I. Szumilewicz, 'Incommensurability and the Rationality of the Development of Science', *Brit. J. Phil. Sci.*, *28*, 1977, p. 348.

32 Putnam, *MMS*, p. 21.

33 I have written a book about this strategy, *Progress and Its Problems*, California, 1977.

34 Putnam, *MMS*, p. 37. After the epistemological and methodological battles about science during the last 300 years, it should be fairly clear that science, taken at its face value, *implies* no particular epistemology.

35 Hooker, 'Systematic Realism', p. 409.

36 Cf. Putnam, *MMS*, pp. 20, 123.

37 Laudan, 'Two Dogmas of Methodology', *Philosophy of Science*, 43, 1976, pp. 467-72.

38 This matter of limiting conditions consistent with the 'reducing' theory is curious. Some of the best-known expositions of limiting case relations depend (as Krajewski has observed) upon showing an earlier theory to be a limiting case of a later theory only by adopting limiting assumptions *explicitly denied by the later theory*. For instance, several standard textbook discussions present (a portion of) classical mechanics as a limiting case of special relativity, provided c approaches infinity. But special relativity is committed to the claim that c is a constant. Is there not something suspicious about a 'derivation' of T_1 from a T_2 which essentially involves an

assumption inconsistent with T_2? If T_2 is correct, then it forbids the adoption of a premise commonly used to derive T_1 as a limiting case. (It should be noted that most such proofs can be reformulated unobjectionably, for example, in the relativity case, by letting $v \rightarrow$ o rather than $c \rightarrow \infty_i$)

39 Cf. Adolf Grünbaum, 'Can A Theory Answer More Questions than One of Its Rivals?', *BJPS*, 27, 1976, pp. 1–23.

40 Putnam, *MMS*, p. 20.

41 As Mario Bunge has cogently put it: 'The popular view on intertheory relations . . . that every new theory includes (as regards its extension) its predecessors . . . is philosophically superficial, . . . and it is false as a historical hypothesis concerning the advancement of science'. (M. Bunge, 'Problems concerning Intertheory Relations', in P. Weingertner and G. Zecha (eds.), *Induction, Physics and Ethics*, Dordrecht, 1970, pp. 309–10.)

42 Putnam, *MMS*, p. 37.

43 K. Popper, *Objective Knowledge*, Oxford, 1973, p. 23.

44 Laudan, 'Ex-Huming Hacking', *Erkenntnis*, Dordrecht, 1978.

45 I owe the suggestion of this realist response to Andrew Lugg.

46 I find Putnam's views on the 'empirical' or 'scientific' character of realism rather perplexing. At some points, he seems to suggest that realism is both empirical and scientific. Thus, he writes: 'If realism is an explanation of this fact [viz., that science is successful], realism must itself be an over-arching scientific *hypothesis*' (*MMS*, p. 19). Since Putnam clearly maintains the antecedent, he seems committed to the consequent. Elsewhere he refers to certain realist tenets as being 'our highest level empirical generalizations about knowledge' (*ibid.*, p. 37.) He says moreover that realism 'could be false', and that 'facts are relevant to its support (or to criticize it)' (*ibid.*, pp. 78–9). Nonetheless, for reasons he has not made clear, Putnam wants to deny that realism is either scientific or an hypothesis (cf. *ibid.*, p. 79). How realism can consist of doctrines which (1) explain facts about the world, (2) are empirical generalizations about knowledge, and (3) can be confirmed or falsified by evidence and yet be neither scientific nor hypothetical is left opaque.

10 *In Defence of Truth*

W. Newton-Smith

1. *The whole depressing story*

VIEWED *sub specie aeternitatis* scientists are a fickle lot. Newton has his brief hour of flourishing with enthusiastic universal allegiance and then is gone to be replaced by Einstein who receives in turn the same degree of accord. Unhappily the picture that emerges from our God's eye perspective on this fickle mistress is most depressing. Think of poor Thales (everything's made of water!); of the alchemists; of the steady state model of the universe. These theories are false. Or, think of the aether drift theories of the last century. If a physics student cannot give a convincing refutation by the end of his first term or two of study, it is gently suggested he might consider changing to history. Indeed, this graveyard of falsified theories provides inductive evidence for a generalization to the effect that any theory will be found to be false within, say, 200 years of first being propounded. I will call this the *pessimistic induction.*[1] Since there is nothing special about the present, this inductive argument gives a good reason for holding that our current, most cherished theories are false and that any theory that ever will be propounded is false.

Prima facie, this induction, if granted, does more than a little to tarnish the image of science as the very paradigm of institutionalized rationality. On this image, scientists are seen as possessing their special tool, the scientific method, which they dispassionately and disinterestedly apply, each application of which takes them nearer the much esteemed goal of TRUTH. But if we have inductive evidence that that goal is not ever to be reached, how can it be rational to continue to pursue it? As Laudan (1977, p. 129) has put the problem:

If rationality consists in believing only what we can reasonably presume to be true, and if we define 'truth' in its classical non-pragmatic sense, then science is (and will forever remain) irrational.

It is, if not downright irrational, certainly pretty unpalatable to play a game which you have reason to believe cannot be won.[2] In such circumstances, the reasonable man may well opt to change the rules of the game. And much recent work in the philosophy of science amounts to attempts to reconstruct the aim of the scientific enterprise in the hope of delivering a more accessible target. The least radical of these attempts to take the sting out of the pessimistic induction do so by making what will be called the *Animal Farm Move*. True, it is said, all past and present theories are false and, indeed, the evidence is that any theory which is the product of finite minds like ours will turn out to be false. However, some theories are falser than others. In Lenin's words, 'we draw closer and closer to objective truth (without ever exhausting it)'. While the historically generated sequence of theories of a branch of a mature science are all, strictly speaking, false, the theories are increasing in verisimilitude; that is, in the degree to which they are approximately true. In this case, we have progress after all for the theories are progressively capturing more and more truth about the world. This thesis, to be examined in detail below, will be called the *thesis of verisimilitude* or *TV*. On this account of the matter, rationality consists in believing in those theories which it was most reasonable to presume have the highest degree of verisimilitude among their available rivals.

This attempt to maintain a conception of rationality linked to truth in the face of the pessimistic induction is most closely associated with Popper. Unfortunately, however, his own particular attempt to do this is a dismal failure. For on Popper's analysis of verisimilitude, no pair of false theories can be ranked in terms of comparative verisimilitude.[3] Even setting aside the intractable difficulties involved in his analysis of the notion of verisimilitude, Popper has not given (and in view of his horror of 'pernicious inductivism' cannot consistently give) any reason for thinking that the methods of science as he construes them are taking us in the direction of the goal of increased verisimilitude. His ban on all inductive argumentation precludes him from giving a reason for thinking that the systematic replacement of falsified theories by as yet unfalsified theories of greater content will increase truth-content without increasing falsity-content. Hidden away in a footnote (Schilpp, 1974, pp. 192–3, fn. 165b) is an indication that Popper has some realization of this problem. There Popper notes that the principle (his assumption of a particular form of realism) which will establish a link between his posited goal (verisimilitude increase) and his anti-inductivist methodology involves a *'whiff of inductivism'*. No mere whiff will turn this mill. A full-blown storm of induction is needed. This 'whiff' represents the bankruptcy of the Popperian enterprise. For if in displaying the rationality of science we have to argue inductively, there is no reason not to accord induction a role right from the start and thus the anti-inductivism which is constitutive of what is unique in Popper's approach to science has been abandoned *ex cathedra*.

For the sake of argument I assume that this footnote represents a momentary lapse of vigilance and in light of this I shall characterize the Popperian strategy (modulus the footnote) as a *transcendent strategy*. For it involves positing a goal—increasing the verisimilitude of our theories—which is simply not accessible by the methods it takes to be constitutive of science—bold conjectures and refutations. Perhaps the strategy is nonetheless a step forward in the face of the pessimistic induction. For science is no longer seen as positively irrational. However, it is hardly the paradigm of a rational activity given that we can have no reason to think that its methods will take us towards its goal.

I will return to the thesis of verisimilitude following a discussion of the strategy deployed in Laudan's *Progress and its Problems*. However, before doing this, I note for the sake of completeness the most radical response offered to date. This is what we might call the *atheistic response* of Feyerabend. 'And as regards the word "truth",' Feyerabend advises us, 'we can say at this stage only that it certainly has people in a tizzy, but has not achieved much else' (Feyerabend, 1975, p. 230). So we are advised to let 'Reason join the other abstract monsters—Obligation, Duty, Morality, Truth' (*ibid.*, p. 180), and to slay the lot with gay abandon. We thereby save ourselves from the task of facing the problem through the simple expedient of jettisoning the concepts in terms of which it is formulated. Taken on its own, Feyerabend's position is not nearly so attractive as it comes to appear when compared with Popper's. For if Truth is utterly inaccessible, as Popper holds, what point is there in assuming that there is any truth at all? And if no reason can be given for thinking that the method (conjecture and refutation) is a way to make progress, why assume that there is any method? Seen in this light, Feyerabend's atheism amounts to the application of Occam's Razor to Popper's transcendentism. Space precludes a critical assessment of Feyerabend's attack on method (on which his attack on truth depends). Indeed, he is a somewhat elusive quarry even given space for the only criticism of an ideology which he countenances as legitimate is inconsistency (mere implausibility or falsehood are not enough). However, it is, I would argue, a straightforward matter to show that his position is inconsistent in that his attack on method presupposes method.[4]

2. *The agnostic strategy*

On Popper's transcendent strategy, the goal is otherworldly and it is unobtainable. For that more worldly, village atheist, Feyerabend, the goal is worldly, obtainable and the pursuit ought to be fun. Or at least I take it that it is if we indulge in what we are enjoined to do; namely, flippantly 'initiating joyful experiments'. Recently there have been attempts, most notably by Laudan, to interpose between these strategies an *agnostic position*. Laudan (1977, p. 127) remarks that setting up truth or verisimilitude as goals for scientific inquiry:

may be noble and edifying to those who delight in the frustration of aspiring to that which they can never (know themselves) to attain; but they are not very helpful if our object is to explain how scientific theories are (or should be) evaluated.

Laudan is no atheist. He does not wish to deny the existence of truth. Rather, he simply has no need of that hypothesis—the thesis of verisimilitude. For he holds science to be essentially 'a problem solving activity' and regards progress in science as a matter of increasing the problem solving capacity of research programmes (hereafter cited as *RP*). His crucial assumption (to be examined below) is that judgements of the problem-solving capacity of a theory are logically independent of judgements of its truth or degree of verisimilitude. However, as shall be argued, his strategy fails. First, I shall argue that his notion of problem-solving capacity is not neutral with regard to truth and verisimilitude in the way he requires. Second, I shall point out that his own position is vulnerable to certain objections he advances against those who have used a notion of verisimilitude.

First, what is problem solving? We are told (Laudan, 1977, p. 25) that:

any theory, T, can be regarded as having solved an empirical problem, if T functions (significantly) in any scheme of inference whose conclusion is a statement of the problem.

Progress is not simply a matter of solving problems, it involves in addition avoiding anomalies and conceptual problems. Progress is a matter of increasing problem-solving effectiveness where this is determined:

by assessing the number and importance of the empirical problems which the theory solves and deducting therefrom the number and importance of the anomalies and conceptual problems which the theory generates (Laudan 1977, p.68).

As Laudan notes, this account of problem solving is reminiscent of the deductive-nomological account of explanation. However, we are warned against the temptation to 'translate the claims I shall make about the nature and logic of problem solving into assertions about the logic of explanation' (Laudan, 1977, pp. 15–16).

On the deductive-nomological model (hereafter cited as the *DN* model), it is a necessary condition of a deductively valid argument's providing an explanation that the premises be true or well-confirmed (depending on the particular version of the *DN* model). In this regard, Laudan's account of problem solving diverges radically from the *DN* model. For Laudan takes it that questions as to whether a theory solves a problem can be settled without settling issues as to the truth or well-confirmed-ness of either the theory or the statement of initial conditions or the statement whose querying generates the problem.

If one were to focus exclusively on the problem-solving capacity of an *RP* (that is, the ability of the *RP* to solve empirical problems) without regard to its problem-solving effectiveness (that is, its ability to both solve empirical problems and avoid anomalies and conceptual problems), this would make science so easy that we could all become Laplacian super-scientists. All you need to do is take your favourite proposition and formulate a theory whose only postulates are that proposition and its negation. Let Q be a statement of any problem you like. Since 'P and not $-P$' entails 'Q', the problem is solved. The fact that any contradiction entails any proposition means that this theory solves any empirical problem. Laudan is saved from this promise of instantaneous success. For he holds that displaying a non-localizable contradiction within a theory provides conclusive grounds for refusing to accept the theory (Laudan 1977, p.49). I make this blatant misconstrual of his position to stress a point with which he agrees and which emerges if we ask why we are inclined to lay down a constraint excluding inconsistent theories. The answer is quite simply that we think that theories are to be evaluated through the categories of truth and falsehood and a theory which is inconsistent is to be rejected because it cannot be true. And unless we are intuitionists, to reject 'p and not $-$p' is to embrace 'p or not $-$p'. Hence our rejection of a theory for being inconsistent is tantamount to embracing the claim that the theory is either true or false. The reason that Laudan will not disagree is that he is quite emphatically not an instrumentalist (Laudan, 1977, p. 126). Above the modest claim was made that we think of theories as being true or false. In assuming with Laudan that logical inference can obtain between theories and statements of problems we are committed to thinking of theories as being true or false. For without applying a notion of truth to theories and statements of problems, we cannot apply a notion of entailment or logical inference to theories and statements of problems. Thus I take it that we are agreed that theories are either true or false and the question before us concerns the role to be accorded to that fact in the evaluation of RPs.

Having reached agreement that theories are true or false even though we may not be entitled to say of any given theory which it is, I turn to the *problem of problems*. It must be remembered that for Laudan a theory solves a problem if and only if the theory entails a statement of the problem. Questions concerning the truth or warranted assertibility of the theory or the statement of the problem are simply beside the point. Suppose that I, having read Laudan, decide to set up in business as a scientist solving a range of problems. Suppose further that I am going to work on such problems as: why won't sugar ever dissolve in hot water? why are swans green? why does matter repel? why do freely moving bodies accelerate in the absence of force? and so on. Certainly I have a problem, but not the right sort of problem. One wants to respond that these are not genuine problems because the proposition queried is in each case false and known to be false. Even if I had some grand theory that enabled me to derive statements of a host of these and other problems, no Nobel prize would be forthcoming. Our untutored inclination is to assume that our concern ought to be with what we might call *non-spurious problems*. That is, with problems whose corresponding statement is such that we have good reason to believe it to be true or to believe it is more likely to be true than false.

My concern in this chapter is not to challenge Laudan's conception of what counts as a problem. Let us be generous to the point of allowing, as he does, that the *esse* of problems is their *percipi*. The point of my caveat is that in the assessment of theories credit should be given only for solutions of non-spurious problems. Laudan would reject any caveat restricting the evaluation of a theory to an assessment of its capacity to solve non-spurious problems (and to avoid non-spurious anomalies). For instance, he writes:

Certain presumed states of affairs regarded as posing practical problems are actually *counterfactual*. A problem need not accurately describe a real state of affairs to be a problem: all that is required is that it be *thought to be* an actual state of affairs by some agents (Laudan, 1977, p. 16).

I take it that Laudan means by 'counterfactual problems' simply a problem whose statement is false and not one whose statement has the form of a counterfactual. If Laudan were rejecting the caveat because he holds that there are counterfactual problems in this latter sense of the term and that as counterfactuals lack truth-conditions, it would be a simple matter to modify the caveat as follows: counterfactual problems count as non-spurious only if we have reasonable grounds for asserting the counterfactual (where having grounds for asserting it does not mean having grounds for asserting it to be true).[5]

Given that we would not prize and, indeed, would not even be interested in, a theory which solved only spurious problems and avoided spurious anomalies why does Laudan want to take into account all problems where for problems *esse est percipi?* We are told:

If factuality were a necessary condition for something to count as an empirical problem then such situations [the speculations concerning the behaviour of hypothetical sea serpents by early members of the Royal Society] could not count as problems. So long as we insist that theories are designed only to explain 'facts' (i.e., true statements about the world), we shall find ourselves unable to explain most of the theoretical activity which has taken place in science (Laudan, 1977, p. 16).

But there is certainly something unhappy about the endeavours of the early members of the Royal Society in the face of the tales of sea serpents. Undoubtedly our ideal (formulated within the rhetoric of problem solving) is a theory that solves non-spurious problems. We want to count it against our sea serpentologists and in favour of, say, Harvey that in the former case the problems were spurious and that in the latter case they were not. Any tenable model of science must allow for this sort of differential assessment. The problem-solving model can aspire to do this only if the only solved problems which count in favour of an *RP* are problems we have reason to believe to be non-spurious. Adding a caveat to this effect in no way precludes us from doing justice to the laudable endeavours of our sea serpentologists. To see this we need only remind ourselves of the fact that the rational assessment of belief has two dimensions. Given that someone has a belief, p, we want to ask both whether the belief is true (judged from our own perspective) and whether on the evidence available to the person it was more reasonable for him to believe p than to disbelieve p or to suspend belief. The prize in the rational assessment stakes goes to the one who scores on both points. Of course there are consolation prizes for those who score on one or the other dimension without scoring on both.

Our sea serpentologists certainly had a problem—a spurious problem. However, let us suppose that it was reasonable for them to think it was a genuine problem so they can score on the other dimension. Unhappily but reasonably they expended their energies on a spurious problem. Happily they coped admirably (or can be imagined to have) in producing a theory designed to deal with this problem. If the theory arrived at meets our criteria for being a good theory we can give them credit for this. We can explain in this way their activity and represent it as rational, while noting the unhappy feature of their activities which precludes them from admission to the Scientific Hall of Fame. They were rational to the extent to which they had reasonable grounds on the basis of the available evidence for thinking their problem to be non-spurious, and to the extent to which they had reason to believe that their theory did entail a statement of the problem.

It might be thought that my spurious theory could be rejected within Laudan's framework by reference to its anomaly-generating capacity without appeal to the caveat that problem-solving capacity is to be restricted to the solution of non-spurious problems. Laudan rightly employs a generous notion of an anomaly. He is correct in holding that one wants to take into account not only the generation of false predictions but also the generation of conceptual problems under the heading of 'anomaly'. Laudan's view that a false prediction counts as an anomaly only if another theory solves that problem, means that with ingenuity I could generate a spurious theory which was anomaly free by constructing a theory from which I could derive a large number of falsehoods, the negations of which were not the consequences of any known theory. However, let us leave aside this more outlandish speculation and consider a pair of theories, T_1 and T_2, which are such that, by and large, if a statement of a problem is entailed by T_1, its negation is entailed by T_2. Suppose further that, by and large, we are inclined to believe the consequences of T_1 and disbelieve the consequences of T_2. We can explain our inclination to prefer T_1 either by saying that T_2 solves only spurious problems (problems whose statements we have reason to believe false) or, equivalently, by saying that T_2 generates anomalies (generates false predictions). Either way we have to admit accessible truth and falsity into the picture. The expression 'accessible truth and falsity' is meant to refer to statements which are such that we can have reasonable grounds in certain contexts for thinking that they are true (or are likely to be true) and reasonable grounds in other contexts for thinking that they are false (or are likely to be false).

If we refuse to do so, Laudan's model of science simply does not latch on to the world. Unless truth plays a regulative role, we can each select on the basis of our whims our own set of sentences which are statements of problems for us just because we so chose to regard them. We each then erect our own theories for solving these problems. Never mind how the world is, just solve your own problems! We would be faced with the unedifying spectacle of a plurality of free-floating sets of problems and their associated theories where some of the theories would rate equally well on the theory assessment scale. It is utterly implausible to suppose that progress could arise through a developing sequence of theories solving ever more spurious problems. This model makes nonsense of the entire scientific enterprise. For truth does play a regulative role in the sense that theories designed to solve problems the corresponding statement of which has been shown to be false (or likely to be false) are condemned for that very reason. Of course, while we might condemn the theory for this reason we may nonetheless laud the theoretician if he had reasonable grounds for his false beliefs, and erected a theory that would have been reasonable had those beliefs been well-grounded.

If we are to latch our theories onto the world using a problem-solving model of science, we have to admit what I shall call *an empirical basis*. This is a range of sentences which are such that we can have reasonable beliefs (in principle at least) about their truth-value. If we can at the level of the empirical basis distinguish between spurious and non-spurious problems, we can avoid the problem outlined above. In this case the solution of non-spurious problems will count in favour of a programme and the solution of spurious problems will count against it. At some points Laudan seems to admit the need for such an empirical basis:

If we ask, 'How fast do bodies fall near the earth?', we are assuming there are objects akin to our conceptions of body and earth which move towards one another according to some regular rule. That assumption, of course, is a theory-laden one, but we nonetheless assert it to be about the physical world. . . . Empirical problems are thus *first order problems*: they are substantial questions about the objects which constitute the domain of any given science. Unlike other higher order problems . . ., we judge the adequacy of solutions to empirical problems by studying the objects in the domain (Laudan, 1977, p. 15).

This suggests that the 'solution' of the problem—why *p*?— obtained by deriving '*p*' from a theory is to count for the theory only if we have good reason to think, on the basis of a study of the objects in the domain, that '*p*' is true or more likely to be approximately true than not.

It turns out that Laudan is not referring to the low-level empirical problems which arise when we ask, 'why *p*?' where '*p*' is an observation sentence. The qualification 'empirical' is intended to differentiate between empirical and such *conceptual* problems as, say, the question of the intelligibility of absolute space. Examples given by Laudan of empirical problems include Brownian motion, the null result of the Michelson-Morley effect and the photoelectric effect.

Laudan is on the horns of the following dilemma. If, on the one hand, we do not consider when assessing a theory from which one can derive a sentence, '*p*', whether or not we have reasons to believe that '*p*' is true, is likely to be true, is probably approximately true, etc., he faces the *problem of problems* outlined above and his model is no model of science as it is practised or as it should be practised. If, on the other hand, we are to take such judgements into account in evaluating a theory and count only the solution of non-spurious problems in favour of a theory, he cannot contrast his position with that of one who takes it that the goal of science is the production of good *DN* explanations. For requiring that *p* not only be derivable from a theory but that the theory be true or corroborated is just what a *DN* model of explanation requires. On this construal of Laudan's intentions, he cannot consistently maintain the thesis that it is more important to ask whether theories 'constitute adequate solutions to significant problems' than it is to ask whether they are 'true', 'corroborated', 'well-confirmed' or otherwise justifiable within the framework of contemporary epistemology'. For in asking whether they provide an adequate solution, we shall have to ask these sorts of questions of the sentences of the theories which are used in the derivations which constitute the solution of problems.

Furthermore, if we can make assessments of the reasonableness of believing in the truth of any empirical sentence, why should we not make assessments of theories which are just conjunctions of such sentences? Laudan's answer no doubt will be that the pessimistic induction gives us good reason to assume that all theories are false. And, as there is no viable notion of verisimilitude, we cannot take the sting out of the induction by making the Animal Farm Move. Thus Laudan is committed to giving a different sort of assessment of individual sentences and theories. However, as we shall see in section 4 below, Laudan's method for assessing theories faces precisely the same problems that are involved in analyzing the notion of verisimilitude.

3. *The transcendental strategy*

Laudan and others have been far too swift in rejecting the thesis that the goal of the scientific enterprise is to be understood in terms of progress towards increasing verisimilitude and that we can have reasons (on occasion at least) for believing that we have indeed made progress. Unfortunately, some of those (Popper) who hold this position have been ill-equipped, given their anti-inductivism, to argue for *TV*. My strategy, which will be called the *transcendental strategy*, involves arguing for *TV* using what Popper would regard as 'pernicious inductivism'. Until the argument has been advanced, I am not going to consider the qualms that some may have concerning the notion of verisimilitude.

The contemporary trend in the philosophy of science is to take science seriously. Kuhn, Feyerabend, and others urge us (in their differing ways) to set aside our rational reconstruction of scientific theories and our philosophers' conceptions of method and look closely at the scientific process with the intention of learning and not instructing. In view of this, it is surprising how rarely philosophers of science (including those cited above) attempt to employ in their philosophical writings the patterns of inference standardly employed in science. This is particularly surprising in view of the additional fact that the methods of science and philosophy are not as distinct as philosophers once fancied. One thinks not only of the general approach of Quine but also of the illustrations of the difficulties of separating empirical and philosophical considerations in the evaluation of particular theories to be found in, for example, Sklar's study of absolutist-relativist controversy concerning space and time, (Sklar, 1974). The particular style of argumentation whose time has come in the philosophy of science is inference to the best explanation (Harman, 1973). Within physics we frequently find a particular hypothesis about, say, the constituents of protons supported by the claim that that hypothesis provides the best explanation of the observed phenomenon. To take science seriously is to admit as legitimate such a style of argumentation. Admittedly, like all inductive argumentation, it has its risks. For it may be that lack of ingenuity has left unarticulated a better explanation of the phenomenon in question. However, this possibility does not undercut the grounds for tentatively adopting the proffered hypothesis.

In the present context, the phenomenon that calls out for explanation is the undeniable fact that in a mature science like physics, contemporary theories provide us with better predictions about the world than their predecessors and have placed us in a better position to manipulate that world. The impressive technological spin-off of contemporary physics is just one measure of this increased predictive and manipulative power. Interestingly, this phenomenon is acknowledged both by hard-line rationalists, such as Popper, soft-line non-rationalists, such as Kuhn, and hard-line non-rationalists such as Feyerabend. Of course, Feyerabend is given to adding the quite compatible claim that there are areas in which magic, traditional medicine and forgotten science had particular achievements not encompassed within contemporary science. He also retorts that there are other fun things to do beside predicting and manipulating the world.

The problem whose solution we seek is: how is it that contemporary theories are more useful in doing what they manifestly are more useful in doing? If *TV* is true we have an answer. If theories are increasing in truth-content without increasing in falsity content, one would expect an increase in predictive power. Indeed, it would be totally mystifying that this increase should occur if it were not for the fact that theories are capturing more and more truth about the world. Thus I suggest we have more reason to believe in *TV* than in its denial, and that we should consequently tentatively adopt that hypothesis.[6] If someone is able to offer a better explanation, we shall have to withdraw the hypothesis.[6] However, as things stand, we do not find any available alternatives whatsoever.

In developing this argument I have sought to derive support for *TV* from a premise common to all parties in the rationalist/non-rationalist controversy. For Popper, Lakatos, Kuhn, Laudan and even Feyerabend agree that within a mature science like physics there has been an impressive improvement in the predictive power of theories. To argue from this phenomenon to *TV* we need the following crucial premise: if a theory T_2 is a better approximation to the truth than a theory T_1, then it is likely that T_2 will have greater predictive power than T_1.

This premise has a strong intuitive appeal. For if a theory has latched onto more theoretical truth about the world, one would expect it to give better predictions. However, in view of the crucial role played by the thesis of *TV*, one would wish to do better than rely on an appeal to mere intuition by providing a justification of the premise based on an analysis of the notion of verisimilitude or approximation to the truth. My attempt to do this is presented elsewhere.[7]

The most sensitive of the Achilles' heels in this argument is the cavalier manipulation of the unanalyzed notion of verisimilitude. Laudan, for instance, objects that 'no-one has been able even to say what it would mean to be "closer to the truth", let alone to offer criteria for determining how we could assess such proximity, (Laudan, 1977, pp. 125-6). On the first point it must be conceded that no one has given a satisfactory analysis of the notion of verisimilitude and that Popper's spirited attempt to do so is a dismal failure. However, that in itself is not a telling objection. Here again we can learn something from the practice of science. It is quite standard to introduce a concept in a theoretical context even if one cannot at the time give a philosophically satisfactory analysis of it. Indeed, such a concept can have a fruitful scientific career while the seas of philosophical controversy wage endlessly around it. Think, for instance, of the concept of spacetime, and the semantical controversies concerning it (that is, is a reductive or non-reductive analysis appropriate?) Or, to take an historical example, think of the controversies about the meaning of 'field' which waged alongside the development of successful field theories. If the concept of verisimilitude is required in order to give a satisfactory theoretical explanation of an aspect of the scientific enterprise, why not use it and leave to Locke's 'under-labourers' the matter of analysis? No doubt some will feel that this is letting the side down, as philosophers are supposed to be exemplary in subjecting concepts to rigorous scrutiny. While there is something in this, the following two points should be noted. First, it should be noted that this concept is not completely *recherché*. It has antecedents in notions commonly employed in ordinary language. If Ichabod answers three questions out of ten correctly on a test and Isabel answers seven correctly, she is nearer the truth. If Ichabod says of the cup which is at the centre of the table that it is near but not at the centre, he has said something nearer the truth than Isabel, if she has said it to be nearer the edge than the centre. I fully recognize that there is a vast shadow between these simple examples and the notion of verisimilitude needed in the present context. In attempting to generalize from the first example, we face the problem of measuring the content of non-finite sets of sentences. The plausibility of the second example turns on a readily available metric for measuring the distance between where an object is and where an object is said to be. It is admittedly hard to see how to generalize this to a fully-fledged scientific theory. However, one might even cite as a merit of the approach being advocated that it generates a nice research programme (namely, the development of a content measure) which, if successful, would have applications elsewhere. Of course, if in time all attempts to analyze the notion face intractable difficulties, one would wish to rethink the position. This is the second way in which I would wish to mute the heresy. While it is certainly legitimate to introduce in a philosophical context (as elsewhere) a concept for which one does not have a satisfactory analysis, this amounts to offering a promissory note that must be redeemed in finite time (unlike the British Government's perpetual war bonds). The fact that one does not have a satisfactory philosophical analysis of a concept does not give a good reason for not employing that concept. It would have been reasonable for a logician writing prior to Tarski to characterize valid rules of inference for a first-order language as truth-preserving transformations even though no philosophically satisfactory analysis of truth for first-order languages was available at the time. In a similar way, it is entirely respectable to use an unanalyzed notion of relative versimilitude (that is, being more approximately true) at this stage. Its utility in accounting for the scientific enterprise provides an incentive to seek an adequate analysis. As noted above, a failure to produce in due course a theory of verisimilitude should prompt us to explore the possibility of building a theory of science that does not employ this notion. However, the time is not yet ripe for despair in this regard.

The second point made by Laudan in the passage quoted above is the problem of providing criteria for assessing relative verisimilitude. If by criteria is meant some algorithm or binding set of rules, none will be forthcoming (just as his own assessment procedure does not provide this). However, once we have adopted *TV*, we can aspire to articulate general guidelines. For, given that the scientific community has been successful in increasing the verisimilitude of their theories, all we need to do is to isolate the principles that have been actually employed in theory choice. We shall then have some reason for thinking that these principles by and large provide tentative, fallible guidance as to the relative verisimilitude of rival theories.

4. *Laudan's metrical problems*

My second major objection to Laudan is a form of *tu quoque*, I press in order to reinforce my argument for operating within the traditional framework of verisimilitude. One of the advantages Laudan claims for his model is that

(1) *it is workable*: unlike both inductivist and falsificationist models, the basic evaluation measures seem (at least in principle) to pose fewer difficulties (Laudan, 1977, p. 109).

His measure was defined as follows:

the overall problem-solving effectiveness of a theory is determined by assessing the number and importance of the empirical problems which the theory solves and deducting therefore the number and importance of the anomalies and conceptual problems which the theory generates (Laudan, 1977, p. 68).

Laudan gives us some principles which it might reasonably be held ought to guide our judgements as to the importance of problems and analogies. However, we are a millenium away from having anything like a technique for measuring the importance of a problem or of an anomaly. It seems bold (to say the very least) to claim that his evaluation measure poses fewer problems in principle. In any event there is an even more serious problem. Just how do we assess the number of problems solved by a theory? Laudan does not provide any principle of individuation of problems and lacking that we are in no position to count up the number of problems. Why should one assume (in the absence of such a principle of individuation) that the number of problems solved by a theory is even finite? Let us suppose for the sake of argument that there are an infinite number of particles. One might be inclined to say that a physical theory which predicted the motion of each body in an infinite subset of the set of all particles solved an infinite number of problems. Suppose further that we have a rival theory which also provides an account of the motion of an infinite subset of all bodies—a subset that overlaps with, but is distinct from, the subset with which the other theory deals. In this case, how are we to compare the theories as to problem-solving capacity? One might think that the example is far-fetched on the grounds that there is not an infinite number of particles and, consequently, there are no actual situations in which we have to face the problem of comparing theories which have an infinite problem-solving capacity. However, one can simply take any two rival theories and regard them as solving an infinite set of problems given that time is either dense or continuous (Newton-Smith 1978). If, for instance, the theories make predictions about the state of a physical system at each instant of time, they will solve an infinite number of problems. For, for each instant, there is a problem concerning the state of the system at that instant. This means that the rhetoric of problem-solving fails to evade what Laudan regards as the crucial challenge to the Popperian approach. Measuring the problem-solving capacity of a theory is too intimately related to measuring the content of a theory for us to be optimistic that the former is a less intractable problem than the latter.

It might be objected that I am using too fine a specification of the notion of a problem. To this one might rhetorically respond that as Laudan regards the *esse* of problems to be their *percipi*, it is enough that I feel that these are all problems. That alone makes them problems. More seriously, the actual state of a system at each instant of time is a potential falsifier of the theory (to put the point in Popperian terms) and thus it is a potential anomaly. Why should not each prediction of the state of the system at a moment of time count as a solved problem? Perhaps Laudan would seek to solve this problem by introducing a coarser notion of a problem so that, for instance, we only consider the theory as solving the single general problem—how does the system evolve through time?—and not the infinite set of problems of the form—what is that state of the system at instant t for each t? In which case the onus is on him to provide some criterion for the individuation of problems and the development of this is likely to prove as difficult as the development of a content measure. So one might retort that as no one has even told us what we mean by 'greater problem-solving capacity', let alone how to measure it, we ought to be wary of using the notion.

Laudan, when pressed on this point,[8] claimed that there is general agreement among members of the scientific community about the individuation of problems. However, it is far from clear that they do agree in the case of theory clash as to whether one theory solves more problems than another. In any event, what is required is an articulation and justification of the principles they do use or ought to use in individuating problems for the purpose of comparing theories as to problem-solving capacity. And one can object *ad hominem* that if this sort of appeal to the ordinary discourse of practising scientists is in order, the defenders of the *Animal Farm Move* can, with equal justice, appeal to the fact that scientists do talk of some theories as being more approximately true than other theories.

These problems do not exhaust the difficulties in Laudan's approach. Perhaps the deepest problem concerns the constraints his position places on the theory of meaning. For if meaning is to be given in terms of truth-conditions, and if truth-conditions cannot be transcendent, if, that is, it must be possible in principle at least to have evidence for and evidence against any statement that can be true or false, there will be insurmountable problems for Laudan and any other non-instrumentalist who holds that neither the truth nor the well-confirmedness of theories is accessible in specifying the meaning of theoretical propositions. Interestingly Popper seems aware of this difficulty, one which has driven him to embrace a Platonic scientism about meaning, whereby understanding a sentence is not a matter of grasping the evidential conditions of the sentence but of being in a quasi-causal relation to the proposition in the Third World earmarked by the sentence in question.

Finally, Laudan seems to have forgotten that we accept theories as a basis for action. Plainly the reason we do so is that we assume the theories on which we act capture, to some degree, important truths or approximate truths about the world. But if the rational acceptance of a theory is to be determined on the basis of its problem-solving capacity; the problem-solving capacity of a theory can be determined without reference to the truth or falsity of its constituent hypotheses; and, the success of a theory as a problem-solver provides no evidential support for the truth or truthlikefulness of a theory, it would be irrational in the extreme to act on a theory which turned out to be acceptable on Laudan's model. To rationally accept a theory as a basis for action is to accept it as telling us something or other about the world, and that is to accept the theory as being more or less true.

5. Conclusion

I began by distinguishing four possible strategies that might be deployed in face of the dilemma that the pessimistic induction generates for the conception of science as rational:

(1) *Transcendent Strategy.* This is the Popperian move of construing the goal of science as that of increasing the

verisimilitude of our theories. Within the Popperian framework, science appears to be about the least rational of all human activities. For there is no reason whatsoever for thinking that the methods of science are methods for reaching its goal.

(2) *Atheistic Strategy*. This is the Feyerabendian game of offering a final solution by jettisoning the entire family of concepts in terms of which the problem arises. We are to give up agonizing for gardening (at least, if we are to take seriously his (and Mao's) advice to 'let a hundred flowers grow').

(3) *The Agnostic Strategy*. This is the approach of Laudan who aspires to give us an accessible notion of progress defined in terms of problem-solving without recourse to the notions of truth and verisimilitude. I argued that his attempt to dispense with truth fails and that his own appraisal measure faces problems of the same ilk as those faced by the traditional strategy.

(4) *The Transcendental Strategy*. I argued that there are respectable reasons for adopting the thesis of verisimilitude notwithstanding the problems involved in giving a satisfactory analysis of the notion of verisimilitude. The goal of science is increasing verisimilitude, and the methods standardly employed by the practising scientist (whatever they may be) are methods for achieving that aim. So rationality in the scientific context is a matter of being guided in our beliefs by the outcome of the applications of these methods, on the grounded assumption that we will thereby enhance our chances of making progress towards the goal.

Notes

1 See in this regard Putnam (1978), p. 25.
2 Laudan talks of 'weakening our notions of rationality and progress' so that we can 'decide whether science is rational and progressive' (Laudan, 1977, p. 127).
3 For a lucid presentation of this difficulty in the Popperian notion of verisimilitude, see Ackerman (1976) pp. 90-1.
4 See, in this regard, Newton-Smith (1980) and Newton-Smith (forthcoming).
5 This caveat would be required if one adopted, for instance, the account of counterfactuals favoured by J. Mackie in his 'Conditionals' (Mackie, 1973).
6 This argument is in the wind. One finds hints of it in Popper's notorious 'whiff of inductivism' footnote, and Putnam attributes a version of it to Boyd. See Putnam (1978) p. 21.
7 See Newton-Smith (forthcoming).
8 In reply to an earlier version of this paper read at the University of Aarhus, Denmark, in August 1978.

References

R. J. Ackerman, *The Philosophy of Karl Popper*, Amherst, University of Massachusetts Press, 1976.

P. Feyerabend, *Against Method*, London, New Left Books, 1975.

P. Feyerabend, 'Changing Patterns of Reconstruction' (review of W. Stegmüller: *Theorienstrukten und Theoriendynamik, Brit. J. Phil. Sci.*, 29, 1977, 351–69.

A. Grünbaum, 'Is the Method of Bold Conjecture and Attempted Refutations, Justifiably the Method of Science?', *Brit. J. Phil. Sci.*, 27, 1976, pp. 105–36.

A. Grünbaum, 'Ad Hoc Auxiliary Hypotheses and Falsificationism', *Brit. J. Phil. Sci.*, 27, 1976, pp. 329–62.

G. Harman, *Thought*, Princeton, Princeton University Press, 1973.

T. S. Kuhn, *The Essential Tension*, Chicago, Chicago University Press, 1977.

T. S. Kuhn, *The Structure of Scientific Revolutions*, 2nd ed., Chicago, University of Chicago Press, 1970.

I. Lakatos, *The Methodology of Scientific Research Programmes*, Cambridge, Cambridge University Press, 1978, J. Worrall and G. Currie (eds.).

L. Laudan, *Progress and Its Problems*, Berkeley, University of California Press, 1977.

J. Mackie, *Truth, Probability and Paradox*, Oxford, Oxford University Press, 1973.

W. Newton-Smith, 'The Underdetermination of Theory by Data', *Proceedings of the Aristotelian Society, Supplementary Volume LII*, 1978, pp. 71–91.

W. Newton-Smith, 'Contre la Méthode?', *Critique*, août-septembre 1980, pp. 774–90.

W. Newton-Smith, *The Rationality of Science*, London, Routledge & Kegan Paul, forthcoming.

K. R. Popper, *Conjectures and Refutations*, London, Routledge & Kegan Paul, 1963.

K. R. Popper, *The Logic of Scientific Discovery*, London, Hutchinson, 1968.

K. R. Popper, *Objective Knowledge*, Oxford, Oxford University Press, 1972.

H. Putnam, *Meaning and the Moral Sciences*, London, Routledge and Kegan Paul, 1978.

H. Putnam, *Mind, Language and Reality*, Cambridge, Cambridge University Press, 1975.

P. A. Schilpp, (ed.) *The Philosophy of Karl Popper, Book I and Book II*, La Salle, Illinois, Open Court, 1974.

L. Sklar, *Space, Time and Spacetime*, Berkeley, University of California Press, 1974.

The conditions for applying an evolutionary model to the development of science: commentaries on Mittelstrasse, Laudan and Newton-Smith

R. Harré

IF science is an activity wholly determined by social forces and formations, any idea of an autonomous evolutionary process in which theories develop out of each other under the pressure of observation and experiment would have to be abandoned.

The first chapter in this section, that by J. Mittelstrasse, addresses this basic issue and presents an argument for resisting the sociological reduction in its most extreme form. Mittelstrasse develops a distinction between an effectual history of science, how theories and practices were related to the way science as an institution developed within circumambient social formations, from foundational science, the interpretation of the history of science as an intellectual enterprise. The latter has a history—that of the interaction of theory and practice allowing for 'methodological reflection upon the foundations of knowledge'.

This distinction between kinds of history is not to be identified with that proposed by Lakatos, between internal and external histories. The latter presupposes a distinction between scientific and non-scientific rationalities which cannot really be sustained. Denying the distinction between forms of rationality means that a foundational history of science must include history of theory and history of practice in one whole, since methodologies have developed to subserve theoretical interests, as well as out of non-scientific praxis. So a concept of progress can be sustained, if we admit that there is both better orientation-in-the-world *and* more systematic understanding. So we can have an evolutionary model, a *constructive* model, as Mittelstrasse calls it.

Two comments seem to be in order. Though a crude sociological reductionism is resisted by this argument, if it is successful, the criteria with which Mittelstrasse finds himself working are compatible with any one of the main contenders for an interpretation of the intellectual enterprise of science, realism, positivism, or conventionalism, if we open up anti-realism into it two major forms. We could profitably see Mittelstrasse's contribution as setting the scene for the debate between Laudan and Newton-Smith, which addresses the question of truth-for-theories through a consideration of one of the arguments for realism. Second, there seems to be a tension in Mittelstrasse's paper, if I have understood it aright, between the early sections in which the efforts of Sneed and Stegmuller to retain a logicist mode of analysis are described (with approval?) and the argument of the later sections relating scientific rationality to non-scientific rationality. Much contemporary philosophy of science has been devoted to showing that many intellectual 'moves' in scientific thinking are unintelligible on logicist principles, most particularly the way that new concepts are bred. It seems to me that Mittelstrasse misses an opportunity to take the anti-logicist argument a step further.

The idea of an evolution of scientific knowledge will appear very differently when set in realist or non-realist approaches to the interpretation of science. In a realist view, evolution will involve the selection of theories which more and more accurately 'reflect' the way the world is structured, and the growing pragmatic success of science is explicable as a simple consequence. A person is a better watchmaker in so far as he understands the mechanism of the watch better. Non-realist views must content themselves with two main sets of criteria for scientific advance—that the discourse of a more developed science is in some way more economical, and that its practice is more effective in prediction and control. In the simple and basic contrasts of this paragraph, we have, I think, the fundamental standpoints of what has proved to be a most persistent debate. In one form or another, it can be traced for some 2000 years. Does science give us an evolving representation of reality, or does it give us an evolving practice? Realism can admit that it does both: anti-realism must be satisfied only with the latter.

Put in these stark terms, the debate can be clearly seen to rest upon a yet deeper distinction. Realist philosophy of science has an explanation for the pragmatic success of more developed theories, while anti-realism does not. Realism is thus rationalistic while anti-realism is irrationalistic. By turning the argument round, realists believe they have a proof, of a sort, for the realist interpretation of science. The best explanation for pragmatic success is relative truth to the world, according to the realist, so it should follow that the evolution of progressively more pragmatically successful theories should also be marked by their greater representational quality, however that is to be understood on further analysis. And this looks like an empirical issue about the history of science.

Newton-Smith's central argument is that addressed to the setting up of a principle according to which the argument that well-established theories could be said to be nearer the truth than more tentative ones can be supported. The argument is simple: in the natural sciences the argument to the best explanation is frequently used. Why should not some form of that argument be used in philosophy? So transposed, it would sanction the principle that a theory's pragmatic success is due to its relative truthlikeness because that is the best explanation of its pragmatic success.

Laudan's criticism of Newton-Smith's argument uses a rather narrow selection of examples of scientific work. For instance, while much play is made with theories such as electric fluids, aethers and so on, there is no mention of Terra Australis, blood capilliaries, bacteria, Neptune and the like. In this way Laudan succeeds in ignoring central features of realist theory of science, in particular the place of existential demonstrations in contemporary theories of experiment, such as, for instance, Bhaskar's recent study.[1] The result is that the argument is conducted within a logical empiricist framework, the very framework in which a coherent account of ontological, epistemic and semantic realism cannot be set up. By presuming that kind of account, a caricature of realism is presented whose refutation is easily accomplished.

Only by ignoring the non-logicist theories of what would, in logicist terms, be called 'approximate truth', that is, the theory of open texture (Waismann[2]), of metaphor and relative epistemic access (Black,[3] Boyd[4]) and the changing balance of positive and negative analogy (Hesse,[5] Harré[6]), can Laudan say that there is no account of approximate truth. But since such a concept could not be formulated in logicist terms anyway, that remark is neither here nor there.

Laudan suggests that because in many cases a theory which was based on a certain ontology was for a time unsuccessful pragmatically, but later came to be amplified so that it was taken seriously, the idea that pragmatic success is a good inductive guide to representative quality fails. But that is to make a simple confusion between short-term and long-term success or failure. Long-term success is just the requirement that is built into Putnam's and other's[7] versions of the principle of referential conservation. And that makes sense only in a non-logicist context, since it depends, I think, upon the idea of an ultimate possibility, in some key illustrative cases, such as Terra Australis, anthrax, etc. of existential demonstration.

Laudan's claim, that there are no empirical studies of science that clearly show that retention of referential confidence is an important practical principle, can only have been made by virtue of a confusion between the rationality of retention *within* an existential frame and the irrationality of retention *across* frames. Now this point is partially conceded by Laudan in his section 6. But once it is conceded even in a weak form, it renders the argument about successor and predecessor theories invalid. A sequence of theories will form a lineage only on condition that their referential terms are operating within *an* articulated ontology. It is no part of the realist position to claim that whatever anybody ever thought was real must determine what is thought real for evermore. But if one ignores the central role that sophisticated realists assign to existential tests in their epistemology one might very well father some such naive consequence on the principle of charity.

It seems to me important to see that were Laudan's arguments to be counted successful, they would eliminate *all* evolutionary models for scientific change. Success or failure of individual theories (if we could finally put together adequate criteria of identity and difference of theories) would be independent of that of their predecessors. Success of a past theory would give no credence to any of its successors, since in the absence of any conservation of reference of like terms, there

294   *The Philosophy of Evolution*

could be no use for the idea of a lineage of theories. This argument would apply whether or not referents are supposed to be observable or unobservable, for familiar Wittgensteinian reasons. If conservation of reference fails for unobservables, it must fail for observables, since the same sceptical argument that would separate the experienceable from the unexperienceable would separate the present referent from those in the future and the past. It follows from this that Laudan must be committed to some form of conventionalism, so that rival theories are just alternative ways of talking about a neutrally apprehended experience. Yet the theory of science as problem-solving, to which he is committed, surely requires that there be at least conservation of reference to *a* real world problem situation (token or type) while its solution is being sought and tested.

References

1 R. Bhaskar, (1978), *A Realist Theory of Science*, 2nd ed., Harvester Press, Hassocks, Sussex.
2 F. Waismann (1968), *How I see Philosophy*, Macmillan, London, Ch. 2.
3 M. Black, (1962), *Models and Metaphors*, Cornell University Press, Ithaca, N.Y.
4 R. Boyd, (1979), 'Metaphor and scientific theory', in A. Ortony, *Metaphor and Thought*, Cambridge University Press, Cambridge.
5 M. B. Hesse, (1963), *Models and Analogies in Science*, Sheed and Ward, London.
6 R. Harré, (1972), *The Principles of Scientific Thinking*, Macmillan, London.
7 M. Bunge, (1973), *Method, Model and Matter*, Reidel, Dordrecht.

Index of Names

Index of Topics

abductive arguments, 261–263
acts v. actions, 162
adaptation, 66, 88–90, 176ff, 201
  calculative, 183–184
  concepts of, 177–181
  developmental, 186
  homeostatic, 185–186
  natural function, 199
  populational, 186–187, 190, 191, 202
  social 182–183, 192–193
Aristotelian theory of generation, 12–14

causal-genetic history, 219
consciousness, individual, 143, 152, 153

Darwinian v. Lamarckian theory, 167, 202, 203
Darwinism, 3–5
dialectical resolutions, 165
differentiation, social, 82–84
discourse(s), 1, 17–18

effectual history, 220–221, 222, 228–229
environment, 56–60
evolutionary change, 8–9, 155
evolution, scientific, 214, 217, 218, 219, 293
expressive v. practical order, 157, 161, 164, 165, 166

foundational history, 216, 220, 221, 228–229
functions, 54, 71–72, 126, 199–201

gene selection, 7, 11, 46, 48, 55, 64
groups as individuals, 36–40

history of science, 213, 214

inductivism, 271, 280
information transmission, 76–77, 84–86
interactors, 30–36, 61–63, 204
internal v. external history, 222–223, 290
irrational praxis, 217

labour, 134, 135, 140, 145, 152, 156–157
lineages, 26–29, 41, 63
logical empiricism, 215
logic of discovery, 216
logico-historical analysis, 141, 142, 146–148

materialism, historical, 120–124, 125, 127, 129
maturity of science, 248–249 281
mechanisms, preservation of, 253–257
metaphysics (of genes), 9–11, 12, 24–25
mirroring reality, 17–19
misapplications, 86, 87, 116, 117, 156
model theory, 218
moralization of law, 130–134
mutation-selection, 77, 81, 156, 164, 167, 174–175

organisms, 24, 25

paradox of evolution, 45, 49
pessimistic induction, 269, 280
philosophy v. science, 2–3
political power, 130
populational thinking, 4–5, 45, 64
predictive power, increase, 282
principle of charity, 238

298